EVERYDAY UNDERSTANDING

INQUIRIES IN SOCIAL CONSTRUCTION

Series editors
Kenneth J. Gergen and John Shotter

This series is designed to facilitate, across discipline and national boundaries, an emergent dialogue within the social sciences which many believe presages a major shift in the western intellectual tradition.

Including among its participants sociologists of science, psychologists, management and communications theorists, cyberneticists, ethnomethodologists, literary theorists, feminists and social historians, it is a dialogue which involves profound challenges to many existing ideas about, for example, the person, selfhood, scientific method and the nature of scientific and everyday knowledge.

It has also given voice to a range of new topics, such as the social construction of personal identities; the role of power in the social making of meanings; rhetoric and narrative in establishing sciences; the centrality of everyday activities; remembering and forgetting as socially constituted activities; reflexivity in method and theorizing. The common thread underlying all these topics is a concern with the processes by which human abilities, experiences, commonsense and scientific knowledge are both *produced in*, and *reproduce*, human communities.

Inquiries in Social Construction affords a vehicle for exploring this new consciousness, the problems raised and the implications for society.

EVERYDAY UNDERSTANDING

Social and Scientific Implications

EDITED BY

GÜN R. SEMIN
and
KENNETH J. GERGEN

SAGE Publications

London • Newbury Park • New Delhi

Chapter 1 and editorial arrangement
© Kenneth J. Gergen and Gün R. Semin 1990
Chapter 2 © Norbert Groeben 1990
Chapter 3 © Jan Smedslund 1990
Chapter 4 © Amedeo Giorgi 1990
Chapter 5 © Jochen Brandtstädter 1990
Chapter 6 © Kenneth J. Gergen, Gabriele Gloger-Tippelt
and Peter Berkowitz 1990
Chapter 7 © Felice F. Carugati 1990
Chapter 8 © Gün R. Semin 1990
Chapter 9 © Adrian Furnham 1990
Chapter 10 © Catherine Lutz 1990
Chapter 11 © Hanns-Dietrich Dann 1990

First published 1990

 SAGE Publications Ltd
28 Banner Street
London EC1Y 8QE

SAGE Publications Inc
2111 West Hillcrest Drive
Newbury Park, California 91320

SAGE Publications India Pvt Ltd
32, M-Block Market
Greater Kailash – I
New Delhi 110 048

British Library Cataloguing in Publication Data

Semin, C. R. (Gün R.)
    Everyday understanding: social and scientific implications.
    – (Inquiries in social construction series).
    1. Knowledge. Sociological perspectives
    I. Title   II. Gergen, Kenneth J. (Kenneth Jay), *1934–*
    III. Series
    306.42

    ISBN 0–8039–8236–4
    ISBN 0–8039–8237–2 pbk

Library of Congress catalog card number 90–60266

Typeset by Photoprint, Torquay, Devon
Printed in Great Britain by Billing and Sons Ltd,
Worcester

Contents

Notes on Contributors

Peter Berkowitz was a student at Swarthmore College, Pennsylvania (USA) and is now attending the Yale Law School.

Jochen Brandtstädter is Professor of Psychology at the University of Trier (FRG). He has diverse publications on developmental and educational psychology, psychological prevention, theory of action and psychology of science.

Felice F. Carugati is Professor of Developmental Psychology at the University of Parma (Italy). Among other contributions to psychology and developmental psychology he has co-authored *Social Representations of Intelligence* with Gabriel Mugny.

Hanns-Dietrich Dann is Professor of Psychology at the Friedrich-Alexander University at Nürnberg (FRG). He has published and edited a number of books, the most recent of which is *Das Beobachtungssystem BAVIS zur Analyse von aggressionsbezogenen Interaktionen im Schulunterricht* (with W. Humpert, 1988).

Adrian Furnham is Reader in Psychology at University College, University of London (UK). He has a very broad range of interests in applied, medical, economic, personality and social psychology. He is author of several books including *Lay Theories: Everyday Understandings of Problems in Social Science*.

Kenneth J. Gergen is Professor of Psychology at Swarthmore College, Pennsylvania (USA). As the author of *Towards Transformation in Social Knowledge* (1982) he is a central exponent of the social constructionist movement in modern psychology.

Amedeo P. Giorgi is Professor of Psychology at the University of Quebec, Montreal (Canada) and at Saybrook Institute, San Francisco (USA). He is the author of *Psychology as a Human Science* and founding editor of the *Journal of Phenomenological Psychology*.

Gabriele Gloger-Tippelt is Associate Professor (akademische Rätin) at the University of Heidelberg. Her research domains are life-span developmental psychology and family psychology. She is author of *Schwangerschaft und erste Geburt: Psychologische Veränderungen der Eltern* (1988).

Norbert Groeben is Professor of Psychology at the University of Heidelberg (FRG). His particular interests include the philosophy of science, subjective theories and psycholinguistics. Among other contributions in these areas, he is co-author of *Das Forschungsprogramm Subjektive Theorien* (1988).

Catherine Lutz is Associate Professor of Anthropology at the State University of New York at Binghamton. She is author of *Unnatural Emotions: Everyday Sentiments on a Micronesian Atoll and their Challenge to Western Theory* (1988). Her work has focused on cultural discourses on emotion and on cultural models of ethnicity in popular photography.

Gün R. Semin is Professor of Social Psychology at the Free University of Amsterdam (The Netherlands). He is co-author of *The Accountability of Conduct* (with A.S.R. Manstead, 1983) and his current work is on the relationship between language and social cognition.

Jan Smedslund is Professor of Psychology at the University of Oslo (Norway). He has published broadly in diverse areas in psychology and the culmination of his more recent thinking can be found in his book *Psycho-Logic* (1988).

1

Everyday Understanding in Science and Daily Life

Kenneth J. Gergen and Gün R. Semin

The focal concern of the present volume is with people's everyday understanding of the world, and more directly, their understandings of themselves and others. Yet, as we focus on this critical domain, it is also apparent that we as scientists are engaged in the very process that is central to our concerns. We are in the process of generating everyday understanding within the profession, and the results of our work may play a vital role in fashioning the future contours of life, both within the science and within the culture more generally. Thus a range of interesting and important questions present themselves. What is the status of lay understandings; how are they generated; how are they to be assessed; and how do they influence or insinuate themselves into science? Are the processes we as scientists hope to elucidate in the arena of daily life identical to those we employ within the science? If so, what does this say about the traditional advantage accorded to the scientist over the layman? If the processes are different, in what ways is this so, and what implications does this have for both science and social policy?

There are well-wrought answers to these questions that have emerged and become progressively sharpened over the years. A massive range of research has attempted to elucidate lay under-standings, including, for example, common beliefs about the body (Jodelet, 1984), health and illness (Herzlich and Pierret, 1987; Pennebaker and Epstein, 1983; Sontag, 1989; Leventhal, Meyer and Neranz, 1980), intelligence (Sternberg, 1985), love and personal relationships (Davis and Roberts, 1985; Oppenheimer and deGroot, 1981; Sternberg, 1988), political life (Ibanez, 1988), emotion (Wagner, 1988), gender (Kessler and McKenna, 1978), lesbianism (Kitzinger, 1987), sexuality (Tiefer, 1987), the concept of the person (Gergen and Davis, 1985; Sampson, 1985), psychoanalysis (Moscovici, 1976), and mental illness (Jodelet, 1988). In many of these cases the research places scientists in a clearly advantageous role; scientists function so as to elucidate the previously unarticulated conceptualization of the layperson, thus exposing the foundations of social life. At least implicitly, scientific understandings are superior; they appear as true reflections of what the layperson understands only feebly. And, as a result, a top-down educational system – where knowledge flows from science to society – is provided additional justification.

Yet certain participants in this dialogue have begun to speak in new ways, both persistent and disquieting. For them the difference between everyday understanding and scientific beliefs is less compelling than heretofore. In certain respects the scientist may even be placed in a position of dependency on the social milieu more generally. What is suggested is a broadscale reconsideration of scientific practice along with existing processes of education. At stake, then, is the traditional conception of human understanding, of science and of education. It is the tension between these opposing positions around which the present volume is constructed.

The aim of the present chapter is to lay out the theoretical context of the debate, to articulate central dimensions of disagreement, to isolate major locations occupied along these dimensions, and to raise questions concerning the viability of contending positions. At the same time, we shall endeavour to locate within these debates the various contributions of the present volume, because each of these contributions provides a more detailed picture of the promises (and problems) inherent in the various positions.

Let us proceed by outlining first what may be regarded as the traditional view of human understanding, and the relationship between lay and scientific accounts. We shall then consider what many regard to be critical problems inhering in the traditional position. This will set the stage for examining two alternative orientations, both attempting to answer criticisms inherent in the traditional view, and offering disparate and challenging perspectives on everyday understanding.

Understanding as Cognitive Representation

That understanding is a process occurring in the mental world of the individual is a view widely shared at least since the Enlightenment. It is a view to which both empiricist and rationalist thinkers – each with their own particular emphasis – have contributed over the centuries. It is also a view that resurfaces in the present century in logical empiricist philosophy. Interestingly, while psychology as a profession has been largely committed to a logical empiricist view of science, theories of knowledge as mental representation were not readily forthcoming. While behavioural scientists believed in their own powers of reason and observation, so keen were they to ground their theories in observables that propositions about the mental states (or cognitive representations) of persons were hazarded only as hypotheticals (if at all), and couched in formalities tied closely to an observation language. The theories of Thorndike, Hull, Spence, Tolman, Skinner and Watson are all apposite.

In this regard, perhaps the most significant effect of the more recent 'cognitive revolution' was to reinstate the traditional commitment to knowledge as individual representation of the external world. While psychologists more generally were inspired by theorists such as Chomsky, Piaget, Bruner, Miller and Fodor, social psychologists could draw more directly from seminal work of Kurt Lewin and such protégés as Festinger and Schachter. Heider and the attribution movement added further impetus by focusing more directly on the manner in which social understanding occurs. Much intergroup-relations research is also based on a model of the individual as cognizer of himself and others. Such assumptions become crystallized and formalized further in the enormous literature on social cognition. Traditional languages of 'ideas', 'thoughts', 'categories', 'attributions' and 'representations' are converted to and homogenized by the pervasive metaphor of the mind as a form of computer or computational device.

Although impossible to capture the rich variations in emphases and assumptions within this diverse group, it is possible to isolate a series of broad assumptions that characterize the majority view. It is useful to elucidate these assumptions as they apply to the problem of everyday understanding – both in science and in society. At the outset, there is a shared commitment to the view that the cognitive world is in some way sensitive to, correspondent with or reflective of events within the objective world. In this sense, knowledge or understanding of the real world is carried within the cognitive system, and it is in the degree that this system is correspondent with the world that one can speak of correct understanding or accurate knowledge.

A second generally binding assumption is that the cognitive system plays a major role in the production of behaviour. Ideally, behaviour should be guided by accurate representation on the cognitive level. One should build up knowledge of the world, and act on the basis of this knowledge. To the degree that cognition is correspondent with reality and behaviour is dictated by cognition, we may speak of behaviour as adaptive (or, in Darwinian terms, as possessing survival value).

A third rudimentary corollary is that language, as a form of behaviour, is guided by cognition. If the categories in language reflect or are systematically linked to the features of the cognitive system, and this system is tied to the real world, we may speak of the communication of knowledge or understanding. In any case, language itself represents a secondary or derivative process. It is useful as a conveyance of knowledge, but does not constitute knowledge itself.

Such assumptions pervade much of the literature on social cognition. Experimental research is often centred on factors that determine the nature of the cognitive system, its operation across time and its influence on behaviour. In the present volume the chapters by Groeben (Chapter 2) and by Dann (Chapter 11) most fully express the traditional views, although their sophistication in doing so takes them well past the metaphor of the mind as computational device. Groeben's account of 'subjective theories' calls attention to the close parallel between lay and scientific forms of cognition. Cognitions of the world exist, for him, as complex aggregates with an implicit argumentational structure. To assess these aggregates requires an elaborate and detailed form of dialogue between scientist and subject. The degree of accuracy of such knowledge structures is open to subsequent assessment. Dann's paper carries such assumptions into the applied arena. For him it is essential to tap the subjective theories possessed by teachers of their management practices with students. In particular, by assessing their understanding of student aggression, the hope is to furnish the kind of feedback that will improve their capacities for problem-solving. In effect, cognition functions in both cases to represent the world and to enable the individual to act effectively. Research in both cases typically relies on the subject's language as an inferential guide to the locus of knowledge and action within. In effect, language operates as a conduit or vehicle for expressing the state of the individual's cognition.

Embedded within this minimal array of agreements is also a set of assumptions concerning the relationship of everyday understandings at the lay level with those of the scientist. First, at the level of real world representation, it is generally presumed that, while similar in their reliance on cognitive structures, the observational skills of the scientist (phase 1 in Figure 1.1) are more rigorous and systematic than those of the lay person (left column). It follows that the cognitive system of the scientist is more accurately reflective of real-world properties than that of the lay person. (It is for this reason that Dann feels the results of the scientific work can enhance the skill of teachers.) This claim to the superiority of scientific understanding is most fully explicated by Furnham (Chapter 9).

A similar advantage to the scientist is often traced to the linkage between cognition and behaviour (phase 2). The lay person is under

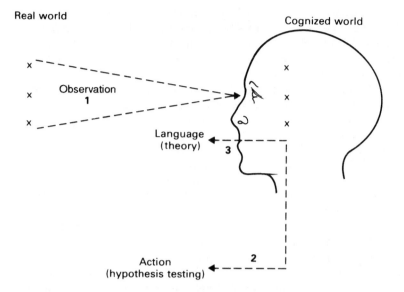

Figure 1.1   *Classical view of human understanding*

little constraint to evaluate the goodness of fit between inner representation and outer reality; the process is haphazard and piecemeal. In contrast, the central activity of science is that of hypothesis-testing. Thus the everyday understanding of the scientist is linked systematically to his/her behaviour and subjected to empirical test.

A third advantage accorded to the scientist can be traced to the link between cognition and language (phase 3). The layman is not obliged to formulate his/her ideas for expression in language. And if converted to linguistic currency, there is little pressure to communicate with others in a clear and consistent manner. In contrast, it is held, the major challenge for the scientist is to communicate his/her ideas in as transparent and rigorous a manner as possible. This process will not only press the scientist towards greater coherence and clarity at the cognitive level, but will enable other scientists to test the propositions in independent settings. The results of these tests can further be used to elaborate the knowledge systems of scientists, thus rendering them yet again more accurate and adaptive.

From these latter assumptions, in turn, one can derive the major challenges for programmes of science and education. To wit: (1) It is essential for the scientist to assay the everyday understandings of the lay person, for knowledge of these understandings is the key to predicting human conduct. (2) It is essential to compare everyday understandings on the lay level with those generated by science. Because in this way it is possible to determine domains of deficiency on the lay level – areas in which the lay population fails to understand the world in a competent way and thus fails the task of adaptation. (3) The educational process should be used to transmit scientific understanding to the lay level. In this manner, understanding in daily life will be improved and life choices rendered more effective.

A Tradition in Trouble

For most readers the preceding account may seem both modest and unnecessary. In one form or another this network of assumptions has been with the profession (if not the culture) for many years, and is in little need of such simplistic clarification. However, this preliminary sketch is useful because it enables us, first, to isolate various ways in which the assumptive structure is proving unwieldy and, second, to understand more clearly the quest for alternatives. Various problems inherent in these rudimentary assumptions have had a long and complex history within philosophic circles. However, it is only within the confines of specific theoretical debates in the profession, that psychologists have begun to appreciate the profundity of the problems with which they grapple. Let us consider four of these problems as they have emerged within recent debates.

The Generation of the Representational System
Whereas it is traditionally assumed that the optimally functioning cognitive system stands in a reflective relationship to objective reality, it has become increasingly difficult for investigators to specify how, in any simple way, this could be possible. Within experimental psychology Chomsky's (1959) critique of Skinnerian theory of language development served as a signal invitation to reconsideration, because, as his critique compellingly demonstrated, knowledge of language could not simply be the product of external inputs. For the richness and flexibility of language use to be understood, it was essential to consider the innate potentials (knowledge) of the language-user. This conclusion was magnified in a broad number of nativist accounts of animal learning and in Gibson's (1966; 1979) work on perceptual affordances. In each case it was argued that organisms bring to situations dispositions determining the individual's sensitivity to or strategies for searching the environment.

    On the one hand these various lines of thinking and research contributed importantly to the cognitive revolution. They all pointed to the essential capacities of the individual to organize, select, attend to or otherwise act upon the environmental givens. It is not the environment as such that determines the individual's beliefs or understandings, but what the individual brings to the environment in terms of cognitive predilections. Yet, while favouring a shift of attention to the cognitive level (and more specifically to top-down functioning), such conceptions simultaneously laid to rest the traditional empiricist assumption that the internal world is a replica of the external world. Precisely how cognitive structure (ideas, concepts, categories) were 'built up' from environmental inputs became problematic. These concerns with the bottom-up conception of knowledge now resonate throughout the literature on social understanding. Within the present volume Brandtstädter's (Chapter 5) contribution first reflects such concerns. As he sees human development, the individual is continuously in the process of monitoring, selecting and constructing the world. Such an argument also has implications for science as well, for, as he argues, the propositions of the developmental psychologist 'do not rely on empirical regularities, but rather on formal and conceptual structures, which in turn can be regarded as cultural constructions'. In a similar manner Gergen, Gloger-Tippelt and Berkowitz (Chapter 6) argue against the notion that parents can build up their everyday understandings of children from observation. 'Whether children are believed to possess "fear" . . . and what behaviours constitute manifestations of fear are not given through observation of the child. They are not read off the surfaces of the body.'

The Internal Determination of the Real
Confronted by the array of problems inhering in a representational or bottom-up conception of knowledge, many psychologists (aided by a host of AI specialists) have turned their attention to the top-down alternatives – theories emphasizing the inherent capacities of the person to organize, store and retrieve information. Rather than reality driving the conceptual system, the conceptual system is said to determine what is taken as real. Thus, depending on the availability or salience of a given schema, the environment is scanned for certain information and memory-biased (Wyer and Srull, 1985) so as to sustain or maintain the schema. In this sense, Greenwald (1987) has characterized the cognitive system as 'totalitarian' – operating so as to maintain its own position of strength. Or, as Kruglanski's (1989) theory of lay epistemology proposes, there is no foundational rationality underlying the individual's attempt to test hypotheses. What the individual takes to

be knowledge is based on his/her motivational system and capacities for memory.

Yet, as many begin to see, by avoiding the Scylla of everyday understanding as built up or produced by the environment, theorists run headlong into the Charybdis of knowledge as internally generated. First, if the individual understands the world on the basis of existing schemas, how is the theorist to account for their origins? Environmentalist accounts (bottom-up) of concept-acquisition are the obvious choice, but such accounts have already been abandoned as unworkable and replaced by top-down accounts. Or, to put it another way, if one understands reality through schemas, how can reality ever produce a schema? Nor are nativist accounts, stressing *a priori* schemas, an inviting alternative (Gergen, 1989). In addition to this problem, in the end the top-down characterization forces the theorist into a solipsistic position: there is no world other than a cognized world. Thus realities outside cognition cease to count as realities at all (Graumann, 1988). And finally, the view of the totalitarian ego is peculiarly anti-Darwinian and anti-scientific. If organisms seek only to sustain their existing beliefs, they would be impervious to environmental variations, and thus incapable of survival both in daily life and as professional scientists. It is perhaps for these reasons that virtually none of the contributions to the present volume has selected a top-down orientation to everyday understanding.

The Identification of Internal Structure
A central question for many investigations of everyday under-standing is the methodology of measurement. Of critical concern is how to determine whether one's measures are valid indications of internal states of individual understanding. As we have seen, it is generally assumed that understanding is more or less propositional in nature, or at least minimally, that its structure can be revealed through language. Yet these presumptions are without justification save through western dualistic tradition that views the mind as present and revealed within language (or, as Derrida has put it, a 'metaphysics of presence'). Further, even those who accept the dualistic presumption are beset by considerable doubt concerning the validity of any given interpretation of the language. There are not only the classic problems treated by hermeneutic theorists such as Gadamer and Ricoeur, problems concerning the capacities of the interpreting agent to 'see beyond the forestructure'. Is it possible, they ask, to understand another's words (the text) in any other way than by duplicating or sustaining the array of understandings one brings to the text (the vicious form of the hermeneutic circle)?

There are also problems in determining whether and how speakers understand their own mental states, that is whether they can report accurately on what they know. Thus in his chapter Groeben explores, for example, how individuals are often ignorant of their own motivational states. Presumably, they could also be ignorant of their states of cognition, thus reporting what is publicly acceptable rather than their actual beliefs. And, as Groeben finds, it is difficult to generate standards of accuracy for interpreting the individual's reports. It is inappropriate to rely on the third-person views of the scientist–observer. Rather, scientists must work co-operatively with their subjects toward a 'dialogic consensus'. In effect, there is little to warrant the traditional claim that specimens of language furnish accurate or transparent indications of the internal world.

The Influence of Understanding on Action
A final array of problems arises in determining how and under what conditions understanding, as a set of cognitive states, determines action. At a basic level, the problem shares much with the preceding issue – whether cognitive states are or can be expressed in language. Present-day psychology inherits a tradition in which this presumption is a significant entry into the commonsense make-up of scientific procedure. However, the presumption that cognition influences action shares all the problems of a dualistic worldview – as confronted by philosophers from Descartes to Ryle and Rorty (see Gergen's summary, 1989). Yet, even when the presumption is accepted, psychologists have not rested sanguine with its implications. There are perennial problems in determining how intentions (as cognitive activities) can be translated into bodily movements, whether attitudes as cognitive states determine behaviour, and whether actions are not often driven by motivational sources beyond conscious comprehension. Again, Groeben's chapter raises such concerns in his analysis of lay subjectivities. Individuals may not understand the motivational sources underlying their actions; and, if this is so, then their actual states of cognition may have little to do with their behaviour. In the worst case, individuals may only furnish rationalizations for acts whose sources they cannot comprehend.

Understanding as Socially Based Cognition

Informed by these and other problems in the cognitive representationist position, many investigators have begun to explore alternative conceptions of understanding, as occurring in both daily life and science. Two significant departures may be discerned, the one a substantial modification of the cognitive view, and the second a radical abandonment. The modified view is based, for many, on a discontent with the socially disembodied character of the cognitive orientation. For most cognitivists, processes of human understanding are intrinsic to the organism, thus more or less universal and transhistorical. While the contents and targets of cognition may vary across time and culture, the fundamental processes remain fixed. In this sense there is nothing importantly social about social cognition, and no significant role to be played by the social psychologist in elucidating the nature of mental life.

As also surmised, the cognitive representationist confronted difficulties in accounting for the origins of cognitive categories or schemas. This incapacity has invited an important alteration in theory. Specifically, if cognitive categories are not inductively derived from the actual conditions of the world, then is it not compelling to view such categories as social in their origins? It is this possibility that has fostered a virtual renaissance in interest in the works of Vygotsky (cf. Wertsch, 1985), and to a lesser degree Schutz, Whorf, Durkheim and Goodman. Vygotsky plays a central role because, as he proposed, not only are the cognitive categories social in origin, but so are the forms of ratiocination in which these categories are embedded. Thus everyday understanding is inherently a social rather than a biological act; it cannot be cut away from the socio-cultural circumstances of the agent.

Within social psychology, Festinger's (1954) concept of 'social reality' along with the intrinsically social nature of the comparison process, and Schachter's (Schachter and Singer, 1959, *inter alia*) distinctly social treatment of emotions prepared the way for the social alternative to the cognitive representationist view of understanding. A key role is also played by the work of Moscovici (1984; Farr and Moscovici, 1984) and his colleagues on social representation. In Moscovici's early work (Moscovici, 1976) social representation took on a sociological character. It referred primarily to the broadly shared and publicly represented perspectives of a culture. Thus psychoanalysis as a movement was less important in itself than the way in which it was presented in the various media. That is, social representations were regarded as:

> systems of values, ideas, and practices with a two-fold function: first to establish an order which will enable individuals to orient themselves in and master their material world, and second, to facilitate communication among members of a community by providing them with a code for naming and classifying the various aspects of their world and their individual and group history. (Moscovici, 1973: xiii)

As Moscovici (1984) has more recently emphasized, publicly shared understandings are also represented on the cognitive level. In effect, private cognitions may properly be viewed as the internalized by-products of publicly shared discourse.

Within the present volume, the chapters by Semin (Chapter 8), Carugati (Chapter 7), Brandtstädter (Chapter 5) and Furnham (Chapter 9) are most directly expressive of the social view of personal understanding. As Semin holds, language is a culturally produced medium in which, among other things, the domain of personality is configured. He then argues that work in the person-perception tradition and in psychometric models of personality has relied on the same knowledge reservoir that everyday knowledge is drawn from – the terms that we use in everyday life in describing and classifying persons and their behaviours. Consequently, the presumed difference between lay and scientific understanding and representations of the person presents an artificial separation; scientific representations of the person do not supersede everyday understandings. Carugati in a similar vein treats 'intelligence' as a social representation largely responsible for scientific conceptualizations (for example, Sternberg, 1985). His main purpose is to show how the concept of interindividual differences in intelligence are negotiated by interested parties, that is parents and teachers. Adopting a social-representational perspective he illustrates the social practices that interested parties employ in evolving a working notion of intelligence in everyday life. It is not only a negotiation between the parties engaged in everyday practices (parents and teachers) in their attempts to create a consensual universe but also a negotiation between a consensual and reified symbolic universe, namely science.

In terms of the initial array of assumptions concerning the relationship between everyday and scientific understandings, the move towards a social account of human understanding has profoundly different implications, because, as this account suggests, both the layperson and the scientist draw from roughly the same pool of everyday understandings. The scientist is first and foremost a member of his/her culture, and as a result will import into the scientific arena the shared categories and modes of thought learned within the culture more generally. It is from this perspective that Semin questions whether 'scientific' models of personality in the person-perception and psychometric traditions can be different since they always have to resort to the same everyday understanding to become intelligible. Furnham examines the same question, namely contrasting lay theories of personality with 'scientific' theories. In doing so he focuses on the issue of individual differences with a view to elucidating the differences behind the implicit assumptions governing everyday theories of personality and contrasting them with the explicit assumptions underlying 'scientific' theories in general. Essentially, the point that emerges in Furnham's contribution is an emphasis on the differences between social practices in everyday life and social practices in science. He argues that, despite the common ground and necessary convergence between lay and scientific conceptions of individual differences, the scientific practice leads to specific constructions which are not as yet available to everyday knowledge.

As we find, then, from the perspective of socialized understanding, the advantage of the scientist over the layman is less clear-cut. The scientist might continue to take a keen interest in lay conceptions, but in all likelihood he/she will locate within these networks an array of assumptions that appear much like those within the science. The results of such research thus invite a reflexive posture towards the science. If lay conceptions guide the psychologist, for example, in establishing various lines of research and modes of data-interpretation, can science do anything more than reify the existing forms of cultural understanding? And, in the case of education, can the scientist ever truly inform the culture of a reality that does not in some way correspond with the array of existing understandings? Because if the scientific proposal could not be incorporated into the network of everyday understandings, would it not simply appear as mystifying or nonsensical? From this perspective, what advantage would there be in educating people concerning social science knowledge? Would education not simply serve to reify further the existing categories of understanding? All are questions deserving the most careful attention.

Understanding as Discursive Construction

Although the shift towards a social basis for individual understanding is a refreshing and provocative one for many, there is still a third and more radical orientation that stands in contrast to the cognitive tradition. Earlier we outlined several problems inhering in the cognitive position, problems concerning the inductive basis for cognition, the impasse of top-down theorizing, and the means by which cognition makes its way into both language and action. All are problems engendered by a dualistic commitment – to a real world on the one side and a mental world on the other. The move to social understanding did begin to encroach on this array of problems. Specifically it offered an alternative means, other than induction, of accounting for the origins of individual conception.

Yet, as many feel, the questions of top-down processing and the relationship of mind to language and action are still left unsolved. Further, it is ventured, although the social-understanding orientation appears to solve the question of concept origin, under closer examination the riddle reappears. Because, if conceptual structures are said to be social in origin, then how did the individual come to understand the initial inputs from the social world? The infant could not understand parental signs or language on the basis of socially engendered categories; there had not yet been a social input. Yet, if the child's understanding did not proceed on the basis of socially engendered understandings, then there must be non-social cognitions – precisely those which the social position wishes to displace. This question remains as yet unsolved.

For a number of scholars these various problems have suggested a radical departure from traditional conceptions of understanding, namely an abandonment of the dualistic presumption. This possibility was initially proposed within the social sciences by phenomenological theorists. Drawing from the works of Husserl, Heidegger and Merleau-Ponty, it is proposed that the separation of the experiencing agent from the object of experience is an artificial and misleading one. Subject and object are inextricably fused. This position is adopted in the present volume by Andy Giorgi (Chapter 4). For Giorgi this means that scientific understandings of the person should not deviate sharply from those of the lay person. For scientists to embark on empirical assessments of abstract hypotheses concerning the nature of mental life (for example, processes of illusory correlation or cognitive priming) is to miss the point. To understand the individual is to gain access to his/her lived experience. The function of the scientist in this case is to clarify and elucidate the nature of the individual's understandings. Giorgi's chapter illustrates such a process.

Again, however, many scholars do not rest easy with the phenomenological alternative to traditional dualism. At the outset it is difficult to see how the scientist can proceed once subject and object have been collapsed in this way. If there is no world outside one's own private experience, then what precisely is one doing as a scientist? Science as a reflection on experience seems insufficient, as one can scarcely presume the existence of others outside one's experience who can understand the reflections. Further, the methodological procedures of the phenomenologist seem inevitably to reinstate the dualism, with an experiencing subject whose experience the scientist is attempting to comprehend. In carrying out research, the phenomenologist does seem to grant the existence of another person, independent of his/her experience. And that individual is presumed to have private experiences separate from those of the phenomenologist. Further clarification of the phenomenological position is required.

More recently, however, a further group of scholars has embarked on a second alternative to dualism, namely the alternative of discursive construction. The central focus in this case is on the language used by persons to describe or explain their world. Everyday understandings, as it is proposed, exist in the language of the culture. No presumption is made concerning the nature of the mental processes of the language-user, including the user's 'experience', 'cognitions', 'meanings' and 'intentions'. Indeed, all such terms are fundamentally integers within the western language system, and it would be a mistake to presume that the existing vocabulary of mind reflects actual conditions or states. Further, it is ventured, words gain their meaning primarily from social interchange. From this Wittengensteinian perspective, language is thus no longer an outer expression of inner states, but is social in its origins, uses and implications. Thus the constructionist joins with those concerned with the social bias of understanding against traditional cognitivism, but abandons the dualism in which both the preceding movements are grounded. In doing so, the constructionist attempts to avoid the array of intractable problems deriving from attempts to link worlds of mind and material.

Within the present volume the constructionist orientation is most fully represented in the chapters by Smedslund (Chapter 3), Lutz (Chapter 10) and by Gergen and his colleagues (Chapter 6). Smedslund's contribution is a crystallization of a perspective he has developed over a decade, namely the examination of a psychology that is based on the explication of conceptual relationships entailed in ordinary language or common sense. The assumption here is that commonsense understanding, as an historically and culturally generated artefact, guides not only everyday life but also the structures of psychological theories and the resultant labelling of observations. In drawing out the radical implications of this 'psychologic' Smedslund questions fundamental scientific assumptions that are shared in the psychological community about operational definitions, prevailing notions of contingent causality, and the notion of objective versus subjective reality. He proposes a conceptual analysis of common sense and its explication as a radical alternative to traditional empirical psychology.

Lutz's essay (Chapter 10) shows the intimate connection between social practices and psychological constructs in an examination of the cultural understandings of emotion among the people of Ifaluk. This work not only uses ethnographic materials to combat the universalist tendencies of scientists standing outside a culture, but demonstrates the clash between the culturally embedded understandings of the anthropologists and the everyday understanding of the community they are examining. The point of this chapter is to show how strongly the understanding of an emotion, 'justifiable anger', is a 'cultural and social process involving negotiation, interpersonal evaluation and power struggles'. Presumably a 'science of emotion' for the Ifaluk would have a quite different character from what is currently accepted as emotion theory in the West.

In their chapter, Gergen, Gloger-Tippelt and Berkowitz adopt a language-centred position in their exploration of conceptions of child-development in Germany and the US. As they conclude, there are both substantial similarities and differences between views of development in the two cultures, and these views are related to actual behaviour of mothers towards their children. Conceptions of the child are linked further to properties of the discursive context, such that mothers' beliefs about their children are intertwined with their conceptions of the family and the work place. In effect, what mothers 'know' about their children's psychological states (emotions, intentions, thoughts) is largely a by-product of the culture's linguistic assumptions about the nature of children.

The implications of the linguistic-constructionist position for the relationship between science and everyday understandings stand in dramatic contrast to those of the cognitivist. Because if language gets its meaning from the way in which it is used by groups of persons, then there is no obvious way of privileging the scientists' words over those of the lay person. The scientist's terms are not more rigorously tied to the world as it is, nor are they more predictive of events in the world (for language itself carries no information as to how it is linked to a world of particulars). Rather, lay language and scientific language are used by the two cultures to carry out certain patterns of social interchange. They both gain their utility from the respective social milieus. To be sure, the scientific community may be more engaged in the process of systematic prediction; and a scientific language may be essential to co-ordinate their activities as a scientific community. However, this is not to privilege the language of the scientific culture as somehow being more accurate or objectively true than that of the lay culture.

The constructionist does join with the scholar of social understanding in a concern with the symbiotic relationships between lay and scientific understandings. In both cases, there is reason to anticipate a close relationship between the forms of understanding of the two communities – largely deriving from the membership of the scientist in the community at large. However, from the constructionist perspective, science should be capable of generating modes of discourse that are outside the understanding of the culture more generally. Because there are no cognitive foundations for understanding (rendering 'transcendence' of existing codes impossible), there is little to prevent cultures of scientists from generating strictly local ontologies. And, as especially vivified in the case of mathematics, the scholar may confront considerable difficulty in communicating these ontologies to the culture more generally.

However, this last point raises the question of the functions of social science and of education. From the constructionist perspective the scientist is not engaged in the process of mapping or picturing the world through language. Thus the process of education cannot furnish the layperson with a 'more accurate' understanding of reality. However, because languages of understanding are built into relationships, both sustaining and rationalizing them, existing languages favour certain patterns of cultural life as opposed to others. (Without a language of 'intentions', criminal trials could scarcely proceed; without words of 'emotion', family life would be transformed.) In this sense, the scientist–educator becomes a participant in cultural life. His/her words may enter into the culture, modifying certain lifeforms while sustaining others. The social sciences become, then, vehicles for generating and disseminating languages that may sensitize or render self-reflexive the culture more generally, and potentially emancipate them from the realities from which they see no alternatives.

Yet the emergence of the constructionist alternative can scarcely be viewed as the end of a dialogue. As readers of the present volume should find, it rather marks the beginning. For there are a number of intellectual and cultural values inherent in the traditions of cognitive and social understanding that the constructionist orientation subverts. Standards of scientific detachment and methodological rigour, on the one side, and values of individual responsibility and autonomy on the other – all are threatened by the constructionist approach. Further, the constructionists have failed as yet to render compelling accounts of the origins of discursive practices, the relationship between language and behaviour, and the significant gains demonstrated by the natural sciences. Thus, while the present volume may furnish the kinds of illustrative contrasts essential for debate, they do not presume a fixed end to the colloquy.

References

Chomsky, N. (1959) Review of Skinner's 'Verbal Behaviour'. *Language*, 35: 26–58.

Davis, K.E. and Roberts, M.K. (1985) Relationships in the real world: the descriptive psychology approach to personal relationships. In K.J. Gergen and K.E. Davis (eds), *The Social Construction of the Person*. New York: Springer.

Farr, R. and Moscovici, S. (eds) (1984) *Social Representations*. Cambridge: Cambridge University Press.

Festinger, L. (1954) A theory of social comparison processes. *Human Relations*, 7: 117–40.

Gergen, K.J. (1989) Social psychology and the wrong revolution. *European Journal of Social Psychology*, 19: 463–84.

Gergen, K.J. and Davis, K.E. (1985) *The Social Construction of the Person*. New York: Springer.

Gibson, J.J. (1966) *The Senses Considered as Perceptual Systems*. Boston: Houghton Mifflin.

Gibson, J.J. (1979) *The Ecological Approach to Visual Perception*. Boston: Houghton Mifflin.

Graumann, C.F. (1988) Der Kognitivismus in der Sozialpsychologie – Kehrseite der Wende. *Psychologische Rundschau*, 39: 83–90.

Greenwald, A. (1987) The totalitarian ego: fabrication and revision of personal history. *American Psychologist*, 35: 603–18.

Heelas, P. and Lock, A. (1981) *Indigenous Psychologies*. London: Academic Press.

Herzlich, C. and Pierret, J. (1987) *Illness and Self in Society*. Baltimore and London: Johns Hopkins University Press.

Ibanez, T. (1988) *Ideologias de la vida cotidiana*. Barcelona: Sendai.

Jodelet, D. (1984) The representation of the body and its transformations. In R. Farr and S. Moscovici (eds), *Social Representations*. Cambridge: Cambridge University Press.

Jodelet, D. (1988) *Folies et représentations sociale*. Paris: Presses Universitaires de France.

Kessler, S. and McKenna, W. (1978) *Gender: An Ethnomethodological Approach*. New York: Wiley.

Kitzinger, C. (1987) *The Social Construction of Lesbianism*. London: Sage.

Kruglanski, A. (1989) *Lay Epistemics and Human Knowledge*. New York: Plenum.

Kruse, L., Weimer, E. and Wagner, F. (1988) What men and women are said to be: social representations and language. *Journal of Language and Psychology*, 7: 243–62.

Leventhal, H., Meyer, D. and Neranz, D. (1980) The common sense representation of illness danger. In S. Rachman (ed.), *Medical Psychology*. Vol. 2. New York: Pergamon.

Moscovici, S. (1973) Foreword. In C. Herzlich, *Health and Illness: A Social Psychological Analysis*. London: Academic Press.

Moscovici, S. (1976) *La Psychanalyse: son image et son public*. 2nd edn. Paris: Presses Universitaires de France. (First edn 1961.)

Moscovici, S. (1984) The phenomenon of social representations. In R. Farr and S. Moscovici (eds), *Social Representations*. Cambridge: Cambridge University Press.

Oppenheimer, L. and deGroot, W. (1981) Development of concepts about people in interpersonal situations. *European Journal of Social Psychology*, 11: 209–25.

Pennebaker, J.W. and Epstein, D. (1983) Implicit psychophysiology: effects of common beliefs and physiological responses on symptom reporting. *Journal of Personality*, 51: 469–98.

Sampson, E.E. (1985) The decentralization of identity: toward a revised concept of personal and social order. *American Psychologist*, 40: 1203–11.

Schachter, S. and Singer, J.E. (1959) Cognitive, social and physiological determinants of emotional state. *Psychological Review*, 69: 379–99.

Sontag, S. (1989) *A.I.D.S. and its Metaphors*. London: Allen Lane.

Sternberg, R.J. (1985) Implicit theories of intelligence, creativity and wisdom. *Journal of Personality and Social Psychology*, 49: 607–27.

Sternberg, R.J. (1988) Triangulating love. In R.J. Sternberg and M.L. Barnes (eds), *The Psychology of Love*. New Haven: Yale University Press.

Tiefer, L. (1987) Social constructionism and the study of human sexuality. In P. Shaver and C. Hendrick (eds), *Sex and Gender*. Beverly Hills: Sage.

Wagner, H.L. (1988) The social context of emotion. *British Journal of Social Psychology*, 27 (1) (whole special issue).

Wertsch, J.V. (1985) *Cognitive Development Theory: A Vygotskian Perspective*. Cambridge: Cambridge University Press.

Wyer, R.S. and Srull, T.K. (1985) *Handbook of Social Cognition*. Vols 1, 2, 3. Hillsdale, NJ: Erlbaum.

PART I

EVERYDAY UNDERSTANDING AND PSYCHOLOGY

2

Subjective Theories and the Explanation of Human Action

Norbert Groeben

Advance Organizer

Within recent years, cognitive aspects of human information-processing have become increasingly focal as an object of psychological research (cf. Lachmann et al., 1979; de Mey, 1982); in the course of this development, naive psychology, that is what the 'man in the street' thinks and knows about psychological phenomena and processes within himself or other people, has also been demanding increasing attention. This concern with naive psychology has been explored in many different ways, for example under the heading of concepts such as implicit personality theory, attribution theory, personal-construct theory, meta-cognition, knowledge systems and structures, naive and intuitive theories and so on. In principle, all these conceptualizations are meant to be included when 'subjective theories' are being discussed in the present context (for an explication of the concept see the following section). For me the exploration of 'subjective theories' represents a post-behaviourist research programme which permits the integration of the traditions of empiricism and hermeneutics in psychology, the methods of experimentation and intuitive understanding – a dichotomy that was at least in part initiated by psychology itself (for instance, Dilthey, 1894).

At the same time, this integration of hermeneutics and empiricism within the framework of a research programme on 'subjective theories' offers various starting points for overcoming the dichotomy between monism and dualism in the social sciences in general. In succession to Dilthey, dualism holds that the 'objects' of research in the social and cultural sciences – human beings, that is – possess specific characteristics distinguishing them from the objects of research in the natural sciences. These specific characteristics are in turn supposed to necessitate scientific criteria and research methods different from those employed in the natural sciences. Among these, the method of understanding, instead of the traditional experimental procedure, is considered to be the most important. According to monism, on the other hand, there are no fundamental differences between the objects of research in the natural and cultural/social sciences respectively; hence the monist claim that the criteria and methods of scientific research (namely experimentation) could and should be the same for all sciences.

In my opinion, it is necessary today to speak of a dichotomy between monism and dualism because several recent attempts at a redefinition of the monism–dualism controversy (cf. Apel, 1979) have not led to a rapprochement of the different views. In the following essay I shall try to outline ways in which a research programme on 'subjective theories' can contribute to overcoming this dichotomy of monism and dualism by integrating hermeneutic and empirical methodologies. For reasons of space, this outline can only touch on the fundamental structures of such an integration. Corresponding differentiations have been elaborated elsewhere: Groeben and Scheele (1977) have largely concentrated upon developing a concept of the human being upon which the research on 'subjective theories' is based; further they have shown why the corresponding research programme (on 'subjective theories') can be conceptualized as post- or anti-behaviourist respectively. The methodological basis for the integration of hermeneutics and empiricism in psychology (against the background of the monism–dualism controversy) has been elaborated in detail by Groeben (1986); a summary of the resulting conceptualization of the research programme 'subjective theories' can be found in Groeben et al. (1988).

Construct Explication: An Introduction

The concept of 'subjective theory' is meant to indicate a specific part of the broad area of cognitive phenomena. In the early history of cognitive psychology simple phenomena such as concept attainment or concept formation were, as a rule, central to the discipline. Recently more complex phenomena, such as schemas, scripts or frames, have become focal. But the cognitive processes and products to which these constructs refer do not yet include the structure to which the term 'subjective theory' applies.

In the first place, using the term 'subjective theory' implies the assumption that the cognitive (sub-)systems of understanding employed by the naive psychologist possess structures and functions parallel or analogous to those of scientific theories. This assumption of a parallel or analogy between the naive psychologist's thinking and the scientific psychologist's theorizing was first postulated by Kelly in his personal construct theory (1955). Like Kelly, the research on subjective theories starts from the assumption that the complex, argumentative thinking of the naive theorist fulfils functions comparable to the theorizing of the scientist: namely, those of the explanation, prediction and change (technology) of the world around him/her. Corresponding to reconstructions of the structure of scientific theories developed within the philosophy of science, these functions can be fulfilled only if the respective cognitive system constitutes a complex aggregate with an – at least implicit – argumentational structure. This concept of argumentational structure does not only include deductive–analytical, but in particular also so-called substantial forms of conclusions (Toulmin, 1969); these substantial conclusions constitute a means towards generating 'new' knowledge. Which forms and structures of conclusions can in fact be part of this type of argumentational structure is, at present, deliberately left open as an issue to be investigated in greater detail in the course of the subsequent elaboration of the research programme.

On the basis of the above distinctions, 'subjective theories' can be approximately (in a first attempt) defined as: *cognitions relating to the self and the world constituting a complex aggregate with an (at least implicit) argumentational structure; these cognitions fulfil functions parallel to those of objective 'scientific' theories, namely those of explanation, prediction and technology.*

Secondly, there exists a deliberate connection between this construct of subjective theories and a specific *concept of human being* which may essentially be regarded as an elaboration of Kelly's model of 'man the scientist'. For the core assumption of a structural parallelism between naive and scientific theories implies a further parallel between the respective concepts of the human being: on the one hand the scientists' conceptualization of themselves as scientists, on the other hand their conceptualization of the subjects of their research. Consequently the research programme 'subjective theories' implies a definitive demand upon scientists to – as far as possible – develop and elaborate concepts of the human being which are equally applicable to themselves and the subjects of their research, concepts of human beings, that is, that do not lead to contradictions when applied to scientists themselves (the *tu quoque* argument).

This reproach of leading to pragmatic contradictions of the above kind can, however, be raised against the behaviourist model of the human being inasmuch as its core assumptions of stimulus control and reactivity are unable to explain the scientific process of the accumulation of knowledge itself (see Groeben and Scheele, 1977: 14ff.; Groeben, 1979). While in behaviourist experiments the subject of research (if a person at all) is controlled by environmental stimuli, it is the researcher him/herself who – due to the experimental method – actively controls the (experimental) environment. The research programme 'subjective theories' decidedly rejects and overcomes this contradictory asymmetry between scientists' ways of conceptualizing themselves and their subjects of research respectively. This implies that human beings as the subjects of research are (at least potentially) to be structurally characterized by those same qualities and abilities which the human being as scientist of necessity regards as part of his/her self-concept: verbal and communicational abilities, reflexivity, potential rationality and the competence to act (cf. Groeben, 1986: 63ff.). These characteristics have been summarized by Groeben and Scheele (1977) under the heading 'epistemological model of man'.

This concept of the human being has been developed in explicit contrast to the behaviourist model and the concept of behaving central to this model. Consequently the concept of acting (in contrast to that of behaving) is of correspondingly central importance to the epistemological model of the human being and hence to the research programme 'subjective theories'. Both within the psychology and the more recent (for instance analytical) philosophy of action aspects such as *intentionality, free decision, meaning(fulness), dependence on situation or context, goal-, norm- and so on orientation, planning and process control* (cf. Groeben, 1986: 71ff., 396ff.) are being posited as the defining characteristics of 'action'. These aspects are partially interlocked, any one logically following from the others. The subject's intentionality in particular already implies other aspects such as free choice, planning, goal-orientation and so on. In this sense the concept of intentionality can be regarded as summarizing the remaining characteristics by which actions are defined and has consequently been central to the explication of the concept of action. It is hence appropriate to employ the term 'action' whenever observable forms of behaviour can be described as intentional.

Since intentionality already implies the above aspects such as free choice, goal-orientation or planning, this type of description of an action as intentional always constitutes an interpretation of this same action as well. Actions are not to be viewed, then, as *per se* existent, physically observable events, but as 'interpreted events', or, more precisely, as interpretation constructs (Lenk, 1978: 345). This characteristic of interpretativity applies to the observer's description of another's action as well as to the agent's self-description.

There exists, however, one significant difference between the observer's and the actor's own description of an action: external observers can give a description of an action only *ex post actu* (cf. von Wright, 1974: 110ff.), whereas the agents themselves can furnish such a description even in advance of the action. This means that only the self-interpretative description of an action can be put into practice, that is, become 'operationally effective' (Lenk, 1978: 344ff.). Hence, it follows that in research on action one ought to rely primarily or at least in a first step on the agent's (intentional) self-description as a form of self-interpretation. This self-interpretation refers in the first place in a narrower sense to the intention 'behind' the action, that is the immediate goal which is to be realized by the action. This immediate goal brought about by the action directly is termed the result of an action; further effects, which in their turn depend upon this result, are termed consequences of an action and are as such to be distinguished from its immediate result.

Such an intentional description of an action refers first of all merely to the intention of achieving the immediate result. But at the same time this intention is, as a rule, embedded within a larger context to the extent that the agent attempts to achieve further consequences of the action as goals in a broader sense. Such further-reaching objectives constitute the (motivational) reasons which the agent him/herself regards as relevant to his/her intentions for acting and hence his/her actions. Thus the agent's self-description (or self-interpretation) of his/her intentions in a broader sense also comprises a heuristic concerning the motivational reasons as well as the effects of the respective action.

Subjective theories refer, then, mainly to the reasons and effects of human action (primarily one's own, but also that of others). In this context we find it useful to distinguish further between a motive system and a belief system. Statements within the motive system refer to the reasons for an action (motivational antecedents of the respective action). Statements within the belief system refer to the extent to which the respective result and in particular the broader consequences of the intended action (succedents of the respective action) can in fact be realized.

From this action-theoretical elaboration of the concept 'subjective theory' two additional characteristics of the term can be derived. First, with respect to the concept of human beings outlined above, especially the reflexive subject's potential rationality, it is important to ask whether or not the assumptions of the motive system and the belief system comprising the agent's subjective theories are indeed so rational as to be acceptable to the scientist testing hypotheses, that is as 'objective' theory. Second, such a study presupposes that these, in part highly complex, assumptions (of the agent) have been adequately understood and (linguistically) represented by the scientist. The adequacy of this representation can only be ascertained by establishing a consensus-in-dialogue with the subject of research; for only the agent (subject of research) him/herself has complete and direct access to the interpretative self-description, and can best decide whether or not a description of an action – presented by the scientist (as researcher) – is indeed adequate. Since this description is to function as a heuristic for scientific explanation, it must always be rendered in scientific language; hence, the corresponding consensus-in-dialogue between agent and scientist must necessarily imply an agreement upon a language game composed of both ordinary and scientific language and thus be equally acceptable to both parties. A consensus-in-dialogue upon an adequate description of an action thus always constitutes a reconstruction of the respective subjective theory in the form of a more precise explication of ordinary-language assumptions (cf. in detail below).

Adding these aspects to the characteristics of the concept of 'subjective theories' outlined above, a narrower and more demanding version of 'subjective theories' results (Groeben et al., 1988: 22). Subjective theories can thus be characterized as: (a) cognitions relating to the self and the world, (b) which can be realized and reconstructed through a consensus-in-dialogue between agent and scientist, (c) constituting a complex aggregate with an (at least implicit) argumentational structure, (d) which in parallel to objective (scientific) theories also fulfil the functions of (e) explanation, prediction and technology, (f) the acceptability of which as 'objective' knowledge stands open to exploration.

In comparison to the broader version of 'subjective theory' outlined earlier, I regard this narrower version as the stronger. The broad variant has the greater *potential for integration* insofar as the theoretical approaches mentioned above (such as implicit personality theory, attribution theory, meta-cognition, naive theories) can be subsumed under it. The narrower, strong version of the concept, however, possesses the greater *potential for reform*. For it takes as a starting point separate individual actions; it further assumes that the exact meaning of each of these actions can be adequately represented only through communication between the subject of research and the researcher, through methods of dialogical understanding, that is. This necessity of a dialogue-hermeneutical description of action constitutes a manifestation of the rational core of the dualist position, that is the thesis that the 'object' of psychology is to be understood as a reflexive subject and hence requires a methodology of understanding. Because of its potential of reform for psychology – thus far dominated by the empiricist methods of the natural sciences – I shall base the following analysis primarily upon this strong version of 'subjective theory'.

At the same time the starting point for overcoming the dichotomy between dualism and monism begins to emerge: while dialogue-hermeneutical methods are necessary for the comprehension of subjective theories (conceptualized in the above manner), understanding and the dialogue-consensual description of actions and subjective theories cannot be the final point of scientific analysis. A further question has to be raised as to whether the agent's intentions, motives (and in part the effects of the action as well) as given by him/herself are indeed correct in the sense of guiding his/her actions. Humans, of course, can err, not only the scientist but the naive psychologist as well. It is therefore essential to inquire and test whether the agent's *reasons* are really the *causes* of his/her actions (and in part to ask corresponding questions concerning the effects of the action as well). These questions bring the perspective of the explanation of action into focus; and it is this question of causal explanation which represents the rational core of the monist position. According to the metatheoretical perspective of the empirical sciences, the causes of an action can only be determined from the outside (third-person perspective) on the basis of a falsificationist programme. As a result, subjective theories in the strong version of the concept ultimately require both a dialogue-hermeneutical method for the description of action and a method based on observation (according to falsificationist criteria) for the purpose of the explanation of action. By virtue of thus achieving an integration of hermeneutical methods into the research programme, this joint procedure in my opinion represents, for the time being, the most promising point of crystallization for overcoming the dichotomy between monism and dualism, and is at the same time also an optimal starting point for overcoming the too narrow empiricist–monistic conceptions of science which have prevailed within psychology over the past decades.

Basic Types of Epistemological Explanation: Explaining Action through Subjective Theories

That a discussion about the causes of actions is taking place at all already implies the assumption that it is possible to explain actions within the traditional causal model. This question as to whether or not actions can be causally explained represents a moot point in the most recent phases of the monism–dualism controversy. Traditional exponents of dualism – the so-called intentionalists – assert that causal explanations of intentional phenomena are impossible or even pointless. Exponents of monism – so-called causalists – assume to the contrary that causal explanations of actions are possible as well as reasonable.

According to the intentionalist von Wright (1974) the causal type of explanation may be conceptualized as a covering law or *subsumption model* respectively. This basically means that the phenomena to be explained (explananda) are subsumed under corresponding laws and antecedent conditions specified in those laws (explanantia). The classic basic structure of the subsumption model is represented by the deductive–nomological type of explanation after Hempel and Oppenheim (1948). This model, however, is not applicable to the largely probabilistic laws of psychology; in the course of the past three decades, however, philosophy of science has yielded a wealth of proposals for liberalizing this model, ranging from inductive-statistical types of explanation and statistical analyses to a pragmatization of the concept of explanation and so on (cf. Stegmüller, 1979, 1983; Groeben, 1986: 202ff., 286ff.).

Among these various proposals, one may be considered decisive in the present context: the possibility of regarding, under recourse to a statistical concept of causality, the *weak* as a form of the *statistical–causal explanation* (Beckermann, 1977a). This requires only one postulate which specifies that effective reasons (causes) have to be 'positively statistically relevant' to an event (1977a: 39). This means that the so-called 'causing condition' must take place in advance of the event to be explained and render its occurrence more probable (1977a: 42). This formal explication of a weak concept of causal explanation largely coincides with the structure of the experimental testing of hypotheses in psychology (cf. Herrmann, 1969; Groeben, 1986: 112f.).

Even against the background of such a liberalized concept of causal explanation, intentionalists continue to maintain that causal explanations of human actions are in principle impossible. Among the many versions of this thesis, the classical concept of the teleological explanation constitutes the simplest and clearest example of the type of argument which the causalists consider sufficient evidence for maintaining the concept of causal explanation of action; it further illustrates the type of category into which non-causal (teleological or intentional) attempts at explanation may be translated. As von Wright proposes, the structure of a teleological explanation – which, according to him, is the only kind of explanation adequate to intentional actions – coincides with that of the so-called practical syllogism (1974: 93): '*A* intends to bring about *p*. *A* believes that he cannot bring about *p* unless he does *a*. Therefore *A* sets about doing *a*.' But as causalists point out in their counter-arguments, goals cannot be antecedents of actions because they are, after all, to be achieved by means of these actions; hence, goals are not acceptable as explanatory conditions. To elaborate: the actor may fail to achieve the intended goals, which is to say that in this case the action does not lead to the intended result (of course, the same point can be made even more strongly for the consequences of actions); in such a case it surely would not make any sense to say: 'an event, known to have happened, can be explained through another which will never happen at all' (Stegmüller, 1969: 533).[1]

What is acceptable as an antecedent condition of an action even where the intended result has not in fact been achieved is the setting up of a goal by the agent, which may be regarded as a motive. Since the setting of a goal or motive – as characteristics of the agent – falls within the scope of the model of the dispositional explanation, causal explanations of actions are to be classified as *dispositional explanations by motive*. The causalist assumption behind this classification is that each case of genuine teleology can be 'translated' into such a dispositional explanation by motive. A corresponding 'translation' of the above syllogism can be found for instance in Werbik (1978: 33):[1]

A1: The person is in the situation *S*.
A2: The person has the motive *M*.
L: Each person having the motive *M* will perform the action *A* in a situation of the type *S*.
E: The person performs the action *A*.

Recent discussions among monists (causalists) and dualists (intentionalists) have led to an extensive series of elaborations upon the impossibility of causal explanations of actions (such as the logical-relation argument, the redescription argument, the law argument, the good reasons argument). In my opinion, however, all these arguments can be refuted in a similar way as the above concept of teleological explanation (cf. Davidson, 1963; Bieri, 1981a; Groeben, 1986: 262ff.). In the present context it is more important that the practical syllogism can be regarded as the simplest (slightly reduced in complexity) form of a subjective theory, as a manifestation of the agent's first-person perspective. The practical syllogism may be said to possess an argumentational structure inasmuch as at least one 'deductive step' is made, a step which includes at least one component of both the motive system and the belief system.

If we retain the possibility of a ('weak') causal explanation of human action, the 'translation' of the practical syllogism into a dispositional explanation by motive can also be used to illustrate that and how a scientific ('objective' or causal) explanation of actions is possible with the help of subjective theories. For this purpose it is generally assumed that the dialogue-consensual reconstruction of a given subjective theory will (as a dispositional explanation by motive) possess a structure parallel to that of scientific explanation. In the final analysis, the usefulness of subjective theories for the purpose of 'objective' explanation thus depends largely on the degree of adequacy of the respective subjective theory to reality.

On this basis it is possible to deduce (on a highly abstract level) the most fundamental types of the so-called epistemological explanation as scientific explanation of human action under recourse to subjective theories (cf. in detail Groeben et al., 1988: 70ff.); they result as a combination of the two dimensions of subjective theories outlined above and their respective manifestations: first, the dimension of the relation to reality with the manifestations of adequacy versus non-adequacy to reality; second, the dimension of content where the aspects of the motive system and the belief system respectively are to be distinguished. From their combinations result the following basic types of epistemological explanation:

Type	Motive system	Belief system	
1	v	v	
2	v	$n-v$	*adequacy*
3	$n-v$	v	*to reality*
4	$n-v$	$n-v$	

In this case v stands for 'veridical' or 'valid' respectively; following the terminology of attribution theory (Jones et al., 1971: 16ff.), 'veridical' refers to the degree to which subjective theories, 'valid' to the degree to which scientific theories or explanations, are adequate to reality. In the above diagram only the letter v is used, since epistemological explanation is concerned with precisely the question whether the respective subjective theory is sufficiently veridical as to be acceptable as valid for the purpose of scientific explanation.

The first basic type (1) can be called 'fully motive- and knowledge-rational subjective theory'. This is the ideal case of an optimally rational reflexive subject whose subjective theory or explanation (of his/her own action) is adequate to reality to such a high degree (the motive system as well as the belief system) that it can be adopted unchanged as an 'objective-theoretical' explanation. Let us illustrate, using a fictitious example to demonstrate the differences between the four basic types of epistemological explanation (non-fictitious examples can be found in Groeben et al., 1988).

The structure of the examples is also supposed to illustrate the two central perspectives which will be elaborated below as a two-phase model of the structure of research: the subjective theory represents the agent's own inside view and thus a psychology from the first-person perspective – which is the reason for presenting this inside view in the first person; the adequacy of the subjective theory to reality, however, can only be assessed by means of observation from the outside and thus represents this outside view as psychology from the third-person perspective and will be presented in the third person.

(1) *Fully (motive- and knowledge-)rational subjective theory*

Subjective theory:
  I want to spread my ideas.
  I think I can achieve this by giving a paper at a conference.
  Therefore I shall give a paper there.
  (Because/If I want to spread my ideas and am convinced that I can achieve this by giving a paper at a conference, I shall give a paper there.)

Adequacy to reality:
  Motive system: He really does want to spread his ideas.
  Belief system: He is convinced, and it is indeed the case, that he will contribute to spreading his ideas by giving a paper at a conference.

'Objective' theory:
  If X wants to spread his ideas and is convinced that he will achieve this by giving a paper at a conference, he will give a paper at the conference (and will in this way contribute to the spreading of his ideas).

From the perspective of the subject's potential rationality, such a fully rational subjective theory constitutes no doubt the ideal case; but it is certainly not the statistical norm.

In terms of frequency, the second type of epistemological explanation is far more common. As in the case of type (1), the agent's cognitions concerning his motives are highly adequate to reality; he is, however, mistaken as to the relation between his action and its consequences. A scientific explanation of the action nevertheless has to take recourse to precisely this belief system lacking adequacy to reality. Wearing an amulet of copper, for instance, can only be explained by taking into consideration not merely the wearer's motive of wishing to avoid illness, but also his conviction that he can achieve this goal by wearing this particular amulet. To illustrate, we will again use the above example.

(2) *Motive-rational (but knowledge-irrational) subjective theory*

Subjective theory: as (1).

Adequacy to reality:
   Motive system as (1): He really does want to spread his ideas.
   Belief system: He is convinced that he will spread his ideas by giving a paper at a conference. But instead he does in fact frighten off his listeners by the obfuscating complexity of his statements.

'Objective' theory:
   If *X* wants to spread his ideas and is convinced he can achieve this by giving a paper at a conference, he will give a paper at the conference (and will thus frighten off his listeners by the obfuscating complexity of his statements).

The third basic type of epistemological explanation is the structural complement to type (2), except that in this case it is the motive system which lacks adequacy to reality while the belief system is to be classified as highly adequate to reality. This difference between types (2) and (3) is by no means negligible; on the contrary it demonstrates an asymmetry concerning the function of the motive system and the belief system respectively within an epistemological explanation. This asymmetry is of the highest importance. While in the case of the motive-rational but knowledge-irrational subjective theory recourse to the belief system, though lacking adequacy to reality, is indispensible, this does not apply to the third type of the knowledge-rational but motive-irrational subjective theory. Here no recourse is taken to the motive system which is inadequate to reality. A scientific explanation is always a dispositional explanation by motives. Consequently the scientist must in fact replace the subjective theorist's inadequate motivational assumptions by motivational constructs which correspond better to reality. The individual's inadequate reflections upon his/her own motives demonstrate what has been called 'rationalization' by psychoanalysis. In this case the scientist (in order to arrive at a 'scientific-objective' explanation) must determine the subject's 'real' motives 'from the outside', as the subjective theorist does not have conscious access to this motivational level. To continue the earlier example.

(3) *(Knowledge-rational but) motive-irrational subjective theory*

Subjective theory: as (1).

Adequacy to reality:
  Motive system: In fact he does not really want to spread his ideas but wants to meet his former fellow students.
  Belief system as (1): He is convinced and it is indeed the case that he will contribute to spreading his ideas by giving a paper at a conference.

'Objective' theory:
  If *X* wants to meet his former fellow students and believes that he wants to spread his ideas and that he can achieve this by giving a paper at a conference, he will give a paper at the conference (and will thus spread his ideas) (and in addition will/will not meet his former fellow students).

In the case of the fourth basic type of epistemological explanation, the subjective theorist's rationalized intention also has to be replaced by the motivation which the external observer regards as more 'real'. But, unlike in the case of type (3), the belief system also lacks adequacy to reality. This is the reason why this fourth type is called motive- and knowledge-irrational subjective theory.

The belief system's lack of adequacy to reality has the effect that – because the expectations concerning the consequences of the action are plainly wrong – not even the 'rationalized' motive (or goal) is satisfied (or reached), not even as a side effect. Since the scientific explanation in the case of the motive- and knowledge-irrational subjective theory requires that basically all subjective-theoretical assumptions concerning antecedents as well as succedents of the action be replaced (by 'objective-scientific' ones), this fourth type of epistemological explanation can be further divided into two sub-types. On the one hand (type (4a)) this replacement (parallel to the subjective theorist) can at least continue to employ the language of motivation; on the other hand it may occasion a shift into a behaviourist language game which presupposes a high degree of determination by the environment (type ((4b)). Both sub-types can again be illustrated using the above example.

(4a) *Motive- and knowledge-irrational subjective theory – motivational 'objective' explanation*

Subjective theory: as (1).

Adequacy to reality:
  Motive system as (3): In fact he does not really want to spread his ideas but to meet his former fellow students.
  Belief system as (2): He is convinced that he will spread his ideas by giving a paper at a conference, but instead he does in fact frighten off his listeners by the obfuscating complexity of his statements.

'Objective' theory:
  If *X* wants to meet his former fellow students, and believes that he wants to spread his ideas and thinks that this can be achieved by giving a paper at a conference, he will give a paper at the conference (and will thereby frighten off his listeners by the obfuscating complexity of his statements) (and will/will not meet his former fellow students).

(4b) *Motive- and knowledge-irrational or non-reconstructable subjective theory – behavioural 'objective' explanation*

Subjective theory: as (1) or non-reconstructable.

Adequacy to reality:
  Motive system: In fact he does not want to spread his ideas but needs the social recognition (which is available at any conference in the form of intermittent reinforcement).
  Belief system: He believes that he can spread his ideas by giving a paper at the conference, but in fact this will only create the expectation to be in turn socially recognized (reinforced) with those who reinforce him.

'Objective' theory:
  If *X* needs social recognition (in form of intermittent reinforcement at conferences), he will give a paper at the conference (and thus create the expectation of being reinforced in their turn with those who reinforce him).

These basic types of the scientific explanation of human action under recourse to subjective theories are yet to be elaborated substantially in the course of a corresponding research programme. Explications have so far focused upon subjective theories about one's own actions, but of course subjective theories about the actions, thoughts, emotions and reactions of others also have to be taken into account (cf. Groeben et al., 1988: 88ff.).

It is more important in this context, however, that the above types of epistemological explanation exemplify the possibility, even necessity, of clearly distinguishing between three different units of research in psychology: acting, doing and behaving (Groeben, 1986). Taking into consideration the definition of acting elaborated above, the concept of 'action' is, properly speaking, applicable to cases (1) and (2) only – those cases, that is, in which the actor's own description of his/her intentions makes sense and is justified because it is adequate in relation to his/her motives as they exist in reality. This coinciding of the actor's description of his/her intentions with the observer's dispositional explanation by motives is basic to the above concept of action as consciously chosen, goal-oriented, planned and so on. This implies the postulate that in the case of acting the relevant intentions and motives are recognized by the agent him/herself or are at least recognizable through self-reflection. This postulate is not generally raised in its present strict form within the theory of action; psychologists for instance tend to consider the concept of action to be compatible with only partial knowledge of one's motives, repressions and so on. I personally regard this latter concept of action as so broad as to be void in the final event. The discrepancy between (subjective) intention and (objective) motivation does, after all, represent a unit of research clearly distinguishable from that of action, exemplified by the basic types (3) and (4a) of epistemological explanation. This category of phenomena which ascribes to human activities precisely a subjectively unknown and unwanted motivation has above all been elaborated by psychoanalysis. There is clearly no point to labelling these phenomena 'actions'. Indeed, the supposition of a not-intended intention, of a non-deliberate deliberation, is a contradiction in terms (*contradictio in adjecto*). This contradiction can only be avoided by clearly distinguishing the category of the discrepancy between (subjective) intention and (objective) motivation as a separate unit of analysis from the unit of action. Nor does it seem to make any sense, however, to apply the term 'behaviour' to these phenomena, as the person concerned does have an internal-dispositional motive – and thus exerts a form of active control instead of being controlled by the environment.

In relation to this phenomenon (divergence of intention and motivation) the German everyday language offers an extraordinarily fitting term: that of *Tun* (doing). *Tun* already implies that the agent need not be fully aware of the meaning of what he/she is doing, and, what is more, that the meaning of the respective activity may also be 'not-intended' (involuntary). Inserting such an interim category (of doing) between the units of 'acting' and 'behaving' helps to avoid the unduly broad application of both the latter concepts, not merely that of acting, but also that of behaving. For over the course of time and as a result of methodological behaviourism, the term 'behaving' has come to be applied to nearly all psychological phenomena, ranging from internal (cognitive or motivational) processes to conscious, organized and self-controlled actions (cf. the criticism by Scheele, 1981). Furthermore, the above explication of the units of 'acting' and 'doing' permits us to limit the construct of 'behaving' (as in case (4b)) to its precise core, which was the original starting point proper of behaviourism: that is, to reactions controlled by the environment. These may well fulfil a function such as the adaptation to reality, but in their case no conscious or unconscious intention or motivation on the subject's side is to be assumed.

Distinguishing three fundamental units of analysis in psychology in turn necessitates the explication of three corresponding different modes of description. The *description of action* has already been introduced above as *intentional*. The explication of the other two categories makes it seem appropriate to speak of a *motivational description* in the case of 'doing', and of a *functional description* in the case of 'behaving' (cf. Groeben, 1986: 145ff.).

It ought to have emerged that the degree to which this kind of description of an action is useful or justified depends on the type of explanation that turns out to be adequate and successful respectively. Description and explanation are thus interdependent. This does not merely imply the traditional reconstruction within the philosophy of science (cf. Groeben and Westmeyer, 1981: 78f.) that any explanation is always an explanation on the basis of a description, but further: that any description is a description on the basis of an explanation (Groeben, 1986: 356). In connection with the core assumptions of the research programme 'subjective theories' outlined at the outset (in particular the assumptions relating to the concept of man), a very decided demand emerges as to the sequence of the units of analysis in research. At the beginning stands the attempt to describe and explain human phenomena on the level of the object unit 'acting'; only in case of failure at this level are we to switch to the description and explanation on the level of 'doing'. And only in a potential final step, following yet another failure, are models of 'behaving' to be considered. Only such a sequential structure is able to do justice to the reflexivity of the subject of research in psychology and make the greatest possible use of his/her potential rationality for psychological research instead of just giving it away or – even worse – missing and thereby distorting it, which in the final event leads to and constitutes a form of scientific reductionism of the 'object' of research.

The Two-Phase Model of Research: Communicative and Explanatory Validation

From these various anthropological, metatheoretical and theoretical premises a two-phase model of research methodology follows, a model that achieves an integration of understanding (by description) and explanation (by observation). If we conceive of subjective theories as the most highly complex and most structured form of the agent's reflections upon his/her own acting and doing (or someone else's reactions including his/her behaviour), then the first phase of research on human action must consist in understanding the agent's subjective theories. Since the agent's first-person perspective refers primarily to the reasons, intentions and aims of his/her own actions, the reconstruction of subjective theories constitutes in the first place an understanding through description of the reasons, intentions and aims of the human subject acting in a reflexive manner. This understanding of the reasons and aims given subjectively by the agent him/herself is the perspective which is brought into focus – nearly exclusively – by the dualist position.

At the same time, however, we are also concerned with the question whether the agent's reasons can be considered valid (from the perspective of the external observer) as effective reasons, that is causes of the activities in question – which constitutes the focal point of the monist position. Traditionally these two questions have been treated – unnecessarily so – as mutually exclusive. Both monism and dualism are in agreement as to this assumption, namely that we can only take either the *perspective of the first person* (*reasons* from the agent's inner point of view) or that *of the third person* (*causes* from the observer's outer point of view). They do, however, differ insofar as dualism considers the first-person perspective to be decisive and exhaustive, and monism raises the same claims for the third-person perspective.

It follows from the basic types of epistemological explanation outlined above that such a thesis of mutual exclusion is neither unavoidable nor rational. A psychology that focuses its research upon a subject capable of reflecting, communicating, reasoning and acting on the basis of his/her reasons must of necessity seek to identify and elaborate precisely those areas where the perspectives

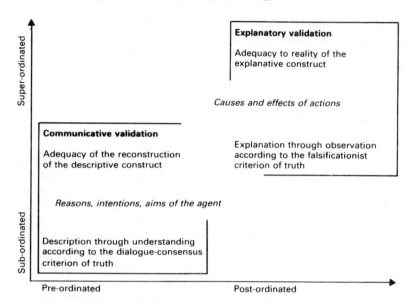

Figure 2.1   *Two-phase model of the research structure for the integration of communicative and explanatory validation (cf. Groeben, 1986: 326)*

of the first and the third person coincide; this psychology must 'elucidate those conditions of acting, which the agent himself may subjectively know to be his reasons and which are also considered effective reasons (causes) by the external observer' (Groeben, 1986: 323). This area where (the agent's) reasons and (the observer's) causes coincide (and likewise the area where intention and motivation diverge) can, however, only be determined if the structure of research in psychology constitutively includes a hermeneutic phase of understanding as well as a falsification phase of observation. The resulting two-phase model of research is illustrated in Figure 2.1 (see also Groeben, 1986: 326).

This model represents an integration of the traditions of hermeneutics and empiricism in psychology inasmuch as it does not merely put the two postulated phases of the research structure into a sequential order, but further succeeds in interlocking the two by separating the dimensions of pre- and super-ordination in a complementary manner. For the dichotomy of monism and dualism – regarding the claim to exclusive validity raised by both positions – has largely been characterized by each considering its preferred perspective (of the first or third person respectively) as pre- and super-ordinated in relation to the competing perspective. The integrative power of the two-phase model of the structure of research presented here rests upon the fact that here the two dimensions of pre-/post-ordination and sub-/super-ordination respectively are being considered as separate. It thus becomes possible to overcome the unduly broad application of the two positions by ascribing to each of them, in accordance with their respective rational core, the more relevant position on the one and – complementarily – the less relevant position on the other dimension.

In accordance with the above conceptualization of the explanation of action, the *phase of understanding* subjective theories through description is at once *pre- and sub-ordinated*. Similarly, the *phase of explanation by observation* is *post- but at the same time super-ordinated*. This separation of the two dimensions and the ascription of a position on those dimensions to both the traditional dualist and monist methods of research respectively constitutes the methodological application of the structural core of the epistemological concept of the human being explicated above. If we want to make use of the potential rationality of the reflexive subject, we must pre-ordinate the understanding of his/her reflexivity to the empiricist-observational testing; since humans can err and psychology hence is to answer not only questions about the agent's subjective reasons but also about the objective causes of an action, the observational phase of research is post- and super-ordinated to the phase of understanding by description. Since, however, this phase of observational explanation largely coincides with the traditional empiricist structure of research in psychology, the potential for reform of the two-phase model rests mainly upon the hermeneutical phase of communicative validation which always precedes that of explanation by observation.

Given the importance of this first phase of correctly reconstructing the respective subjective theories, we now turn to the question of how to ascertain their communicative validity. From our point of view this first phase of understanding the subjective theories has to be one of communicative validation (Lechler, 1982, after Klüver, 1979) for the following reasons. Individual actions are highly complex units of psychological research with individual–subjective dimensions of meaning (cf. in detail Groeben, 1986: 145ff.). An adequate understanding of the voluminous and complex contents and structures of the reflexive subject's first-person perspective, for which subjective theories are paradigmatic, can only be achieved by means of communicating with the reflexive subject as subject of research. Whether or not the scientist's description on the basis of his/her understanding is really an adequate representation of the subject's first-person perspective, only the subject of research him/

herself can decide. This is precisely the meaning of the term *consensus-in-dialogue as hermeneutical criterion of truth*. The scientist (researcher) enters into a dialogue with the subject of research in order to make sure that his/her understanding (for example, of the subjective theories of the subject of research) is indeed adequate. This adequacy may count as achieved if and insofar as the subject of research agrees with (or consents to) the scientist's description. Since a useful description in scientific language always constitutes an elaboration of the subject's thinking in everyday language, an adequacy of understanding (description) must needs be an *adequacy of reconstruction*. Hence, communicative validation consists of a reconstructive description (through understanding, for example, of subjective theories); the adequacy of this reconstruction is determined by establishing a consensus-in-dialogue with the subject of research.

This phase of the communicative validation of subjective theories presupposes that the reflexive subject has access to his/her cognitions, reflections and the like (that is, is capable of supplying accurate information about him/herself). It is precisely this assumption, however, that has been denied by Nisbett and Wilson (1977).

The subsequent controversy concerning these issues (cf. Smith and Miller, 1978; Rich, 1979; Ericsson and Simon, 1980; Cotton, 1980; Kraut and Lewis, 1982; White, 1980; Adair and Spinner, 1981; summarized by Groeben, 1986: 134ff.), however, has shown that Nisbett and Wilson's pessimistic assessment of the human being's capacity to give self-reports is largely to be attributed to the use of inadequate experimental methods and attempts at interpretation. As a consequence of this critique, Smith and Miller (1978) and Adair and Spinner (1981) concede that there might exist certain situations or areas where self-reports are not at all possible (or possible only with certain restrictions) – cases, that is (such as reflexes or automatisms), in which subjective theories might not be developed at all (see below). Of even greater importance, however, is the constructive question, in which areas and under what conditions the reflexive subject is capable of providing information about him/herself and how this information can be optimized. The sheer existence of this capacity – not always and everywhere, but in principle – ought to be beyond doubt; what must be done with regard to a hermeneutic phase of research of communicative validation is to identify and elaborate the conditions under which the reflexive subject's access to his/her own cognitions and reflections (especially in the form of highly complex aggregates) is optimal.

A framework for optimizing those conditions of access is offered by the *dialogue-consensus criterion of truth* (and the resulting regulative idea of the ideal speech situation). This dialogue-hermeneutical criterion of truth has been explicated by the Frankfurt School (especially by Apel, Habermas, Lorenzer) primarily in an attempt to reconstruct the methodology of psychoanalysis. According to Habermas (1968: 193), the reconstructive interpretations by the psychoanalyst will be therapeutically effective only if the client can adopt them as adequate and feels that they fit his/her life history. In the case of the phenomena relevant in this context, that is those relating to the first-person perspective (such as subjective theories), the truth of the respective statements depends upon the degree to which the speaker is rational and truthful.

Normally, the respective degree of rationality and truthfulness can be determined only on the basis of action; the adequacy or correctness of the latter is in turn again decided by consensus between actor and observer. In order to avoid the otherwise inevitable *circulus vitiosus* (effectively an infinite regress), Habermas (1968, 1973) introduces the 'ideal speech situation of discourse' as a prescriptive concept. A speech situation is ideal if system constraints of every kind are neutralized or excluded as far as possible. In this way systematic distortions of the communication can be minimized or avoided altogether. 'That speech situation is to be called ideal in which communication is hampered neither by external contingent influences nor by constraints which result from the structure of the communication itself' (Habermas, 1973: 255).[1]

Communication of the above kind that is free of distortions and constraints permits the communication partners to be truthful and hence justifies employing the concept of consensus-in-dialogue as a (hermeneutical) criterion of truth. This definition, however, explicitly concedes that the ideal speech situation constitutes not only a metatheoretical value concept, but moreover a value concept that will in most cases be counterfactual (Habermas, 1981: 71). The ideal speech situation is thus a regulative idea which implies that it will rarely, if ever, be fully realized in actual research; nevertheless efforts to achieve at least an approximation are possible and in fact necessary (Skirbekk, 1982: 57f.). This quality of counterfacticity, of being approximated but rarely, if ever, fully achieved in reality, is by no means restricted to the dialogue-consensual criterion of truth, but applies equally to the empiricist–falsificationist truth criterion (cf. Groeben, 1986: 97ff.). The elaboration of rules in accordance with speech-act theory for the success of argumentative–persuasive communication (happiness conditions) constitutes a first step in the concretization of the ideal speech situation (cf. Kopperschmidt, 1973: 87ff.; Groeben and Scheele, 1977: 178; Groeben, 1986: 179f.). A paradigmatic example of a method of this type which is especially oriented towards the consensus-in-dialogue as hermeneutical truth criterion is the Heidelberg Structure-Formation Technique (Scheele and Groeben, 1979/1984, 1988).

The second (post- and super-ordinated) phase of research of explanatory validation does not require further elaboration, being based upon the falsificationist truth criterion of external observation which characterizes the empiricist methodology of present-day psychology. Nevertheless it cannot be taken for granted that in this phase of research the currently employed experimental strategies are all equally suitable for determining the veridicality of subjective theories in relation to actions (that is, the degree to which subjective theories guide actions). In particular, the experimental method is contra-indicated for investigating the self-contained intentionality by which acting is defined (cf. Groeben, 1986: 243f.). The investigation of actions according to falsificationist criteria thus requires 'weaker' designs; particularly suitable are *correlation, prognosis and modification studies* (cf. Treiber and Groeben, 1981, 1983). In the case of correlation studies the subject's accounts of his/her cognitions (subjective theories) are correlated with observations of his/her behaviour at approximately the same point of time. In the case of prognosis studies a prediction of an action for a future situation is derived from the subjective theory at a certain point of time $t1$; the degree to which it is adequate to reality is tested at a later point of time $t2$ through observation. Modification studies constitute the closest approximation to classical (quasi-)experimental designs: the subjective theory is modified (at a point of time $t1$) in order to test (by comparing observations at the points of time $t1$ and $t2$) whether the subjective theorist's actions have changed in accordance with the modification of his/her subjective theories (cf. Groeben et al., 1988: 198ff.).

Though these liberalizations of empiricist methodology are by no means trivial, in this context they nevertheless do not constitute the most important aspect of the relation between the two phases of communicative and explanatory validation. The nature and importance of this relation emerges all the more clearly if one takes into account the fact that psychology up to now has been restricted almost entirely to the second phase of research. This phase, which has so far counted as 'standard' (the statistical norm), emerges against the background of the complete two-phase model of the structure of research as a special, reductionist case. This is not to say that this special case never occurs. We concede quite on the contrary that the complete two-phase model cannot be realized in all areas of research; examples such as reflexes, automatisms and so on have already been mentioned above (large parts of the psychology of perception certainly provide further examples; cf. in detail Groeben et al., 1988: 35ff.). Versions of the research structure in psychology falling short of the complete two-phase model are hence permissible by all means. In the case of 'doing', for instance, subjective intention and objective motivation of the actor do not coincide; the corresponding structure of research must fall short of the complete two-phase model inasmuch as the description of the actor's subjective intention is to be replaced by an 'understanding from the outside' on the part of the researchers, that is, a consensus among the researchers only to the exclusion of the subject of research. This latter approach may be termed monological hermeneutics in contrast to the dialogical hermeneutics employed in the complete two-phase model (Groeben, 1986: 124ff.). In the case of 'behaving', the research structure is reduced and limited to the second phase of the two-phase model, that is to explanative validation only.

In spite of the possibility of applying such reduced versions, the complete two-phase structure is to be retained and approximated as a methodological regulative idea of the highest importance. In the case of 'doing', for instance, a hermeneutical phase of reconstructing the first-person perspective in dialogue is indispensible – for how else is the divergence of subjective intention and objective motivation to be detected in the first place (compare the above basic types (3) and (4a) of epistemological explanation)? Of even greater importance, however, are the prescriptive dynamics which emerge as a result of relating the two-phase model to the different units of research. Against the background of the concept of the human being as capable of reflection, communication, rationality and acting, the complete two-phase model is to be considered of higher importance even if the largest part of psychological phenomena and processes were to be classified as behaviour and hence studied employing a research structure lacking the hermeneutical phase of description. Taking this concept of the human being as a starting point, the first step in research always ought to be the attempt to describe and explain psychological phenomena and processes as actions and switch to the lower units of research (lower in regard to the complexity of the respective dimensions of meaning) of doing and behaving only in case of failure on the unit level of acting. For only in this way can one do justice to the reflexivity and potential rationality of the human 'object' and thus achieve a non-reductionist form of psychological research.

Notes

For translation I am indebted to Angelina Meissner and Margit Schreier, and to the support of Kenneth Gergen.
   1 Put into English by the translators.

42　Everyday understanding and psychology

References

Adair, J.G. and Spinner, B. (1981) Subjects' access to cognitive processes: demand characteristics and verbal report. *Journal for the Theory of Social Behavior*, 11: 30–52.

Apel, K.O. (1979) *Die Erklären-Verstehen-Kontroverse in transzendental-pragmatischer Sicht*. Frankfurt am Main: Suhrkamp.

Beckermann, A. (1977a) *Gründe und Ursachen*. Kronberg, Taunus: Scriptor.

Beckermann, A. (1977b) Handeln und Handlungserklärungen. In A. Beckermann (ed.), *Analytische Handlungstheorie*. Vol. 2: *Handlungserklärungen*. Frankfurt am Main: Suhrkamp. pp. 7–84.

Bieri, P. (ed.) (1981a) *Analytische Philosophie des Geistes*. Königstein, Taunus: Hain.

Bieri, P. (1981b) Generelle Einführung. In P. Bieri (ed.), *Analytische Philosophie des Geistes*. Königstein, Taunus: Hain. pp. 1–28.

Bieri, P. (1981c) Materialismus: Einleitung. In P. Bieri (ed.), *Analytische Philosophie des Geistes*. Königstein, Taunus: Hain. pp. 31–55.

Bieri, P. (1981d) Intentionalität: Einleitung. In P. Bieri (ed.), *Analytische Philosophie des Geistes*. Königstein, Taunus: Hain. pp. 139–44.

Cotton, J.L. (1980) Verbal reports on mental processes: ignoring data for the sake of the theory? *Personality and Social Psychology Bulletin*, 6 (2): 278–81.

Davidson, D. (1963) Actions, reasons and causes. *Journal of Philosophy*, 60: 685–700.

Dilthey, W. (1894/1968) Ideen über eine beschreibende und zergliedernde Psychologie. Reprinted 1968. In *Gesammelte Schriften*. Vol. 5. Stuttgart: Teubner. pp. 139–240.

Ericsson, K.A. and Simon, H.A. (1980) Verbal reports as data. *Psychological Review*, 87 (3): 215–51.

Groeben, N. (1979a) Widersprüchlichkeit und Selbstanwendung: Psychologische Menschenbildannahmen zwischen Logik und Moral. *Zeitschrift für Sozialpsychologie*, 10: 267–73.

Groeben, N. (1979b) Normkritik und Normbegründung als Aufgabe der Pädagogischen Psychologie. In J. Brandtstädter, G. Rieviert and K.A. Schneewind (eds), *Pädagogische Psychologie: Probleme und Perspektiven*. Stuttgart: Klett-Cotta. pp. 51–77.

Groeben, N. (1986) *Handeln, Tun, Verhalten als Einheiten einer verstehend-erklärenden Psychologie*. Tübingen: Francke.

Groeben, N. and Scheele, B. (1977) *Argumente für eine Psychologie des reflexiven Subjekts*. Darmstadt: Steinkopff.

Groeben, N. and Westmeyer, H. (1981) *Kriterien Psychologischer Forschung*. Munich: Juventa.

Groeben, N., Wahl, D., Schlee, J. and Scheele, B. (1988) *Das Forschungsprogramm Subjektive Theorien*. Tübingen: Francke.

Habermas, J. (1968) Erkenntnis und Interesse. Frankfurt am Main: Suhrkamp.

Habermas, J. (1973) Wahrheitstheorien. In H. Fahrenbach (ed.), *Wirklichkeit und Reflexion*. Pfullingen: Nieske. pp. 211–65.

Habermas, J. (1981) Theorie des kommunikativen Handelns. Frankfurt am Main: Suhrkamp.

Hempel, C.C. and Oppenheim, P. (1948) Studies in the logic of explanation. *Philosophy of Science*, 15: 135–75.

Herrmann, T. (1969) *Lehrbuch der empirischen Persönlichkeitsforschung*. Göttingen: Hogrefe.

Jones, E.E. et al. (1971) *Attribution: Perceiving the Causes of Behavior*. Morristown, NJ: General Learning Press.

Kelly, G.A. (1955) *The Psychology of Personal Constructs*. Vol. 1 (2). New York: Norton.

Klüver, J. (1979) Kommunikative Validierung – Einige vorbereitende Bemerkungen zum Projekt Lebensweltanalyse von Fernstudenten. In Th. Heinze (ed.), *Lebensweltanalyse von Fernstudenten*. Fernuniversität Hagen. pp. 68–84.

Kopperschmidt, J. (1973) *Rhetorik*. Stuttgart: Kohlhammer.

Kraut, P.E. and Lewis, S.H. (1982) Person perception and self-awareness: knowledge of influence on one's own judgements. *Journal of Personality and Social Psychology*, 42 (3): 448–60.

Lachmann, R., Lachmann, J.L. and Butterfield, E.C. (1979) *Cognitive Psychology and Information Processing: An Introduction*. New York: Lawrence Erlbaum.

Lechler, P. (1982) Kommunikative Validierung. In G.L. Huber and H. Mandl (eds), *Verbale Daten*. Weinheim: Beltz. pp. 243–58.

Lenk, H. (1978) Handlung als Interpretationskonstrukt. In H. Lenk (ed.), *Handlungstheorie – interdisziplinär*. Vol. 2 (1). Munich: Fink. pp. 279–350.

Mey, M. de (1982) *The Cognitive Paradigm*. Dordrecht/London: Mouton.

Nisbett, R.E. and Wilson, T.D. (1977) Telling more than we can know: verbal reports on mental processes. *Psychological Review*, 84 (3): 231–59.

Rich, M.C. (1979) Verbal reports on mental processes: issues of accuracy and awareness. *Journal for the Theory of Social Behaviour*, 9 (1): 29–37.

Scheele, B. (1981) *Selbstkontrolle als kognitive Interventionsstrategie*. Weinheim: Verlag Chemie, Edition Psychologie.

Scheele, B. and Groeben, N. (1979/1984) *Die Heidelberger Struktur-Lege-Technik (SLT)*. Weinheim: Beltz.

Scheele, B. and Groeben, N. (1988) Dialog-Konsens-Methoden zur Rekonstruktion Subjektiver Theorien. Tübingen: Francke.

Skirbekk, G. (1982) Rationaler Konsens und Ideale Sprechsituation als Geltungsgrund? Über Recht und Grenzen eines transzendentalpragmatischen Geltungskonzepts. In W. Kuhlmann and D. Böhler (eds), *Kommunikation und Reflexion*. Frankfurt am Main: Suhrkamp. pp. 54–82.

Smith, E.R. and Miller, F.D. (1978) Limits on perception of cognitive processes: a reply to Nisbett and Wilson. *Psychological Review*, 85 (4): 355–62.

Stegmüller, W. (1969) Probleme und Resultate der Wissenschaftstheorie und Analytischen Philosophie. Vol. 1: Erklärung und Begründung. Berlin: Springer.

Stegmüller, W. (1979) *The Structuralist View of Theories*. Berlin: Springer.

Stegmüller, W. (1983) Probleme und Resultate der Wissenschaftstheorie und Analytischen Philosophie. Vol. 1: Erklärung und Begründung. Revised and expanded 2nd edn. Berlin: Springer.

Toulmin, S. (1969) *The Uses of Arguments*. Cambridge: Cambridge University Press.

Treiber, B. and Groeben, N. (1981) Handlungsforschung und epistemologisches Subjektmodell. *Zeitschrift für Sozialisationsforschung und Erziehungssoziologie*, 1 (1): 117–38.

Treiber, B. and Groeben, N. (1983) Vorarbeiten zu einer reflexiven Sozialtechnologie. In P. Zedler and H.H. Moser (eds), *Aspekte qualitativer Sozialforschung*. Leverkusen: Leske. 163–208.

Weber, M. (1956) *Wirtschaft und Gesellschaft. Grundriß der Verstehenden Soziologie*. Vol. 1. Tübingen: KTB.

Werbik, H. (1978) *Handlungstheorien*. Stuttgart: Kohlhammer.
White, P. (1980) Limitations on verbal reports of internal events: a refutation of Nisbett and Wilson, and of Bem. *Psychological Review*, 87 (1): 105–12.
Wright, G.H. von (1974) *Erklärung und Verstehen*. Frankfurt am Main: Fischer Athenäum. (English original: *Explanation and Understanding*, 1971, Ithaca: Cornell University Press.)

3

Psychology and Psychologic: Characterization of the Difference

Jan Smedslund

A decade ago, I first suggested the possibility of a scientific psychology based on the explication of psychological common sense (Smedslund, 1978a). The essence of the new position was formulated as follows: 'This viewpoint is that valid theoretical statements in psychology are explications of conceptual relationships embedded in ordinary language (common sense). This conceptual network is *anterior* to and organizes both our observations and our theorizing' (1978a: 1). Some analogies between Euclidean geometry and the new form of psychology were pointed out, notably that both consist of a system of logically necessary propositions, and that both are practically useful. They allow one both to predict the outcome of given procedures and to estimate their degree of success, through measuring the deviation from the logically expected outcomes.

This first statement was followed by a series of articles and a debate in the *Scandinavian Journal of Psychology* which has continued up to the present. (See Bandura, 1978; Smedslund, 1978b; Smedslund, 1979; Jones, 1980; Smedslund, 1980b; Smedslund, 1981; Sjoberg, 1982; Smedslund, 1982a; Smedslund, 1982b; Valsiner, 1985; Smedslund, 1986b; Smedslund, 1987c; Ray, 1988; Smedslund, 1988b.) In parallel to the above there have been several articles and discussions in other international publications. (See, for example, Smedslund, 1980a; Lock, 1981; Shotter and Burton, 1983; Smedslund, 1984a; Smedslund, 1984b; Tennesen, 1984; Vollmer, 1984; Wilkes, 1984; Smedslund, 1984c; Laucken, 1984; Smedslund, 1985; Smedslund, 1986a; Brandtstädter, 1987; Gelder, 1987; Smedslund, 1987a; Smedslund, 1987b.) The book *Psycho-Logic* (Smedslund, 1988a) further establishes the new position as an alternative in the international debate.

The term *psychologic* is introduced here to designate the position which in the publications cited was referred to as (explicated) *commonsense psychology*. Propositions in psychologic are explications of psychological common sense and have the form of logical implications. In order to be acceptable, they must be regarded as correct by all speakers of the language in which they are formulated. They indicate what *must* be the case *if* certain conditions have been established. They also mediate the inference that *if* the consequent does not occur, *then* the necessary antecedent conditions cannot have been established.

The aim of the present article is to characterize as precisely as possible the new psychologic, as it differs from current mainstream conceptions of psychology. I will try to characterize the concepts and propositions of psychologic in contrast to those of traditional psychology in terms of their definitional, ontological, epistemic, modal and descriptive versus normative status.

Operational versus Conceptual Definitions

Suppose that you are sitting in your car, waiting for the lights to change, and that the red lights are followed by clear blue ones. You will undoubtedly be surprised by this. I will use the phenomenon of surprise and this very simple example to examine in detail what is involved in changing from the traditional frame of reference of psychology to the position here called psychologic. (For more complex examples, see Smedslund, 1978a; 1981; 1984b; 1988a.)

Surprise is familiar to all of us. Nevertheless, it needs to be formally defined in a manner which makes it amenable to scientific study. Psychologists have traditionally tended to argue that psychological phenomena must be manifested in something observable, and preferably measurable, in order to be legitimate topics for scientific study. This is reflected in the popularity of so-called *operational definitions*. Published articles always contain precise descriptions of the methods and the resulting objective data, whereas it is rare to find formal definitions of the concepts involved and formal derivations from the concepts to the measures used. One seems to take for granted that the readers know what the words mean and what the measures measure.

Can one, then, give an adequate operational definition of surprise? The answer is negative. All efforts to find overt measurable behaviours characteristic of surprise and of surprise only are doomed to fail. The reason is that one may successfully *simulate* surprise and *hide* surprise. A scientific approach must allow one to describe and account for both of these alternatives. Their existence means that no overt behaviour or pattern of behaviours can be identified with surprise.

In order to bypass the possibility of simulation and hiding, one may speculate that there are bodily indicators characteristic of each emotion, witness the use of so-called lie-detectors. However, looking for patterns of bodily arousal which reliably characterize surprise and surprise only, one is faced with the problem of how to decide whether or not a given pattern of measured bodily arousal is correlated with surprise and only with surprise. Measured patterns of arousal do not, in themselves, have any surprise-like qualities. A possible answer could be that a certain pattern of arousal indicates surprise because it is found to be correlated with verbal reports of surprise. Such reports could be taken as reliable under conditions where both simulating and hiding were regarded as unlikely. These are conditions where the person's want to deceive, if any, is taken to be weaker than the person's want to be honest.

However, at this point one encounters the problem of the accuracy of the verbal report, even when it is taken to be honest. The verbal report is *about* something, namely surprise. But how can we know that the person's report of surprise is accurate? This is equivalent to the difficult question of how a person can know that he or she is surprised. This question means that one must distinguish between the reporting of being surprised and the actual state of being surprised. One option is to accept that, if a person is taken to be honest, then a report of surprise or of no surprise means that there *is* suprise respectively no surprise. But, whether or not this is accepted as a diagnostic convention, one must still ask *how* the person knows that he or she is surprised. This question cannot be neglected, because it is linked to another, strictly unavoidable, question: how do individuals acquire the ability to label correctly their own and others' state of surprise? This is a difficult question since one cannot rely on a unique set of necessary and sufficient bodily indicators. The reason is that, even if such a set could be found in the laboratory, it would be inaccessible to observation in the everyday social situations in which children learn to use the term surprise correctly. The preceding is not to deny that there is bodily arousal during surprise. It only denies that these bodily impressions can form the necessary and sufficient conditions for identifying surprise. What, then, can form a basis for learning to identify surprise in oneself and in others?

An obvious possibility is to state that surprise is recognized as being the result of experiencing something unexpected. Hence, surprise may be characterized as the state of a person who has experienced something unexpected. This definition allows us to diagnose surprise independently of overt behaviour and direct verbal reports, as well as of measures of arousal.

However, before accepting this definition, it needs some critical revision. When a car appears on a road which usually has much traffic, a person will not be surprised. This is so because, although the person did not specifically expect a car to arrive at that moment, he or she did expect cars to appear at relatively brief intervals along the road. Hence, the term surprise should be reserved for the case when a person has experienced something he or she has expected *not* to occur. However, this formulation is still slightly unsatisfactory. It is not the case that the person waiting for the traffic lights to change had *expected* that blue lights would *not* occur. More correctly, the person had *taken it for granted* that there would be yellow and green lights, and had not even remotely considered the possibility that the lights would be blue. Hence, a generally applicable definition of surprise should include both cases of definite expectation of non-occurrence and cases where non-occurrence is unreflectively taken for granted. Taking the preceding considerations into account we arrive at the following definition:

> Definition 1. '*Person* P *in situation* S *at time* t *is surprised*' = df 'P *in* S *at* t *is in a state of having experienced something that* P *had expected or had taken for granted would not occur.*'

What can be wrong with this definition? It provides the person with criteria for labelling as surprise his or her own as well as other persons' states. Also, it allows children to learn how to label their own state and the states of others, given that they have mastered the terminology of expectation, or in conjunction with mastering this. Obviously, similar considerations apply to the learning of terms of expectation, linked to other terms and so on. The question of how language as a whole system is linked to the extralinguistic world is left open here. What is asserted here is merely that single terms can and should be defined by their place in the system.

It is well known that the state of being surprised varies in *strength* from being very mild to being very intense. It is also obvious that the degree of surprise is routinely taken to correspond to the degree of unexpectedness of the event. Hence, strength of surprise may be defined as follows:

> Definition 2. '*The strength of* P's *surprise at experiencing* X *in* S *at* t' = df '*The degree of unexpectedness of* X *in* S *at* t *for* P.'

The degree of unexpectedness may, for example, be estimated by asking *P*, in advance, to judge the likelihood that *X* will occur in *S* at *t*.

One may be inclined to try to link strength of surprise to amount of measured arousal. However, again, degree of arousal can only be a symptom of strength of surprise, and presupposes criteria of strength of surprise against which the bodily measures can be validated. In conclusion, surprise and strength of surprise appear to be most usefully definable in terms of unexpectedness and degree of unexpectedness.

The preceding arguments, using the example of surprise, point in the direction of a general conclusion: psychological terms cannot be adequately defined by reference to particular overt behaviours, particular verbal reports or particular patterns of measured bodily processes. They can only be defined through their relationship to other psychological terms, and so on. *Descriptive psychological language forms an interrelated system, and the single terms are only definable through their place in this system.*

The preceding conclusion also summarizes one argument for a change from traditional psychology to psychologic. Traditionally, one has sought to anchor psychological terms, through operational definitions, to specific overt behaviours, verbal reports and/or physiological measures, while neglecting to give stringent conceptual definitions. I have tried to indicate, through one example, that this does not work. Another, very similar, example is the famous frustration–aggression hypothesis, where one has had to move from operational definitions of frustration and of aggressive behaviour, seen as empirically related, to conceptual definitions of lack of respect and of anger, seen as logically related. (See Smedslund, 1984b and 1988a.)

In psychologic, terms are assigned, by definition, to a place in a conceptual system. This use of conceptual definitions allows one to determine what follows or does not follow logically from given propositions, and, hence, to distinguish between logical and empirical relationships. This allows one to recognize the occurrence of *pseudo-empirical* research, that is, research attempting to test logically necessary propositions by empirical methods. In the example used here, this would amount to studying whether or not people who experience something they have expected or taken for granted would not occur, actually *are* surprised. Clearly, this can be known in advance, given the proposed definitions of the terms involved. It is equally clear that, if they appear *not* to be surprised, then something is the matter with one's diagnostic and/or other procedures. Therefore, pseudo-empirical research can always be redefined from being hypothesis-testing to being procedure-testing, that is, comparing the outcome of procedures with what is logically expectable. In traditional psychology, the general absence of sharp conceptual definitions means that one usually cannot decide between what follows and what does not follow from the descriptions used. Consequently, the question of pseudo-empiricality almost never arises and discussions about whether a relation between two variables is logical or empirical are rare. Data are always and automatically treated as empirical. It may even be inconceivable to many psychologists that actual findings *can* be non-empirical. (See, for example, Bandura, 1978.)

In summary, psychologic rejects the traditional psychological custom of relying exclusively on *operational definitions* (descriptions of concrete procedures and observations). Terms in psychologic are always defined *conceptually* and hence belong to an explicitly formulated system.

Objective versus Psychosocial Reality

The difference between psychology and psychologic also involves a difference in the *ontological* status of the domain studied. Ontology has to do with mode of existence. We can ask in what sense psychological phenomena, such as the state of surprise, are taken to exist.

Traditional psychological research is not very consistent in this respect and contains many different approaches. However, in reporting actual research, most of them would probably focus on objective measures such as marks on paper on rating scales and questionnaires, records of button-pushing, physiological measurements and so on. In other words, one gathers *objective* data (existing independently of persons), and treats psychological states as hypothetical constructs or intervening variables linked to these measures.

In contrast to the above, psychologic takes takes a *subjectivistic* position, and defines psychological phenomena as existing *for* persons. The state of surprise is one that exists *for* the person who has experienced something that he or she had expected or taken for granted would not occur. It should be noticed that the subjectivistic position applies also in the case where beliefs, wants, feelings, perceptions and acts are unreflective and automatic. From descriptions of what a person's behaviour is systematically related to (correlated with) in the surrounding psychosocial reality, one may infer something about what exists for and what does not exist for a given person in a given situation at a given time, even though that person does not and perhaps cannot report anything about it. The preceding means that what a person is unreflectively taking for granted is given the ontological status of existing *for* that person. It obviously cannot be said to exist independently of the person.

Psychologic as a system, although referring to what exists *for* persons, is exclusively concerned with what is regarded as correct by *all* members of a given culture or subculture. Hence, it is concerned with what I will call the structure of *psychosocial reality*. This term refers to everything which exists for and is shared by all persons in a given culture.

More specifically, the propositions of psychologic are explications of common sense, which is defined as follows: '*The common sense of culture* C' = df '*The system of logical implications taken for granted to be correct by every competent member of* C.' If proposition *A* is part of the common sense of culture *C*, and if the researcher is a competent member of *C*, it follows that he or she too takes it for granted that *A* is correct. The process of explication of common sense consists of a dialogue within one person or between several persons, in which tentative formulations are checked against what one already knows intuitively. The formulation finally selected ought to be stable over dialogues with successive groups of *informants* (who are judging the explicit formulation), and over trials with successive groups of *respondents* (who are acting according to the proposition without formulating it explicitly).

The preceding means that the development of psychologic consists in exploring a domain which is *well known* from the start. The researcher is at the same time explicating the structure of his or her own and the informants' mental life, and the structure of the psychosocial reality which exists for everyone in the given society. The dialogue leading to a proposition in psychologic is, obviously, another kind of process than the experimental probing leading to a theoretical formulation in psychology. This difference also involves a difference in the conception of the subject matter studied. Psychologic involves a knowledge which is tacitly shared. The explication of psychological common sense to form a system of psychologic is an undertaking which is assured of some success because, by definition, every competent member of a culture and speaker of a language has the requisite knowledge. Without such knowledge, individuals would not be able to manage their daily lives and could not be characterized as competent speakers of the natural language involved. Consider the example used here. From a relatively early age persons acquire the ability to arrange surprises for each other. In doing this, they avoid giving the person to be surprised any information about what is going to happen. In order to surprise someone very much, they try to arrange events which they believe are completely unexpected for the person involved. Thereby, they show in practical action that they have mastered the elementary propositions in psychologic presented in this article.

In summary, the shared character of language ensures that propositions in psychologic will be useful, once they have been perfected through dialogues between competent speakers of the natural language involved. The shared meanings of language belong to an existential realm (psychosocial reality) quite different from the objective one, which is independent of people. The reader who wants some other and richer examples of psychosocial reality may, for example, consider the meaning of the proposition 'it is Friday today'. This is a state of the world which exists for, and is maintained by, people. It belongs to a shared system of accounting for time, which yields innumerable predictions of individual psychological processes. For example, if it is Friday today, then it is Saturday tomorrow, and yesterday was Thursday, and so on.

The social nature of many psychological phenomena needs to be emphasized: consider again the example with the traffic lights. We may safely take it for granted that all the drivers encountering a blue traffic light will be surprised, given our knowledge of their expectancies. However, we may also, and equally safely, take it for granted that all the drivers will take it for granted that all the other drivers too are surprised. Moreover, we may take it for granted that all the drivers will take it for granted that all the other drivers will take it for granted that all drivers will be surprised. Finally, we may take it for granted that all the drivers will take it for granted that all the other drivers will take it for granted that all drivers will take it for granted that all drivers will be surprised. This mirroring effect reflects the thoroughly *social* character of the event. It is expressed in the following three axioms in *Psycho-Logic* (Smedslund, 1988a).

For every proposition X, *valid in culture* C, *there exists a proposition* Y, *valid in* C, *where* Y = '*Every person takes it for granted that* X *is valid in* C *for every person.*'

For every proposition X, *valid in culture* C, *there exists a proposition* Z, *valid in* C, *where* Z = '*Every person takes it for granted that every person takes it for granted that* X *is valid in* C *for every person.*'

For every proposition X, *valid in culture* C, *there exists a proposition* V, *valid in* C, *where* V = '*Every person takes it for granted that every person takes it for granted that every person takes it for granted that* X *is valid in* C *for every person.*'

These three propositions probably cover most of the applications of the mirroring in actual life. Nevertheless, by combining them, one may generate unlimited higher-order propositions, turning the social arena into a true hall of mirrors with successive reflections tapering off into infinity. Among other things, this means that people expect others who want to surprise them to hide information from them, and that they expect a second person to expect a third person who wants to surprise the second person to hide information from that person, and so on. In other words, to the extent that the propositions of psychologic are validly formulated, they describe a shared structure underlying human interaction. You know how to use the term surprise correctly, you know that others know this too, you know that they know that you know it. Psychologic capitalizes on the enormous amount of order involved in psychosocial reality.

In conclusion, whereas traditional psychological research has tended to rely on objective measures, psychologic relies on explications of consensual psychosocial reality, which exists only *for* the community of persons involved.

The Empirical and Contingent versus the *a Priori* and Non-Contingent

Psychological propositions differ in *epistemic* status, that is, they differ in *how* their truth can become known. The main distinction is between *empirical* and *a priori* propositions, and these may be defined as follows:

'P *is knowable empirically*' = df '*It is humanly possible to know* P *only experientially.*'
'P *is knowable* a priori' = df '*It is humanly possible to know* P *other than experientially.*'
(Bradley and Swartz, 1979: 150, following Kant.)

The alternative to knowing something experientially is to know something through *valid reasoning* from given premises. Knowledge arrived at through insight, intuition or revelation must be validated either experientially or logically in order to become scientifically acceptable.

Propositions also differ in their *modal* status, that is, with respect to categories such as *necessary*, *possible* and *impossible*. The main distinction here is between *contingent* and *non-contingent* propositions, and these may be defined as follows:

'P *is contingent*' = df 'P *is possibly true and possibly false.*'
'P *is non-contingent*' = df 'P *is either necessarily true or necessarily false.*'
(Bradley and Swartz, 1979: 14–16.)

In ordinary scientific discourse, disregarding certain philosophical discussions of limiting cases, it is generally accepted that there is a link between epistemic and modal categories such that a proposition is, normally, either *a priori and* non-contingent or empirical *and* contingent. Since there is no interest in necessarily false propositions, this means that there are only two scientifically interesting types of propositions, namely *a priori* and necessarily true propositions, testable by logical methods, and empirical propositions which may be true or false, and which are tested by empirical methods.

Let us now turn to a comparison of the propositions of psychology and psychologic with respect to combined epistemic and modal status. With reference to the example of the traffic lights, one may ask the following question: what is the relation between the perception of the event expected, or taken for granted, not to occur, and the state of surprise? The position of traditional psychology would, I think, frequently be that the perception of the unexpected blue lights *causes* the state of surprise. Accordingly, the actual occurrence of symptoms of surprise in drivers would be taken as *evidence* for the correctness of this allegedly empirical and contingent principle which may be formulated as follows:

Law 1. *If* P *in* S *at* t *experiences an event which* P *has expected, or taken for granted, not to occur, then* P *in* S *at* t *will become surprised.*

With respect to the quantitative aspect of surprise one may also formulate the following allegedly empirical and contingent proposition:

Law 2. *The strength of* P's *surprise at having experienced* X *in* S *at* t *is directly proportional to the degree of unexpectedness of* X *in* S *at* t *for* P.

If a person regards it as absolutely certain that an event will not take place, and that event nevertheless does take place, the person will become maximally surprised. Conversely, if a person regards it as absolutely certain that an event will take place and that event does take place, then the person will be not at all surprised.

Laws 1 and 2 are taken to be empirical and contingent by psychology since they link two operationally clearly different measures, namely judgements of presence versus absence respectively of degree of surprise on the one hand, and judgements of maximal versus minimal respectively degree of likelihood of an event on the other hand. Such focusing on operational measures *without* conceptual analysis is, in my view, typical of much of contemporary psychology. It involves a general lack of recognition of the fact that, even if a proposition is knowable experientially, that is, through data, this does not exclude its being knowable through reasoning too. Hence, it may actually be *a priori* and non-contingent. In other words, findings need not be empirical at all, but may be *pseudo-empirical*. As already mentioned, to do pseudo-empirical research means to attempt to test an *a priori* and non-contingent proposition empirically, which clearly does not make sense. Gergen (1982, 1987) and I (Smedslund, 1978a) have argued that perhaps *all* reasonable psychological propositions are *a priori* and non-contingent and, hence, *all* investigation of such propositions is pseudoempirical.

The difficulty with many empirical interpretations of psychological relationships is best recognized through considering the definition of surprise given above. If the reasons for selecting this definition are valid, then the relationship between the unexpectedness of an event and the strength of surprise takes on a very different epistemic as well as modal status. Inserting Definition 1 of surprise in Law 1 we get:

> *If* P *in* S *at* t *experiences an event which* P *has expected or taken for granted would not occur, then* P *in* S *at* t *will be in a state of having experienced something which* P *had expected or had taken for granted would not occur.*

This formulation is clearly tautological, that is, true in all possible worlds.

Similarly, if we assume that the reasons for selecting the given definition of strength of surprise are valid, and if we insert this definition (2) in the second of the alleged laws (2), we get:

> *The degree of unexpectedness of* X *in* S *at* t *for* P *is directly proportional to the degree of unexpectedness of* X *in* S *at* t *for* P.

Again, we get a tautological formulation, true in all possible worlds.

The preceding means that two principles, which might have been taken by traditional psychology to be empirical and contingent, turn out to be *a priori* and necessarily true, given the suggested definitions in psychologic. These definitions reflect a typical characteristic of the semantics of ordinary language. If a person encounters something which he or she has expected or taken for granted would not occur, then the resulting state is to be labelled *surprise, irrespective of its specific experiential, behavioural or bodily concomitants.* The advantage of this is to have a uniform label for a state which follows a very special type of situation, likely to lead to changes in the person. Children learn to use the label surprise to characterize this state, even though it has no defining characteristics at all, besides being subsequent to an event that was expected or taken for granted not to occur. This, in my view, is typical of the entire system of commonsense psychology embedded in language. Labels are applied relative to other labels on adjoining events, and the links to the content of what is referred to (the extra-linguistic domain), if there are any, are undescribable. Another way of fomulating this conceptual nesting is to say that there is an implicit *psychological calculus* built into ordinary language. The definition of concepts in terms of other concepts in complex structures makes it possible to formulate necessarily true propositions of the kinds presented above about unexpectedness and surprise and about the strength of surprise and the strength of unexpectedness.

It may be concluded that the difference between psychology and psychologic appears to consist, among other things, of a difference between empirical and contingent, and *a priori* and non-contingent propositions. In terms of the present example, this means that, whereas current mainstream psychology will tend to interpret the surprise of drivers upon perceiving the blue lights as an empirical finding (albeit trivial and definitely expected), psychologic will treat it as a necessarily true consequence of the expectations of the drivers.

One consequence of the difference which needs to be emphasized has to do with the interpretation of *negative* findings within the two traditions. In the empiricist tradition of psychology, a hypothetical finding that some drivers apparently were *not* surprised by the blue lights may mean different things. Either it may mean that one has not been able to establish the required conditions properly (for example, these drivers may have been forewarned by a friend that a psychologist had installed blue lights in a certain street crossing), *or* the diagnosis of lack of surprise was incorrect and *all* the drivers were actually surprised, *or* (as a last resort) the empirical law linking surprise to unexpectedness is weakened.

The position of psychologic has the comparative advantage of rendering any negative findings unambiguous as far as truth of the relevant proposition is concerned. If one observes a driver who appears to be not at all surprised by the blue lights, then there *must* be something the matter, either with one's diagnosis of his or her state, or with the arrangement of the conditions. The driver may be faking, or the lights were not really unexpected, and so on. However, not a shred of doubt is thrown upon the link between unexpectedness and surprise. At this point the analogy to Euclidean geometry is perfect. If the measured sum of angles in a triangle does not equal 180 degrees, then the deviation is attributed to a failure to establish the required conditions (faulty measuring instruments, imperfectly constructed triangles and so on), and no doubt whatsoever is attached to the corresponding Euclidean theorem. Proven propositions in geometry and in psychologic are similar in that they are normally taken to be empirically invulnerable. I have no quarrel with critics who, on Quinean premises, and in principle, argue against a completely sharp distinction between logical and empirical truth. However, in actual research one *must* make such a distinction every time one decides whether or not to regard a proposition as invulnerable to outcomes.

The preceding leaves at least one very salient problem unsolved, namely the question of how the *usefulness* of psychologic can be established. In traditional psychology the criterion has been the ability of a psychological theory to predict outcomes successfully. In psychologic the problem may appear less clear. Since propositions in psychologic are *a priori* and non-contingent, they are not sensitive to actual outcomes. How, then, can their usefulness be established? Obviously, logical consistency alone cannot be a sufficient criterion. If that were the case, then any logically consistent system would be equally useful.

Historically, the usefulness of Euclidean geometry was established without any systematic research, through a process of explication of already existing spatial intuitions and concepts. Geometrical theorems had to be proved but, after that, their applicability to practical problems was simply confirmed in actual practice.

What about the propositions of psychologic? How far is the analogy to geometry valid?

One way of checking their adequacy is to test their *correctness* as explications of commonsense psychology through dialogues with informants. Smedslund (1982b and 1982c) reported high degrees of consensus among informants concerning a number of theorems in psychologic. However, there is something peculiar about an undertaking of this kind. On the one hand, it is true that unless there is widespread agreement propositions in psychologic are useless for the purpose of prediction and explanation. On the other hand, the researcher does not expect, nor is he or she prepared to accept, a massive lack of consensus about the formulations. The reason is that formulations in psychologic reflect the researcher's well-tested and practically working understanding of the natural language involved. One knows in advance that, since language is shared, one is bound to get widespread agreement. Words such as 'surprise' and 'expect' simply mean what they mean in English, in given contexts, and it is a criterion of a competent speaker that he or she knows these consensual meanings. Words taken out of context may be more or less ambiguous, but consensus is strengthened when one considers the meaning of terms in given contexts. The more complete the description of the context, the more agreement will there be among informants.

It follows from the above that only two kinds of disagreement are to be expected concerning suggested propositions in psychologic.

One of them reflects a failure of the explicator of common sense to consider all the nuances involved. A good example of this was the revision of the definition of surprise from the simple formulation 'unexpected' to 'expected or taken for granted not to occur'. The correctness of this change is expected to be acknowledged by every native speaker when being reminded of cases such as the one with the blue traffic lights. In general, corrections of the way common sense is explicated into propositions of psychologic may be achieved through *dialogues* with competent informants.

The other kind of disagreement to be expected has to do with misunderstanding due to differences in assumed *context*. The context is the set of all factors which make a difference in the way something is understood. Informants may disagree with propositions in psychologic because they think of contexts in which the words used mean different things. The term surprise is relatively insensitive to context, yet there are contexts within which the definition of surprise given above may appear not to apply. For example, a person may be situated in a setting where he or she expects to be continually surprised. In this setting he or she may state something like 'I didn't encounter anything unexpected at all and I was very surprised by that.' However, it should be clear that, in this case, surprise was relative to a general expectation and not to the individual events. Also, persons hearing this statement will automatically interpret it to mean precisely that the person had expected to be surprised.

The preceding means that although, in principle, propositions in psychologic may be checked with respect to consensus, they probably will usually not be tested except through dialogues between researchers. In this respect too the analogy to ancient geometry appears to hold.

It may be objected to the above that a system of *a priori* noncontingent propositions cannot be used to make predictions in the real world. In the case of geometry Hempel (1949) makes the distinction between mathematical geometry and physical geometry, the latter being seen as a useful, but by the same token empirical, discipline. Hempel (1949: 249) ends by quoting Einstein as follows: 'As far as the laws of mathematics refer to reality, they are not certain, and as far as they are certain, they do not refer to reality.' I believe that Einstein's thesis applies to what I will call *objective reality* (that which exists independently of persons), but it does not apply to what I have called *psychosocial reality*. The reason why a person can know with certainty that *if* another person experiences something which he or she had expected or taken for granted would not occur, *then* he or she will become surprised, is that the person knows, by virtue of being a person in the given cultural–linguistic context, that this is the *correct* way of labelling events. Persons know much about each other because they know that they are *similarly programmed*. Their common conceptual system allows them to predict each other's experiences and acts. The premise for making predictions in psychologic is 'culturally–linguistically you are like me', and the question we ask is 'what would I do if I were in your situation?' In conclusion, a system of *a priori* and non-contingent propositions (psychologic) is predictively useful in the realm of psychosocial reality.

The Descriptive versus the Normative

Propositions in psychology and in psychologic differ in yet another way. In contrast to the *descriptive* propositions (laws) of psychology, propositions in psychologic must be characterized as *normative* (rules). This entails at least three salient differences between psychology and psychologic.

First, a valid natural law cannot be transgressed, whereas a valid rule can be. One *can* say 'I am very surprised, although I have nothing to be surprised about,' but this is an incorrect way of speaking. It does not make sense without additional assumptions. Any proposition in psychologic *can* be negated, but at the expense of its correctness and meaningfulness.

A second difference between laws and rules is that an actual transgression invalidates a law, but does not invalidate a rule. An obligation remains valid even though it is transgressed. A person may say, 'I am very surprised, but I have absolutely nothing to be surprised about,' and yet it is still valid that one cannot be surprised without having something to be surprised about. It is always possible to break a rule, but the result is behaviour which is incorrect. (I am disregarding here the special case in which the breaking of a rule leads to a change in the system of rules. See Valsiner, 1985; Smedslund, 1986b.)

Finally, a third difference between laws and rules is that, when a transgression of a rule occurs, there usually are direct or indirect *sanctions* from others. Laws are valid in themselves, and attempts to ignore or transcend them automatically fail because things are what they are. The propositions of psychologic are valid only by normative consensus and are maintained through sanctions. They reflect what are correct and meaningful ways of speaking and behaving and the criteria of this are thoroughly *social*. The definition of surprise given here is maintained through consensus of English-speaking persons and someone who talks about surprise in unacceptable ways is rapidly corrected. Hence, psychologic owes its predictive success to its being an explication of rules which people regard as correct and live according to. These rules are man-made and maintained by people, and hence are very different from natural laws.

It may be concluded from the preceding that whereas psychology has been looking for a natural order inherent in psychological phenomena in the same sense as physics has been looking for a natural order inherent in physical phenomena, psychologic is concerned exclusively with a *man-made* order. People have developed a system for making themselves intelligible and predictable to each other, and rely on and enforce this order in their daily lives. For example, at any given time each individual in a large city will tend to answer correctly a question about date, time of day and place where he or she is located, and will tend to behave accordingly. This ensures an immense predictability. Persons are constituted by this order and mutually assist each other in maintaining it.

Conclusions

The contrast between psychology and psychologic, described in this article, involves a difference between viewing psychological phenomena as occurring according to originally unknown natural laws, and viewing them as occurring according to tacitly well-known, but originally unformulated, social rules.

The approach of psychologic consists in making explicit the structure of the psychosocial reality which constitutes the individuals participating in it, and is itself constituted by their interaction. The amount of order built into this cultural–linguistic system is very high, and is what makes people describable, explainable and predictable to each other. In this domain, what is studied is entirely *man-made*, and can only be explicated by individuals already socialized into the given cultural–linguistic system. The basic concepts presumably embedded in this system should be defined as explicitly and sharply as possible. Only then will it be possible to know *what* a psychological measure measures, that is, exactly what follows from given observations in terms of the conceptual system. Since psychosocial reality is a human construction, it contains only what has been put into it, and therefore is, at least tacitly, well known to those who are constituted by it and are maintaining it. The truly unknown is encountered only when one moves outside the shared socio-cultural system to study how the individual's experiences and actions are influenced by, and influence, what goes on in the body.

One key to understanding the distinctions developed here lies in contemplation of the difference in publication practices between psychology and psychologic. In psychology, manuscripts containing exact descriptions of the measuring procedures used, but no formal definitions of the set of concepts involved, and no formal derivations of the measures from such definitions, are often accepted for publication.

In psychologic, the presence of rigorously defined concepts and formal derivations of measures from these concepts should be made a requirement for publication. This will lead directly to a general recognition of the following dilemma: either the proposed variables are logically related and, hence, the study is pseudo-empirical, or the proposed variables are logically unrelated and, hence, the outcome of the study is arbitrary as far as general laws are concerned. The latter conclusion follows because, in the domain of psychosocial reality, outcomes will have to be explained in terms of local, historically determined conditions, and history always has an element of chance. (See Gergen, 1973; 1976; Smedslund, 1979.) Also, the necessity of defining one's concepts explicitly will lead to a recognition of the unavoidable normative restrictions on what are correct explications of common sense, and, hence, on what are acceptable definitions.

This article has only described the formal differences between psychology and psychologic as alternative positions. The question of the extent to which these positions are in conflict, may coexist peacefully or may somehow merge has been left open.

References

Bandura, A. (1978) On distinguishing between logical and empirical verification: a comment on Smedslund. *Scandinavian Journal of Psychology*, 19: 97–9.

Bradley, R. and Swartz, N. (1979) *Possible Worlds: An Introduction to Logic and its Philosophy*. Oxford: Basil Blackwell.

Brandtstädter, J. (ed.) (1987) *Struktur und Erfahrung in der Psychologischen Forschung*. Berlin: de Gruyter.

Gelder, B. de (1987) Commonsense mentalism and psychological theory. In F. van Holthoon and D.R. Olson (eds) *Common Sense: The Foundations for Social Science*. New York: University Press of America.

Gergen, K.J. (1973) Social psychology as history. *Journal of Personality and Social Psychology*, 36: 309–20.

Gergen, K.J. (1976) Social psychology, science and history. *Personality and Social Psychology Bulletin*, 2: 373–83.

Gergen, K.J. (1982) *Toward Transformation in Social Knowledge*. New York: Springer.

Gergen, K.J. (1987) The language of psychological understanding. In H.J. Stam,

62   Everyday understanding and psychology

R.B. Rogers and K.J. Gergen (eds), *The Analysis of Psychological Theory: Metapsychological Perspectives*. New York: Hemisphere.

Hempel, C.G. (1949) Geometry and empirical science. In H. Feigl and W. Sellars (eds), *Readings in Philosophical Analysis*. New York: Appleton-Century-Crofts.

Jones, A.J. (1980) Psychology and 'ordinary language' – a critique of Smedslund. *Scandinavian Journal of Psychology*, 21: 225–9.

Laucken, U. (1982) Aspekte der Auffassung und Untersuchung von Umgangswissen. *Schweizerische Zeitschrift für Psychologie und ihre Anwendungen*, 41: 87–113.

Laucken, U. (1984) Von Setzungen und ihren Folgen. Dargelegt an Bespielen aus der Wahrnehmungspsychologie. *Psychologische Beiträge*, 26: 250–62.

Lock, A. (1981) Indigenous psychology and human nature: a psychological perspective. In P. Heelas and A. Lock (eds), *Indigenous Psychologies: The Anthropology of the Self*. London: Academic Press.

Ray, J.J. (1988) Semantic overlap between scale items may be a good thing: reply to Smedslund. *Scandinavian Journal of Psychology*, 29: 145–7.

Shotter, J. (1981) Critical notice: are Fincham & Schultz's findings empirical findings? *British Journal of Social Psychology*, 20: 143–5.

Shotter, J. and Burton, M. (1983) Common sense accounts of human action: the descriptive formulations of Heider, Smedslund and Ossorio. In L. Wheeler (ed.), *Review of Personality and Social Psychology*. London: Sage.

Sjoberg, L. (1982) Logical versus psychological necessity: a discussion of the role of common sense in psychological theory. *Scandinavian Journal of Psychology*, 23: 65–78.

Smedslund, J. (1978a) Bandura's theory of self-efficacy: a set of common sense theorems. *Scandinavian Journal of Psychology*, 19: 1–14.

Smedslund, J. (1978b) Some psychological theories are not empirical: reply to Bandura. *Scandinavian Journal of Psychology*, 19: 101–2.

Smedslund, J. (1979) Between the analytic and the arbitrary: a case study of psychological research. *Scandinavian Journal of Psychology*, 20: 1–12.

Smedslund, J. (1980a) Analyzing the primary code: from empiricism to apriorism. In D. Olson (ed.), *The Social Foundations of Language and Thought: Essays in Honor of Jerome S. Bruner*. New York: Norton.

Smedslund, J. (1980b) From ordinary to scientific language: reply to Jones. *Scandinavian Journal of Psychology*, 21: 231–3.

Smedslund, J. (1981) The logic of psychological treatment. *Scandinavian Journal of Psychology*, 22: 65–77.

Smedslund, J. (1982a) Common sense as psychosocial reality: a reply to Sjoberg. *Scandinavian Journal of Psychology*, 23: 79–82.

Smedslund, J. (1982b) Seven common sense rules of psychological treatment. *Journal of the Norwegian Psychological Association*, 19: 441–9.

Smedslund, J. (1982c) Revising explications of common sense through dialogue: thirty-six psychological theorems. *Scandinavian Journal of Psychology*, 23: 299–305.

Smedslund, J. (1984a) The invisible obvious: culture in psychology. In K.M.J. Lagerspetz and P. Niemi (eds), *Psychology in the 1990s*. Amsterdam: Elsevier Science Publishers BV.

Smedslund, J. (1984b) What is necessarily true in psychology? In J.R. Royce and L.P. Mos (eds), *Annals of Theoretical Psychology*. Vol. 2. New York: Plenum. pp. 241–72.

Smedslund, J. (1984c) Psychology cannot take leave of common sense: reply to

Tennesen, Vollmer and Wilkes. In J.R. Royce and L.P. Mos (eds), *Annals of Theoretical Psychology*. Vol. 2. New York: Plenum. pp. 295–302.

Smedslund, J. (1985) Necessarily true cultural psychologies. In K.J. Gergen and K.E. Davis (eds), *The Social Construction of the Person*. New York: Springer.

Smedslund, J. (1986a) The explication of psychological common sense: implications for the science of psychology. In R. Barcan Marcus, G.J.W. Dorn and P. Weingartner (eds), *Logic, Methodology and Philosophy of Science VII*. Amsterdam: Elsevier Science Publishers BV.

Smedslund, J. (1986b) How stable is common sense psychology and can it be transcended? Reply to Valsiner. *Scandinavian Journal of Psychology*, 27: 91–4.

Smedslund, J. (1987a) Das Beschreiben von Beschreibungen, Erklären von Erklärungen und Vorhersagen von Vorhersagen: paradigmatische Fälle für die Psychologie. In J. Brandtstädter (ed.), *Struktur und Erfahrung in der psychologischen Forschung*. Berlin: de Gruyter.

Smedslund, J. (1987b) Ebbinghaus the illusionist: how psychology came to look like an experimental science. In *Passauer Schriften zur Psychologiegeschichte*, 5, Ebbinghaus-Studien 2: 225–39.

Smedslund, J. (1987c) The epistemic status of interitem correlations in Eysenck's Personality Questionnaire: the a priori and the empirical in psychological data. *Scandinavian Journal of Psychology*, 28: 42–55.

Smedslund, J. (1988a) *Psycho-Logic*. New York: Springer.

Smedslund, J. (1988b) What is measured by a psychological measure? *Scandinavian Journal of Psychology*, 29: 148–51.

Tennesen, H. (1984) What is remarkable in psychology? In J.R. Royce and L.P. Mos (eds), *Annals of Theoretical Psychology*. Vol. 2. New York: Plenum. pp. 273–9.

Valsiner, J. (1985) Common sense and psychological theories: the historical nature of logical necessity. *Scandinavian Journal of Psychology*, 26: 97–109.

Vollmer, F. (1984) On the limitations of common sense psychology. In J.R. Royce and L.P. Mos (eds), *Annals of Theoretical Psychology*. Vol. 2. New York: Plenum. pp. 279–86.

Wilkes, K.V. (1984) It ain't necessarily so. In J.R. Royce and L.P. Mos (eds), *Annals of Theoretical Psychology*. Vol. 2. New York: Plenum. pp. 287–94.

4

Phenomenology, Psychological Science and Common Sense

Amedeo Giorgi

The philosopher . . . does not directly appeal to what the 'plain man' expressly asserts or believes. He finds it necessary to get behind this by a process of constructive interpretation. (G.F. Stout, 1931)

We shall no longer hold that perception is incipient science, but conversely that classical science is a form of perception which loses sight of its origins and believes itself complete. (M. Merleau-Ponty, 1962/1945)

Common sense and disciplined thought have an uneasy if intricate relationship with each other. The relationship is uneasy because the boundaries between them have not always been clear and one side has frequently sought ascendency at the expense of the other; the relationship is intricate because, ultimately, they need each other. Amazingly, the short epigram by Stout that opens this paper either shows or implies all of the complexities of the relationship between common sense and disciplined thought. The necessity for common sense is revealed when the philosopher finds that he must turn to the 'plain man', but its insufficiency is also demonstrated when the philosopher admits that he does not appeal to what the common man expressly asserts. The intricacy is revealed when the philosopher finds that he or she must somehow 'go behind' the explicit assertion, yet the assertion remains the focal point even as he or she tries to go behind it. Finally, a further complexity is uncovered since the process of 'constructive interpretation' is itself something that has to be grounded and common sense may play a role in the grounding, especially if acceptance of the lay community is to be involved.

Of course, the relationship is even more complicated than the above analysis expresses because the process is dynamic. The outcomes of disciplined thought filter into common sense, and thus common sense is influenced by the state of the art of disciplined thought, but rarely ever is such knowledge appropriated in the way that disciplined thought itself understands it. (Obviously, I am using 'disciplined thought' as a generic term for scholarly pursuit whether it be philosophical, scientific or professional.) The knowledge emerging from disciplined thought gets accommodated to the criteria of common sense and it is often forgotten that this switching of context means that the same interpretations usually do not prevail. On the other hand, disciplined thought often begins its specialized elaboration by uncritically taking over meanings that belong to common sense and thus may carry over inadequate hidden assumptions for its more specialized context. Thus Merleau-Ponty's epigram is provided as a reminder that no matter how important science may be as a corrective to common sense, it is not ultimate. Therefore, there is a reciprocal tension between the two perspectives that can never be eliminated even though careful analysis can possibly account for the relative role of each perspective.

A Phenomenological Psychological Analysis of Lifeworld Descriptions

Although there are many available interpretations of such terms as 'phenomenological', 'psychological', 'common sense', 'science' and so on, the present analysis follows the perspectives of Husserl (1931/1913; 1970/1954) and Merleau-Ponty (1962/1945; 1963/1942). I do not claim to follow them literally and I speak about issues which they have not directly addressed. In my view, a phenomenological analysis essentially means an analysis of descriptions from within the perspective of the phenomenological reduction which teases out the essential meanings of the experiential descriptions through a process of free imaginative variation. To do a *psychological* phenomenological analysis means that the descriptions come from others and that psychological essences are being sought rather than philosophical ones, although free imaginative variation is still used. (See Giorgi, 1985, for further details.) Assumed within this process is that the initial descriptions come from naive subjects in the everyday world (lifeworld; commonsense perspective) and the scientific analysis transforms them into psychological (scientific) expressions. Thus the very activity of psychological phenomenological analysis presupposes the relationship between common sense and science. The reason this relationship is so blatant in the phenomenological approach is that from a phenomenological perspective it is clear for theoretical reasons that mainstream psychology has not assumed the most adequate perspective with respect to psychological phenomena and thus the approach to the psychological has to be taken up again.

The easiest way of demonstrating the major point of this article –

how a phenomenological psychologist deals with the relationship between common sense and science – is to draw from a concrete application. Accordingly, presented below is an interview taped by one of my students about the experience of a situation in which someone learned. The phenomenon of learning was the focus of the research even though from an everyday perspective, obviously, a lot more was included. I will present here only the interview itself and the observer's description.

Naive Description

Subject: You know I left my restaurant downtown to come here. All I wanted was a little delicatessen. Just what I needed for my retirement, and I thought I was rid of all the problems. Now, after last night I wonder if I can keep it up.

Researcher: What happened? I thought things were going well for you here.

Subject: They were. That is I thought they were until last night. I learned so much last night and now I don't know what I should do.

Researcher: What did you find out?

Subject: I learned about these girls [waitresses]. Last night with the snow and all, the young crowd came here. This place was packed and business was great. Then I realized the girls were cheating. We must have cooked hundreds of hamburgers, but when I went over the slips only a few people had paid for hamburgers. The girls gave their friends all this food and only wrote them a slip for a coke or a cup of coffee. This has been going on for months. Last night I caught them. I really didn't know what to do. I felt like I wanted to hit them; then I felt like crying because of all my hard work trying to make a go of it here. I learned that after all these months these girls don't have any respect for me. . . . I also found out that they don't give a damn about their jobs. So I fire them, what do they care! All they are concerned about is getting a date for Friday night and giving away my food.

In my restaurant downtown it was different. The girls wanted to work; they needed jobs to keep their families. These kids today don't give a damn about anything. I don't know how much money I've lost. What a fool I have been! I've really been stupid! I learned last night what a foolish mistake it was to come here. I know now that I just can't handle young kids. I could hardly stand to come here today. I talked to them this morning and they just laughed and talked behind my back. Now that I know all of this, I don't know what to do. I guess I started out wrong. I think I need to get some new people and start all over again. This time in the beginning I'm going to be tough. Everyone will know from the start who is boss. We won't have the same problems. This time they are going to respect me. I learned last night that you sure can't run a restaurant unless you are respected.

Researcher: How was it that you learned all this last night?

Subject: I don't know. I guess I was watching more than usual and I knew we had sold lots of hamburgers. I watched and listened to these kids. If I had stayed blind to this whole thing much longer, they would have walked off with the store. I was just too trusting and I wanted to be their friend. That doesn't work – you can't be the friend and the boss. You can't run a restaurant without respect. No sir, old Harry isn't going to be fooled any longer.

General Description of Situated Structure of Learning

Learning is awareness of the necessity to reorganize a personal project based upon the discrepancy between the implicit assumptions brought to a situation vital for the continuance of the project and the perception and understanding of the actions of others in terms of the project in the same situation. It is also manifested in S's discovery of the fact that he is prereflectively and ambiguously living out two conflicting roles with respect to the others involved in the project and in the ability of S to circumvent the difficulty by imagining he can choose to live out the project in terms of the preferred role in an unambiguous way.

I will first make some preliminary comments about some aspects of descriptive research that may be unfamiliar, but then I will concentrate upon the performance of the phenomenological reduction within a psychological context not only because it seems to be a key stumbling block to the understanding of the phenomenological approach but also because it seems to fly in the face of common sense. The overall value gained by this emphasis will be an actual demonstration of how science goes beyond common sense – clarifying and transforming – even while presupposing it.

General Comments

I shall begin with the reasons I have for obtaining descriptions from subjects as primary data. First of all, the phenomenological approach is descriptive and most properly belongs within the context of descriptive science. This means both that the primary data are descriptions of situations which are either experienced by a subject or observed and described by the researcher or a colleague, and that the results provided by the researcher are also descriptive. However, the latter descriptions are written with technical terms and within the perspective of the discipline of psychology. Thus, as mentioned above, phenomenologically motivated research in psychology intrinsically involves the relationship between common sense and science.

Phenomenological terms for common sense are 'the natural attitude' or 'the lifeworld perspective'. The natural attitude refers to the normal pre-reflective attitude within which we do our daily living. It would also include the host of taken-for-granted assumptions underlying most of our activities. The aim of phenomenological analysis would be to understand the natural attitude better than it understands itself, and, in order to accomplish that goal, a break from the natural attitude would be required and for phenomenologists it would mean the assumption of the phenomenological attitude. The idea of the 'lifeworld' is a concept that Husserl emphasized in his later writings and it has multiple meanings (Carr, 1987; Scanlon, 1988). The term has been taken up in several ways, but the ambiguity is in Husserl (Scanlon, 1988). According to Scanlon (1988: 2), the assumption of a phenomenological attitude towards the lifeworld means 'critically, reflectively, achieving a stance that makes it possible to remember the indispensable involvement of experiences and practices of the lifeworld in the technological enterprise of modern science, an involvement that is easily forgotten under the spell of the impressive rational results of that science'. As Scanlon (1988: 6) observes, such a description can be taken to mean a presence either to the 'world of pure experience' or 'to the concrete surrounding world'. One could perhaps relate these two meanings by saying that one must turn first to the 'concrete surrounding world' and then try to be present to it from a perspective of 'pure experience' in order to understand how the concrete surrounding world got to be the way it is.

The restaurant description presented above, for example, is basically a description containing a spontaneous expression about an event in the life of the subject even though it was obtained by means of an interview. Indeed, it is even an event that stands out for the subject and he reflects upon it in a concerned way. The subject reports his experience under the aegis of learning, the theme of the research. However, it should be made clear that the research really implies two meanings of learning: learning$_L$, a lifeworld sense of learning, which is a naive sense because it expresses the way in which learning is lived and implicitly understood in the everyday world; and learning$_P$, a psychological sense of learning, the task of which is to clarify what learning may mean from a psychological perspective with the hope that the latter, in turn, might help clarify the way in which learning is lived or thought about in the everyday world.

In a way, the phenomenological approach makes the beginning of psychological science more transparent, in part because it actually *is* beginning, but also in part because its theoretical orientation values the question of origins. Thus, rather than create a situation in a lab, such as mainstream psychology does (assuming that learning takes place within it if action takes place because the researcher structured a task that with high probability could lead to learning), I decided to get descriptions from subjects about everyday experiences that they would select as learning experiences from their own naive perspective. The difference in point of departure also reflects a difference in outlook. Even though recognizing that it is not perfect, the traditional research psychologist assumes that the behaviour of the subject in a situation is largely determined by the situational variables; the phenomenologist recognizes that the subject's attitude or stance towards the situation is active and that in addition to the behaviour expressed the subject's experienced meanings also have to be taken into account. For example, a researcher could construct a learning task, but a subject may subsume the performance of the task under the rubric of 'frustrating' or 'anxiety-provoking' even if performance did reach criterion. Could such a subject simply be numbered among the learners without qualification? On the other hand, it should be appreciated that in phenomenological research the research question emphasizes a concrete description of the situation, and not the subject's motives for selecting the situation, nor the subject's reflections upon, or opinions about, the situation insofar as it is a learning situation for him or her. In such a way, the description exceeds the subject's own awareness about learning and thus is not reducible to the subject's reflections about it.

As mentioned above, these descriptions become the primary data of the research, which, of course, must be analysed. While the major theme of this essay is to articulate the meaning of the phenomenological attitude for which the reduction is essential, a word about the assumption of the psychological attitude is necessary. Numerous theoreticians in the history of psychology have argued that presence to psychological reality depends, in part, upon the assumption of a proper attitude (see, for example, Titchener, 1929) and phenomenologists accede to that line of thought. The presupposition here is that psychological reality is not 'ready-made', but rather must be constituted. Now, it is readily granted that the precise and comprehensive meaning of psychology is not yet an historical achievement even if one is not entirely mute on the issue (Giorgi, 1982). Nevertheless, it is also admitted that psychological praxis, in a mixed way, does genuinely access psychological reality even though psychological theory lags in its ability to express well this concrete access. Thus the view adopted here is that one should forge ahead with the praxis with the hope that theoretical clarification will follow.

One implication of the assumption of the psychological attitude that should be stated is that a psychological analysis will be more narrow than the lifeworld description because the latter contains much more than merely psychology. However, if the psychological analysis is of value, it is because it deepens lifeworld understanding even though the increased depth is obtained necessarily at the price of breadth. One cannot analyse all of the implications of a description, but one can examine the whole description from the perspective of the psychological attitude that the researcher has assumed.

Now, I want to turn to the phenomenological perspective that informs the psychological praxis. As indicated previously, to be phenomenological, one has to employ the reduction, seek the essence of the phenomenon being experienced with the help of free imaginative variation, and then describe the results. For reasons of space, I shall limit my discussion to issues surrounding the reduction. However, by detailing the issues involved with the performance of the reduction, I will also be demonstrating the phenomenological approach to the relationship between common sense and disciplined thought.

The Reduction
To place oneself within the perspective of the phenomenological reduction means two basic things: (1) to put out of play all knowledge about the phenomenon being researched in order to be fully present to and freshly experience the phenomenon under scrutiny, and (2) to refrain from making existential or ontological claims about what is being experienced so that the sense of the experience can be more precisely clarified.

I shall begin with the second point because it is less problematic. Phenomenologists are concerned with the precise way in which things and events present themselves to consciousness, and because of this concern for the mode of presence, they refrain from saying that things or events *are* the way they present themselves. This attitude is neither one of denial nor one of doubt but precisely one in which nothing is posited even though what is present is explored. Moreover, nothing that was present in the natural attitude is lost within the reduction; on the contrary, since nothing is to be taken for granted within the reduction, the person assuming it should be present to more than the one remaining in the natural attitude. The attitude being described here is not unlike that of the traditional researcher carefully inspecting his or her data before arriving at a conclusion, wherein one tends to weigh all factors before ascertaining their genuine value.

Now, it is obvious that this meaning of the reduction breaks with common sense. Here, what seems strange is that the phenomenologist wants to understand things or events precisely in their relationship to the awareness one has of them. In the natural attitude, things and events are experienced as being wholly independent of consciousness. For the natural attitude, events happen 'out there', and consciousness is somewhere hovering about one's head, and they are two independently unfolding activities that occasionally, by chance perhaps, get correlated in some mysterious way, and then go on their separate ways again. Thus the phenomenological insistence that the sense of things and events are constituted (neither created nor caused) by consciousness seems strange to the natural attitude. Of course, it is the intentional relation that is being described here as a way of accounting for awareness of regular realities in a non-causal way. Even though the scientific attitude may be ultimately responsible for the natural attitude of today, any non-causal relationship would fly in the face of common sense.

I shall now try to clarify the first meaning of the reduction because that seems to be the most problematic point for non-phenomenological scientists and even for many who are sympathetic to phenomenology. The problem is that everyone wonders how one is to empty oneself of one's history, prior experience, language, acquired skills and so on, and go back to a position other than the way one understands oneself in a personal, biographical way. The assumption underlying this perplexity is that one must somehow, existentially, become some kind of 'null point'. This is not Husserl's meaning (cf. Scanlon, 1988). Rather, to assume the reduction means to bracket that knowledge which is relevant to the issue at hand but not yet intuitable in the current situation or its experiential horizons, and to become aware of the senses in which past or other extraneous sources of knowledge might have an effect upon the originary experience taking place at the moment. In other words, one only wants to attend to the ongoing presence to the issue as it forms itself in the consciousness of the researcher, and not to many other concomitant processes that are also going on, such as associative connections (this reminds me of another description), questions (I wonder what will happen next), doubts or hesitations (I'm not sure about how to handle this).

There is a certain sense in which one is functioning in a split way. One allows one's spontaneous responses to the experiential presentations (either perceptually or by means of descriptions) to happen the way they happen, but one is also critically evaluating them rather than simply accepting them. It is not as though one prevents certain types of meanings, images, thoughts and so on from happening. Indeed, one encourages them to take place. However, one does not simply pounce upon them uncritically, nor even merely accept them, but rather slowly and cautiously one tries to clarify, as far as possible, just why these particular meanings or thoughts and so on appear at this moment in the process in order to see what possibilities exist for the resolution of the problem at hand. One also takes the time to give full recognition to the mode of presence of the meanings, ideas and so on so that one can identify them, in terms of both their concrete meanings and their origins.

Another point of clarification should be mentioned. When Husserl speaks of the desire for presuppositionlessness, total presuppositionlessness is not meant. Mere presuppositions are not contrasted with total knowing, but with evidentiary presences, necessary presuppositions and classified taken-for-granted ones. What is allowable are intuitable givens or necessities that obviously belong to the situation. What is not allowable are gratuitous assumptions that will enable one to keep moving on a problem or to circumvent certain types of difficulties merely for the sake of keeping moving or circumventing. One should not even turn to psychological theories with known speculative contents, such as psychoanalysis, for example. If we turn to the example provided above, what would be allowable as 'givens' would be that the subject presents himself as a male living in twentieth-century America who appears to be experienced in running restaurants but who is encountering a problem in his new situation. Everything said thus far is totally supportable intuitively by the description. What would not be allowable would be to presuppose that the subject is unmarried and that he wants younger waitresses about him all day because he is lonely for female companions. Such a presupposition is wholly gratuitous, even if plausible, because there is absolutely no descriptive support for it. What would be equally unsupportable would be to assume a psychoanalytic perspective towards the description and then try to account for the subject's relationship with the waitresses in terms of a fixation in the psychosexual development of the subject according to psychoanalytic theory. The theory itself has speculative aspects and its application to the description is also tenuous. Thus a phenomenologist would not make those moves.

I would like to explore the meaning of the reduction further by referring to the first part of the third statement by the subject in the above example. It is the section where the subject starts by saying 'I learned about these girls [waitresses] . . .' and it goes down to where he says, 'This has been going on for months. . . .' Now, even though I am a psychologist, I am required by phenomenology to put out of play all my psychological 'knowledge about' learning. Thus I do not think about reinforcement, learning curves, sign-Gestalt theory, or any other concept or specific study of which I am aware. I also acknowledge that I have performed many phenomenological psychological analyses of learning similar to this one before, but I also must not let those analyses influence this one. Since I am dealing with a very particular, concrete description of learning from an ordinary person randomly chosen from everyday life it really is not so difficult to bracket the concepts and language of traditional learning theory. The concepts do not readily apply to such lifeworld descriptions (although they could be made to apply).

It is probably harder to convince the non-sympathetic reader of my ability to bracket the previous phenomenological psychological analyses of learning. Yet I believe I do that, and perhaps I can describe the process sufficiently so that one can see how it is possible to do so. First, it should be appreciated that all of the steps of the phenomenological method are deliberately open-ended so that only the content of a description can close off the methodological step and not on *a priori* content criterion. Perhaps it is better to say that the criteria are non-specific and empty and only when an actual intuition is experienced with its specific qualities can one know that the criterion has been fulfilled. Since phenomenology is meaning-oriented, only a grasping of the meaning of a description (or behaviour) will satisfy the methodological step, and these descriptions are usually generated by others. Thus the researcher's consciousness grasps a meaning generated by others, but it is the researcher who discovers the boundaries of the meanings because to establish meaning units (one of the methodological steps), one must experience the transition in meanings provided by the description from a psychological perspective which only the researcher assumes. That is, the subject himself or herself should never consciously be in a psychological attitude. All content possibilities exist in the determination of a meaning unit, from one word to a page. The point for the issue at hand is that one must really get into the description or phenomenon under study in an experiential way to accomplish this step and since the concrete phenomenon is always new, one exceeds what one knows. It is the open-endedness of the method that provides the fresh possibility each time of transcending one's 'knowledge about'. Thus, even though I have determined countless meaning units before, they are of no help now because this is a completely new description. In other words, the criterion 'establish a psychological meaning unit by assuming a psychological perspective towards a lifeworld description' is so empty that only a sensitive presence to the content currently available could genuinely satisfy the criterion.

Now, of course, one can always ask: 'How do I, as an interested colleague, know for sure that you didn't falter, and let a past memory or an uncritical association determine the closure of the task rather than the appropriate fresh attentiveness to content?'

Well, there are no guarantees; there are only checks and balances. When I offer my findings to the appropriate community of scientists, they can criticize my results and *offer counter-evidence* that my findings do not hold up. The counter-evidence of course would also have to follow phenomenological guidelines, but it would take me too far afield to try to spell those out here. The major point is that dialogue with a peer community is possible.

Another way of saying that the bracketing is possible is to recall that one is able to distinguish knowledge from experience. Phenomenology wants to emphasize the concrete experience not the 'knowledge about' the event or the phenomenon. To be sure, there is a close relationship between knowledge and experience and past knowledge more often than not serves as a proximate context for ongoing experience, but nevertheless they are distinguishable. For example, confronted with the Müller-Lyer illusion, one *knows* that the lines of the two figures are equal, but still one experiences the line with arrowheads at the ends as shorter. Or often in going into a test one *knows* that one is wholly prepared, but still *anxiety* can be experienced. It is this differential that phenomenology capitalizes upon in order to bracket knowledge and be present to experience.

Thus far we have been merely treating a particular sense of the reduction, namely the ability to bracket past theoretical 'knowledge about' a phenomenon so that one can be present to a concrete instance of it directly and freshly. But the meaning of the reduction also includes the idea that I should not let particular biographic factors such as my personal history or my first language influence my analysis either.

Consequently, I now want to turn to the difficult areas of history, sociality and language. In what sense can these be bracketed, and in what sense still present? I shall turn to history first, and I immediately find that two histories are present, that of the researcher and that of the subject. Of course, the above statement obviously already implicates sociality and language since a description is the basis of my knowledge of the subject's history. (In general, in the human realm, there is always concomitancy in the sense that when one human dimension is present all others are also at least implicitly present. Thus concrete analyses of human phenomena must proceed by a selective thematization.) I will first deal with the subject's historicity, or perhaps I should say 'temporality' since future references are equally present and important. One has only to read the first paragraph of the subject's description and the fact that the subject has a past oriented towards a future immediately strikes one. He was the owner of a restaurant downtown and he wanted to prepare for his retirement, so he opened a new deli in a different part of town, at which he is currently experiencing problems. It is within this temporal project that the learning occurs.

Of course, I do not know all of the particulars of the subject's project, but only what is revealed and implied within the description. But enough is revealed to provide a sufficient sense of the subject's project so that a minimal, meaningful, contextualized understanding of the learning is possible. One could obtain more information, of course, but, on the other hand, one has to be careful not to fall into the trap of the 'fallacy of completeness' (that is, the expectation that more data will solve a theoretical problem. There will always be an open-ended horizon to a description and the method has to deal with open-endedness as such). In sum, then, the temporality of the subject is unfolded with the description. Within the reduction, one considers it precisely as it presents itself without claiming that it is exactly as it presents itself.

Now I shall consider the historicity, or temporality, of the researcher. Of course, biographically speaking, I was trained as a psychologist and have practised as one for many years. Moreover, I have developed a method of phenomenological analysis and have applied it to descriptions of learning more times than I can enumerate. Yet I am required by the phenomenological procedure to bracket all of the above, it would seem. However, to be more precise, I am required to bracket all of the *past achievements* so that they do not predetermine what I will discover this time, but I could use whatever procedural gains I have acquired from past experience to help me be more open to the present experience so that I can capture it more fully. Thus there is a transfer over from past experience in a sense, but it is meant to be limited to procedural matters. What is prohibited is the thrusting of past achievements on to the contemporary task, but skills acquired in remaining open or in being critical could obviously carry over. It should also be recalled that my role as a psychologist does not exhaust my identity. I am constantly encountering my naivety in everyday life, such as when I read about the federal budget, nuclear weapons or have a car problem explained to me by a mechanic.

But, of course, the objection goes deeper than this. The historicist will legitimately point out that much of my contemporary understanding is something that was learned over time and that it plays a critical role in all of my ongoing openness to the world of experience. Indeed, one might even go so far as to claim that without such a developmental, historical framework there would be no intelligibility whatsoever. That is indeed a common refrain heard from empiricists. But if taken completely literally, as Merleau-Ponty (1964/1961) has noted, it would prove too much since one could never then break out of what has been historically determined and thus 'the new' could never come into history. Because of empiricism's bias on experience, and because experience is primarily backward-referencing, history looms large as determinative. However, the model for the phenomenologist's detachment from experience should be more like the way one is aware of the future. At any given moment how is one open to what is about to come? The typical empiricist answer is to project the past into the future, which, in effect, is to say that there is only the past. But there are experiences in which the unexpected crashes in on our present concerns, or experiences in which one is receptive to 'what is about to come', with only the vaguest outlines in anticipation of the coming event. Now, these outlines, while present, should not be construed as being determinative of the coming event, for clearly they are often unfulfilled (consider a gambler's expectations!). Descriptions of experiences of the future are being used here to show the non-reducibility of present consciousness to historically determined consciousness. If true, then aspects of a given moment of consciousness of a human subject can be non-determinatively constituting, and it is this or these aspects that one tries to reach within the reduction. But this relatively freely constituting consciousness must be forged into a role in order to perform its function. To demonstrate this I'll turn to the example again.

In my analysis of the first paragraph spoken by the subject I said that the psychological meaning was 'S reveals a personal project involved with an experience which makes him doubt if he can sustain the project.' Now, in what sense can one say that that statement is either historically determined or historically transcended? Note, what is being analysed is a description of a constituent in its essential aspect, not its factual aspects. To be sure, to be a restaurant owner and to be mindful of one's retirement by opening a deli does imply a certain moment in world history, before which it may not have been conceivable. But I can imagine numerous historical epochs in which a human might have a personal project that begins to be doubted. But how did I come up with that statement? To my knowledge, I have never written a statement precisely like that before. One can appeal to the unconscious, of course, but I would say the burden of proof is on those who would want to construe such an interpretation. Rather, I would say that I opened up to the psychological meaning of the statement, intuited it and then described what was intuited in such a way that it withstood critical evaluation. It is also a meaning that transcends my personal consciousness in the sense that what emerged was based entirely upon the descriptive data and not my own opinions. Again, of course, without a background of language, socialization, enculturation and so on, I would not have been able to utter or describe the sentence. But one has to distinguish between 'conditions that make possible' and the actualization of any possibility. The recognition of this fact seems to be the heart of the matter. Subjectivity plays a role in actualization even if historical dimensions are at work in making the conditions of subjectivity possible. It would be reductionistic to claim that all human phenomena are always reducible to their conditions exclusive of subjectivity.

Ironically, even as I reflect and meditate and try to see in which way I may yet be historically determined, I experience myself as transcending historical determination, but of course, not historical limits. For example, if I try to project myself to 100 years from now and try to imagine myself analysing the same description, I find that I am, at least initially, somewhat paralysed. I do not know what the conscious structure of a late-twenty-first-century psychologist will be. I find that I can only answer the question speculatively, and I want to avoid that. But I can imagine that such a psychologist will understand 'entertaining doubts about a personal project based upon a certain experience'. Similarly, if I project myself back into the late nineteenth century, I have a better feel, of course, for how a psychologist might relate to the same description based upon historical knowledge, readings and so on, and again I recognize that the twentieth-century language used in the description might be a bit curious for a nineteenth-century psychologist and that some words (for example, a Coke) might be puzzling, but I can easily imagine that the psychologist could understand 'having doubts about a personal project'. Thus the essential description does not require that one gets into the actual historical structure of other times, but precisely one which is relatively liberated from such concerns. Thus I am able, to a certain extent, to detach myself from historical conditions even as I recognize historical limits (I can't get into twenty-first-century consciousness, and I can only vaguely assume the attitude of nineteenth-century consciousness). One could perhaps summarize this point by saying that there are indeed empirical constraints to the transcending powers of consciousness, but the empirical constraints are not totalizing; they can be transcended.

The above discussion of history has already led to sociality and so I will take up that issue next. Doesn't the social precede, succeed and surround me? Isn't it larger than I am? So in what sense can it be said to be bracketed?

The first relatively liberating move, of course, is the very assumption of a social perspective so that the extensive trans-personal organizing power of the social is brought to awareness. Again, there are two socialities, the subject's and my own. When I read the subject's descriptions, I recognize that delis are organized by others in a very special way and that other people that come in may have myriad motivations entirely different from mine and that the successful running of a deli implies, behind the scenes, countless jobbers, tradesmen, deliverymen and so on, all operating within their own spiralling network of interpersonal and social relations. I can imagine the network spinning increasingly outward and I realize that I can never get to the absolute starting point of these social relationships. By a kind of imaginative transfer, I then realize that something similar is true for me, the researcher. I am wearing clothes made by others, using pencils and papers manufactured by others and, again, I don't really know that I could get to the precise source of these relationships. I also recognize that in both cases it would be worthwhile to get at the origins of the social relations, in the sense that such knowledge would be beneficial for my understanding, but I realize that it cannot be done. Consequently, I become aware that my knowledge must be gained against the ground of this factual indeterminacy. Then the thought occurs that I must try to see to what extent social factors may be determining what I am responding to in the subject's description and perhaps contingently affecting what I want to say. I would want to bracket such contingencies so that only essential or relevant contingent factors play a role.

For example, it is clear that both the subject and I share a North American context when it comes to understanding the description. Moreover, I immediately know what a deli is – a peculiarly American type of eating place which, ironically, often features European foods but, unlike Europe, has tables so that the food can be eaten on the premises. Thus, factually speaking, it is important to share social and cultural factors to understand a 'deli'. But once I express the importance of the first paragraph insofar as it is essentially relevant for psychological learning, I say that the subject is embarked on a 'personal project which gets challenged'. Thus all of the specific meanings of deli are no longer relevant, even though I initially had to know what it meant in order to express the first part of the subject's description in terms of a 'personal project'. Factually speaking, I do have to know what a deli is, and perhaps some appreciation of the type of eating place that is connoted by the term is helpful, but I do not necessarily have to know its social origins in order to make sense of the subject's relation to it in terms of the research perspective, which is the meaning of the deli with respect to the subject's experience insofar as it is a learning experience.

The same is true with respect to my own social origins. Whatever influence my parents, my peers, my childhood relationships may have had upon me, when I try to grasp the subject's relationships with his current waitresses in an essential way, I do not let those factors influence me. While I may experience my biographical contingencies determining my sympathies for either the subject or the waitresses, my judgement is based not on those sympathies, but on essential matters. Thus I may feel sorry for the subject because his employees are cheating him, and let us assume that these sympathies are felt because I come from a working-class background and I really can appreciate what it is like to work hard and then see no return for it. Nevertheless, my intuition into the essential meaning of the subject's relation to his waitress insofar as it is revelatory of learning has to be based upon evidence relating to the description which is there for all to see and not upon my sympathies based upon biographical contingencies. After all, this is no different from what we expect judges to do. An older southern judge, for example, may be prejudiced against blacks because of his upbring-ing, but if a black accused of a crime is brought before him, one expects him to decide the case based upon the evidence and not his contingent biographical background. What is required theoretically is that an attitude of consciousness can be assumed that can apprehend the objective aspects of the phenomenon under study. A denial of this possibility is a denial of all science, not just its phenomenological form.

Now I'll turn briefly to language, even though the argument will follow the same pattern. Of course, I can agree that in many instances the language one speaks shapes and determines percep-tions, feelings, opinions and so on, but it is not wholly determinative. If it were, how could one even utter something new, or how could translations occur, not only between languages but also between language and other modes of expression, such as music, for example?

In those moments when language is transcended it is because a meaning or event evokes an expression that accurately characterizes the state of affairs being observed. Language is both an open-ended system and a dynamic one. It evolves and changes, but it can only do so through speakers, who must be responding to something non-linguistic in order to be able to contribute to the evolution of a language. A language that changed only because of internal pressures would soon dry up. In the case at hand, for example, that is, the description of constituents of the psychological essence of a concrete description, in each case I find myself confronted with a gap that is filled with tension. I often must express myself in a way that I initially find to be puzzling. I concentrate on the problem, I read the appropriate section of the concrete description again, I then think of the task before me, and then I begin to wonder how I can express the intuited meaning. More often than not, certain forms of expression come to my awareness and I compare them, sometimes, with the 'tense gap' and I find them lacking, until at last words form and I find them fitting. Sometimes this is done with genuine excitement as I discover expressions I never believed could be realized, and other times I begrudgingly accept modes of expression that I hope I will be able to improve upon later. The point of this description is to show that I am being guided by a non-linguistic presence that language is being called upon to express through me. If true, not all linguistic expressions are completely determinative. The process is more dialectical than that.

The arguments presented above against social, historical and linguistic determination, as opposed to influence, are all based upon subjective initiative. That is, the claim is made based upon intuitive evidence that subjectivity is active and constituting with respect to the world and that, while it is influenced and modified by all sorts of factors, it is always capable, in principle, if not factually, to take a stand with respect to these factors.

Thus the above reductions show that an absolute starting point in the sense of total conditionlessness is not demanded, as well as that a totality of understanding is equally not necessary. What *is* necessary is a transcending of the many forces that modify subjectivity and the establishment of relevancy boundaries. Thus I do not know the historical origins of all of my biases – the point is that I am to approach the description according to a clarified perspective, but not a bias. Or if I accept a bias, then the results must be accepted as correlated with the bias. Thus, the issue is not the origin of my biases, but my ability to rise above them. The same would be true of social relations, linguistic usages and all other influential factors.

Concerning the Relationship between Common Sense and Science

I shall try to draw some conclusions with respect to the science–common sense relationships in a phenomenological vein. The epigram by Stout more or less expresses the conventional wisdom with respect to the relationship between science and common sense. While common sense may hold sway in daily life, it is ultimately held to be insufficient and thus the motivation for a scientific perspective is introduced. It is then held that the scientific perspective completes the commonsense one, even if this involves an overturning of the results of common sense. Thus Stout's cautions with respect to the opinions of common sense are deserved. Since science, within its own perspective, is superior to common sense, the implication here is that over the long haul scientific understanding should replace commonsense understanding. Thus Skinner's (1948) concept of psychological Utopia is based upon this premise.

Merleau-Ponty's epigram, however, expresses a different vision and it would imply all that I have tried to explicate in terms of the reduction. To conceive of science as a form of perception is, in a way, to reintroduce an Achilles' heel into the process and to throw doubt upon the completeness of science. The first viewpoint does indeed suggest a Utopian vision: science will correct and complete all the limitations of everyday life. The second viewpoint suggests that such a vision is illusory because it is forgetful of its grounding in the same processes of perception that function in everyday life. To be sure, there is a difference between lifeworld perception and scientific perception, but that is due to the context of understanding that operates within science which is more explicit, clarified and universally uniform. However, the increased precision is obtained through a narrowing of perspective. To assume that there can be a perspective that assumes all perspectives, that is, a view that could be as comprehensive as everyday life but as precise as science, is the illusion that tempts all that hold the first view. Science, in that sense, cannot replace common sense.

In the second view, science, too, is dependent upon perceptual processes of a subjectivity that can be either veridical or false – the same processes that lifeworld perception is dependent upon. The implication here is that both science and common sense have their ways of overcoming the limits of perception, but, of course, differently. Since most thinkers do hold that perception is limited, Husserl's call to return to the 'world of pure experience', one of the meanings of the reduction mentioned above, is precisely to try to clarify the nodal point of vulnerability in the realm of experience, and this nodal point is operating in science as well as everyday life. The clear implication here is that these subjective perceptual processes can never be avoided, even if they can be transcended when truth is achieved, and, insofar as science will always presuppose them, it will always be vulnerable in this sense because the achievement of truth is not guaranteed. Thus it behooves science not to be forgetful of them.

References

Carr, D. (1987) The lifeworld revisited: Husserl and some recent interpreters. In D. Carr, *Interpreting Husserl*. The Hague: Nijhoff. pp. 227–46.

Giorgi, A. (1982) Issues relating to the meaning of psychology as a science. *Contemporary Philosophy: A New Survey*. Vol. 2. The Hague: Nijhoff. pp. 317–42.

Giorgi, A. (1983) Common sense and science: adversaries or friends? A comment on Luckmann. *Phenomenology and Pedagogy*, 1: 80–6.

Giorgi, A. (ed.) (1985) *Phenomenology and Psychological Research*. Pittsburgh, PA: Duquesne University Press.

Gurwitsch, A. (1974) *Phenomenology and the Theory of Science*, ed. L. Embree. Evanston, IL: Northwestern University Press.

Husserl, E. (1931/1913) *Ideas*, trans. W.R.B. Gibson. New York: Macmillan.

Husserl, E. (1970/1954) *The Crisis of European Sciences and Transcendental Phenomenology*, trans. D. Carr. Evanston, IL: Northwestern University Press.

Luckmann, T. (1983) Common sense, science and the specialization of science. *Phenomenology and Pedagogy*, 1: 59–73.

Merleau-Ponty, M. (1962/1945) *The Phenomenology of Perception*, trans. C. Smith. New York: Humanities Press.

Merleau-Ponty, M. (1963/1942) *The Structure of Behavior*, trans. A. Fisher. Boston: Beacon Press.

Merleau-Ponty, M. (1964/1961) Phenomenology and the sciences of man. In J. Edie (ed.), *The Primary of Perception*, trans. J. Wild. Evanston, IL: Northwestern University Press.

Scanlon, J. (1988) The manifold meanings of lifeworld in Husserl's *Crisis*. Unpublished paper.

Skinner, B.F. (1948) *Walden Two*. New York: Macmillan.

Stout, G.F. (1931) *Mind and Matter*. New York: Macmillan.

Titchener, E.B. (1929) *Systematic Psychology: Prolegomena*, ed. H.P. Weld. New York: Macmillan.

PART II

THE CULTURAL CONSTRUCTION OF DEVELOPMENT

5

Development as a Personal and Cultural Construction

Jochen Brandtstädter

Developmental psychology as a scientific endeavour presumes that human development over the lifespan is governed by certain universal and invariant nomological principles. Developmental researchers try to reduce the diversity of developmental patterns to a more parsimonious set of basic generative processes, to establish causal connections between ontogenetic events, and so on. However, such attempts to bring out lawful order are seriously hampered by the fact that developmental trajectories observed in different biographical, cultural and historical contexts usually exhibit a broad range of variation. As Brim and Kagan (1980: 13) have put it: 'growth is more individualistic than was thought, and it is difficult to find general patterns.'

Given this state of affairs, it is not surprising that there is a growing tendency among developmental psychologists to consider the search for nomological order in human development as futile *in principle*. Arguments in favour of such a stance refer, for example, to the chance element in any biography (cf. Bandura, 1982), to the transitory and emergent nature of developmental phenomena (cf. Kagan, 1983), to the fundamental plasticity of developmental processes (cf. Lerner, 1984), and to the resulting historical relativity of developmental trajectories (cf. Gergen, 1980). Obviously, difficulties in extracting order from the diversity of developmental phenomena may reflect not only a fundamental feature of development, but also theoretical deficiencies. As a fact, however, the traditional ideal of establishing general and invariant laws of development is no longer unanimously accepted.

The thesis underlying this chapter is that lifespan development is in essential respects a *personal and cultural product*. Developmental phenomena are linked not only by causal laws, but also by culturally regulated personal actions. Consequently, developmental psychology can in some ways be regarded as belonging to the realm of the 'sciences of the artificial' (cf. Simon, 1969). The corollary to this thesis is that the 'emerging crisis' (Gergen, 1980) in lifespan developmental psychology is largely due to problems in combining the causal–nomological stance with an explanatory perspective that accounts for human development as a process that is subject to social and personal control. To elaborate this argument, I will first consider some conceptual and functional relationships between development, culture and action.

Development, Culture and Action

The notorious contextual specificity of developmental patterns reflects not only an inherent 'plasticity' of human development, but also the fact that developmental processes are subject to personal and cultural control. The regulation of development over the lifespan is both a precondition and a central task for any social and cultural system. The strategies and goals of development-related control, which are partly institutionalized in systems of education and socialization, depend on theoretical beliefs and accumulated knowledge about human development, as well as on culturally shared conceptions of successful living and coexistence. As these contextual conditions undergo historical change, so do the modal patterns and constraints for individual development. The common textbook formula which holds that development is the co-product of genetic and environmental factors thus needs to be qualified to include the notion that environment has to be conceived largely as an artificially arranged ecology that has the tacit or explicit function of enhancing or impeding certain developmental outcomes. This, however, should not be read to imply that the cultural ecology of development is constructed (or could be reconstructed) according to some pervasive rational design or masterplan. The untenability of such an assumption becomes obvious if one considers the fact that cultural structures result from a cumulative, long-term process that by far transcends the experiential and cognitive horizon of any single individual (cf. also von Hayek, 1979). Likewise, if we consider development as shaped by personal and social action systems, we should account for the 'bounded rationality' of human agents, that is, the fact that decisions and actions usually have unanticipated and unintended side effects (cf. Simon, 1957).

Culture is sometimes defined so as to imply the perfection of an object that is capable of improvement, and in particular the perfection of human development and life activity itself (cf. Hofstätter, 1977; Klaus and Buhr, 1971). This definition highlights the close relation between the concept of culture and the notion of developmental control. The cultural setting, however, should not plainly be conceived as a superficial arrangement that may be abandoned in favour of some more 'natural' mode of living, as it has often seemed in the alienation literature since Rousseau. The functional interdependence between culture and development is captured more precisely if one conceives of culture as an indispensable 'exosomatic means of adaptation' (Rudolph and Tschohl, 1977), which in the evolutionary course has come to replace, and compensate for, narrow and rigid adaptive automatisms. The behavioural and developmental potentials which have made possible the construction, maintenance and change of cultural systems thus at the same time necessitated the culturation of development. The basic idea can already be found in Herder's *Abhandlung über den Ursprung der Sprache* (1772); it has been theoretically elaborated in the anthropological systems of Childe (1956) and, particularly, of Gehlen (1971). As Geertz (1973: 44) pointedly puts it: 'We are . . . incomplete or unfinished animals, who complete or finish ourselves through culture.' The institutions, knowledge systems and problem solutions that are established and transmitted in the process of cultural evolution permit a greater variation in behavioural and developmental patterns (cf. Chiszar, 1981), but at the same time impose new tasks on individual development. The complexity of these tasks corresponds to the considerably prolonged phase of dependency which characterizes human development and socialization. From a phylogenetic point of view, increase in brain size and capacity, delayed speed of maturation and prolonged childhood along with the evolution of family and group structures constitute a complex of synergetic factors, which have probably reinforced each other in the evolutionary course (cf. Bruner, 1972; Gould, 1977; Lerner, 1984; Scarr-Salapatek, 1976).

These considerations already suggest that cultural and 'natural' aspects of human development are functionally interdependent (cf. Boesch, 1980; Lewontin, 1982). Developmental processes are constrained by cultural regulations insofar as they involve the shaping of individual development in accordance with normative standards and age-graded developmental tasks; but as these processes always involve changes on subpersonal (biophysical, biochemical, neurobiological) levels, they are at the same time subject to fundamental laws of nature, which in turn constrain the range of effective intervention into development. This, however, should not be taken to imply that an explanatory stance that conceives of development as a cultural and personal construction could be reduced to, or replaced by, a subpersonal–physicalistic type of analysis. These two levels of developmental analysis correspond not to different segments of reality, but rather to different explanatory strategies which generate their own specific research questions and problem solutions (cf. also Dennett, 1971).

The Individual as Co-producer of his Development

Aside from distinct modes of heteronomous control, which predominate during earlier, dependent phases of socialization, the cultural regulation of human development also involves processes of self-organization and self-formation. Such processes are guided and motivated by beliefs, expectancies and value orientations related to personal development over the lifespan, which typically become more articulate in adolescence and early adulthood. The adult person generally conceives of his or her development as a process which, for different phases of life, involves gains and losses in different areas and functional domains (cf. Heckhausen, Dixon and Baltes, 1989), and which is more or less amenable to change and optimization. Such implicit models of development, and related control beliefs, determine the emotional quality of one's developmental perspective, as well as the motivation actively to shape the course of personal development. There is considerable individual variation with regard to this point (cf. Bandura, 1982; Brandtstädter, 1984a). The person's life themes and identity projects (cf. Harré, 1983; Wollheim, 1984) already provide an organizing framework and motivational source for everyday actions and life. To be sure, in everyday routines one usually does not reflect these basic meanings; they may remain latent until critical events or life transitions necessitate the revision and readjustment of prior developmental options and life perspectives.

This outlines some basic tenets of an 'actional' perspective on development, which lends greater emphasis to the individual's active contribution in shaping and optimizing personal development over the lifespan. This theoretical stance partly differs from current interactionist and organismic views in that it regards development not only as a by-product of person–environment transactions, but more specifically as a target field for control and optimization. It is worth noting that this point of view is by no means incompatible with biogenetic approaches; it may on the contrary contribute to a deeper understanding of the interplay between environmental and genetic factors in development. Developmental genetics increasingly recognizes the import of selective and constructive activity as a mediator between the genetic bases and phenotypic manifestations of development (cf. Lewontin, 1982). The individual (to the extent that it has freedom of choice) selects and shapes its environment according to personal preferences and competences, which in turn are more or less closely related to genotypic conditions. It creates developmental niches with specific affordances and limitations, and thus selectively exposes itself to specific influences, the developmental impact of which is moderated again by genotypically based reaction norms (cf. the concept of genotype–environment covariation; Plomin, 1986; Scarr and McCartney, 1983).

An action-theoretical developmental perspective is not a new one, despite the fact that its broader reception is of a more recent date (cf. also Brandtstädter, 1981a; Lerner and Busch-Rossnagel, 1981). The theme of self-formation is already prominent in Aristotelian action theory, where the concept of rational action appears as intimately connected with the ideal of a 'good life' (cf. Müller, 1982). In early German developmental psychology – one has to mention here particularly Dilthey (1894) and Spranger (1914) as proponents of a so-called 'geisteswissenschaftliche Psychologie' – development was conceived explicitly as a process of self-formation. However, this concept was heavily fraught with anti-causalist notions of freedom and spontaneity, and thus did not fall on a fertile soil in an era when psychology increasingly began to model itself as an experimenting natural science.

Today, as an 'intentional stance' (cf. Dennett, 1971) has experienced a comeback in different branches of psychology, developmental psychologists are no longer deterred, but are increasingly attracted by the idea that individuals are producers of their development (cf. Lerner and Busch-Rossnagel, 1981). However, this notion entails a certain danger of overstatement. First of all, any life history can be seen as a mixture of actions and unanticipated and uncontrolled events. The impact of quasi-random events and chance encounters on the individual's life course is particularly emphasized in 'aleatorical' conceptions of development (cf. Bandura, 1982; Gergen, 1980). Again, this insight is not a recent one; as Schopenhauer notes, 'the course of a man's life is in no wise entirely his own making; it is the product of two factors – the series of things that happened, and his own resolves in regard to them, and these two are constantly interacting upon and modifying each other' (1851/1951: 197).

The view that persons are the sole producers of their development is already rendered questionable by the more fundamental fact that an individual's action space is constrained by, and subject to, heteronomous influences. We decide and act within a macrosystem of norms and institutions which is largely pre-given, even though it may be open to criticism and change in many respects. More subtly, we cannot influence the 'internal' context of our actions *ad lib*. For instance, we do not *decide* to have a specific emotional reaction, we usually do not *decide* to find some argument convincing, and we certainly do not *decide* to have a sudden insight; these things rather happen to us (we can of course make arrangements to raise the probability that they happen to us). Admittedly, one can cultivate one's emotions, opinions and volitions to some extent (cf. the concept of 'second-order volitions'; Frankfurt, 1971). Nevertheless, we have to recognize that actions are constrained by subpersonal and transpersonal control mechanisms which are not subject to personal agency, but rather reflect our cultural and evolutionary heritage. This fact is sometimes given short shrift in psychological and philosophical theories of action, which thus have produced no less a skewed image of human behaviour and development than, on the other side, mechanistic–behaviouristic approaches have done.

The Construction of Coherence and Continuity in Human Development

The Causal–Nomological Approach

There is a widespread view that the construction of continuity and coherence of developmental phenomena is coterminous with the detection of causal links. The concept of causal linkage is usually explicated with reference to the scheme of deductive–nomological explanation (*DN* explanations; Hempel and Oppenheim, 1948). According to the *DN* model, an event of type E is explained by deducing the statement describing E from a set of premises which comprises, first, the description of an antecedent event A and, second, a deterministic law formula stating that events of type A are invariantly followed by events of type E.

The project of representing even limited domains of development as a causal structure in terms of the *DN* scheme encounters considerable difficulties. Some more technical difficulties become obvious when we consider the format of *DN* explanations, which basically covers only two events (the antecedent and the consequent). To extend the *DN* scheme to developmental sequences which encompass multiple events or time series, one would have to construct an explanatory chain where each link in the chain would constitute a *DN* explanation, and these links would have to be connected so that the consequent event within the preceding link simultaneously figures as the antecedent event of the next link in the chain (causal–genetic explanation; see Stegmüller, 1969).

Apart from being rather cumbersome, such a construction seems problematic for the following substantial reasons. In a developmental system, sequences of states can be modelled as a continuous causal chain only if the system – for all phases evolving from the initial state – can be treated as *closed*, that is, as independent of exogenous factors. The developing human organism however has to be conceived as an *open* system, the states of which depend not only on preceding states, but also on stimulation, information and alimentation from extraorganismic sources. The developmental researcher adhering to a causal–deterministic stance may try to deal with this complication in two basically different ways. The most obvious move perhaps would be to extend the scope of causal analysis, according to Nagel's rule (1957: 17): 'if determinism is assumed, alternatives in a system which do not appear to occur as the consequence of the presence or operation of antecedent factors . . . must be regarded as belonging to a more inclusive system which is deterministic.' By this strategy – we may call it the *holistic* strategy – the researcher may try to approximate the ultimate causal ideal of a closed system in which nothing remains unexplained or accidental. An opposite strategy which in certain respects appears to be more realistic – call it the *focusing* strategy – consists of centring selectively on those aspects or subsystems of development which for all practical purposes can be treated as closed, because exogenous influences seem negligible or can be bracketed as quasi-constant factors. For instance, if the researcher is interested in the development of optical illusions, he may perhaps choose to omit socio-economic and historical variables from consideration.

Despite their different thrust, both strategies strive towards the ideal of establishing causal coherence. Their respective strengths and weaknesses are defined by the methodological tension between scope and precision of theoretical systems (cf. Bunge, 1967). Whereas the focusing strategy tends to generate a manifold of precise but context-blind and dissociated miniature theories, the holistic strategy typically produces panoramic but detail-blind theories with limited predictive power.

In the currently popular debates about developmental 'paradigms', the adequacy of a causal–nomological stance is an issue of continuing controversy (cf. Reese and Overton, 1970; Overton and Reese, 1981; Lerner and Kauffman, 1985). A common objection is to be found in the argument that developmental processes can at best be conceptualized probabilistically. Probabilistic–genetic explanations differ from causal–genetic ones in that they involve probabilistic or statistical instead of deterministic law formulas. This difference is not fundamental as long as statistical hypotheses are conceived as provisional quasi-laws that simply reflect a limited insight into the relevant causal mechanisms, and can eventually be replaced by strict deterministic laws. The case is different if the relationships under consideration are regarded as *irreducibly* probabilistic. Some proponents of a probabilistic conception of development explicitly endorse the latter view, claiming that this posture is in harmony with the world view of modern physics (cf. Kagan, 1980). We hold this to be misleading. If, for example, the indeterministic format of predictions in quantum physics is considered as irreducible and reflecting an ontological property of the micro-physical world, then this view is supported by the overwhelming predictive success of quantum physics laws. There is no comparable theoretical background for a probabilistic stance in developmental psychology. On the contrary, the assumption of irreducibly pro-babilistic developmental laws is heuristically counter-productive if it brings the search for coherence to a premature halt. We should not calm ourselves by attributing predictive failures to a fundamentally probabilistic nature of development. Rather, we should consider the possibility that our theories and observations may be deficient – and that the individuals under investigation, as personal agents, may have their reasons for not behaving as predicted.

From a Causal to an Action-Theoretical Stance
How far is an action perspective focusing on the personal, social and cultural control of human development compatible with a causal–nomological stance?

   The action perspective suggests that, before we attempt to interpret any seemingly regular relationship in causal–nomological terms, we generally have to consider the possibility that this relationship is mediated or moderated by regularities in social and cultural action patterns. It suggests that, as a general heuristic attitude, propositions about developmental contingencies ('If A, then B') should be qualified by pragmatic provisos, such as 'If A, then B – as long as nothing is done to prevent the occurrence of B after A,' or '. . . as long as the occurrence of A induces activities to bring about B', and the like. A closer inspection leads one to the conclusion that many propositions framed in developmental research are suitable candidates for such pragmatic provisos: memory functions decline in old age – but there is no *a priori* reason to assume that this decline is an invariant natural process that cannot be counteracted (for example, by mnemonic training programmes, pharmacological treatments); genetically determined metabolic disorders such as phenylketonuria or maple syrup disease lead to intellectual retardation – as long as available methods of early diagnosis and dietical treatment are not applied; presumably 'unfavourable' developmental conditions in early childhood may have detrimental and lasting effects only in a social context with scarce resources for prevention and treatment; and so on. The field of prevention naturally provides the most striking examples, as preventive actions, by definition, aim at making the occurrence of predicted behavioural and developmental disorders less probable (cf. Brandtstädter and von Eye, 1982). The developmental prognoses that motivate preventive interventions obviously cannot be conceived as causal–nomological arguments; a proposition that can be negated by active intervention should not be taken as a law of nature (cf. van Inwagen, 1975). It is important to note that the reverse of this argument is not necessarily valid: event sequences that, at a given time in a given context, cannot be modified do not by virtue merely of this fact qualify as causal or nomological laws. Limited modifiability may simply reflect temporary epistemic or technical limitations; the imputation of causal or nomic necessity, however, implies the strong assumption that the relationships in question can *under no circumstances* be altered by active interventions. For many, if not most, of the regularities that developmental research has unearthed in its search for causal relationships, it is highly questionable that this could be definitively demonstrated.

The Problem of Developmental Universals Reconsidered

One might be tempted to conclude from the considerations above that research and theorizing in developmental psychology can only frame quasi-laws which are valid in specific historical and cultural contexts alone (cf. Looft, 1973; Gergen, 1980). This conclusion, however, may be premature. I will now consider examples of propositions in developmental theories for which stronger validity may be claimed. Such stronger propositions are not hypothetically inferred from the observation of empirical regularities, but rather derived from formal and conceptual structures. Before elaborating this argument, I will consider some current uses, or rather misuses, of the notion of universal developmental laws.

According to common lore, universal principles of development can be established by demonstrating that certain developmental phenomena are manifested in the same manner across a variety of social, historical and cultural contexts. Thus, for example, Kagan (1976, 1981) considers the development of separation anxiety as a universal sequence, since this phenomenon is seen to unfold among children in the United States in essentially the same way as in, for example, Guatemala, Israel or Botswana. Similar claims of universality have been made for developmental sequences in perception, memory, language acquisition, moral judgement, social–cognitive development and many other functional domains (for example, see Munroe, Munroe and Whiting, 1981; Warren, 1980).

I do not intend to question the value of comparative developmental research in any way. The observation that certain developmental phenomena manifest themselves in similar manner over a broad range of contextual conditions may, for example, yield valuable insights into the genetic buffering or canalization (Waddington, 1957) of developmental trajectories. Such canalization effects, however, only refer to the typical range of environmental influences realized in phylogenetic history; they do not extend to the universe of potential environments. This already renders problematic any attempt to infer the invariance or universality of a developmental phenomenon from observed transcontextual stability. Such inductive generalizations, however, are unwarranted for more basic epistemological reasons. Comparative investigations can only span a finite range of contextual variation; claims of universality apparently need a stronger base than a finite series of observations.

This, of course, is the well-known problem of induction. There appear to be two classic answers to this problem. The first one suggests that theoretical propositions should be considered as conjectures which cannot be definitively verified, but only refuted by empirical evidence (cf. Popper, 1963). According to this view, claims of universality can be made only in a tentative sense. A different answer which was already formulated by Kant (1781/1969) suggests that strict universality must, and can only, be based on principles the validity of which can be ascertained *a priori*. Both answers have their well-known problems, which I do not intend to discuss here. It should be noted, however, that they converge in rejecting the inductivistic illusion that claims of universality could be founded on purely observational grounds. Thus the question arises of whether a *non-inductivistic* account of developmental universals might be conceivable. In searching for such an account, we obviously have to look for propositions in developmental research that (in a sense that remains to be explicated) are stronger than simple empirical hypotheses. In the following, I shall try to show that there are in fact 'a priori elements' (Brandtstädter, 1982) in developmental research programmes, which however are often clothed in the dress of empirical hypotheses. Further, I will try to show that these *a priori* elements arise from formal or conceptual structures, upon which any meaningful empirical study must rely.

Universal Developmental Sequences as Structural Implications

Developmental sequences often involve a stepwise construction where higher or more complex achievements are built up from more basic ones in an ordered progression. Paradigm examples can be found in the acquisition of skills and competences. To solve complex mathematical problems, one must first acquire basic arithmetics; to play chess competently, one must first learn the elementary rules of the game; to use a concept correctly, one has to learn the basic distinctions that are implied by that concept, and so on.

Such sequential postulates are obviously not derived from experimental studies, but rather from a *structural analysis* by which a given developmental task is decomposed into its constitutive elements. Parenthetically, this is also the typical approach used by didactics to devise instructional or learning sequences. Such structural analyses may have to be complemented by empirical or experimental studies in order, for example, to transform them into an instructional programme that corresponds to the learners' aptitudes. Nevertheless, it should be clear that sequential postulates of the mentioned type are not hypothetical conjectures that can be hounded to death by counter-evidence. Rather, they have the quality of *structural implications* (cf. also Lenk, 1987). This does not mean that the analyses performed to unfold an implicational structure are fail-safe. But, at least as far as they can be shown to be logically or conceptually correct, they are resistant against refractory evidence: if, for example, anybody pretended that there are competent chess players who did not know how to move a knight or bishop, or children who competently use the concept of 'lying' without having acquired the notion of truth, we would advise him to re-examine his observation methods or his concepts.

Obviously, relationships which are implied by formal or conceptual structures are epistemically stronger than purely empirical generalizations. I would like to go one step further and argue that sequential postulates in developmental psychology can claim universal validity only to the extent that they can be reconstructed as structural implications.

We can roughly distinguish three different types of structural implications (cf. Brandtstädter, 1984b).

Formal Implications This type of implication is derived from formal (for example, logical or mathematical) structures. As a simple example, let us consider an artificial calculus with elements x

and o and the following two production rules (cf. also Berztiss, 1975; Lorenzen, 1974): (R1) Given any figure F (that is, any string with elements x and o), generate Fx ($F{\rightarrow}Fx$)! (R2) Given any F, generate xFo ($F{\rightarrow}xFo$)! (The sequence in which R1 and R2 are applied is not fixed.) This production system generates specific figures or strings (let the starting element be o). By executing, for instance, the production sequence R1, R2, R2, R1, we obtain the following succession of strings: *ox, xoxo, xxoxoo, xxoxoox*. Note that certain strings *cannot* be generated by the given production system (for example, *oox, oxoo, ooxx*). Let us now extend the production system by the following rules: (R3) $F{\rightarrow}xFxo$, (R4) $F{\rightarrow}oF$. It can be shown that, by adding R3 to the production system, we can produce no new figures beyond those that can be generated by the original system. To prove this, we only have to demonstrate that the transition from F to $xFxo$ prescribed by R3 can also be achieved by applying first R1 and then R2. In contrast, by adding R4 to the original production system, we can generate new figures, because the transition from F to oF cannot be achieved by the original production rules. Thus we have demonstrated that R3 is not a 'genuine' extension, but simply a formal implication of the original calculus. This may not be self-evident, but it can be made evident by certain analytic steps.

Paradigm cases of formal implications are tautological statements which are implied by the logical system of statement calculus, or Boolean algebra. Implications derived from logical or mathematical structures – though devoid of empirical content – may nevertheless yield non-trivial insights, as has been amply documented in the history of logics and mathematics. There are also numerous examples for formally true propositions which initially were considered as empirical generalizations, and only later were shown to be strictly provable (cf. Klix, 1980).

With respect to developmental research, it is important to note that certain competences or developmental tasks also exhibit a well-defined formal structure. As paradigm examples, we may consider the kinds of tasks and cognitive competences analysed in Piagetian research. For instance, to solve equilibrium tasks on a beam balance, the objects suspended on both sides of the balance have to be compared with regard to weight, distance from the centre and so on; to solve seriation tasks, the sticks to be seriated have to be compared with regard to their length, observing certain formal properties such as the transitivity of asymmetrical relations and so on. The necessity of these requirements can be demonstrated by considering the formal structure of the task in question. Generally, if some developmental task A formally implies some developmental achievements *B*, then *A* cannot be accomplished before, but only later than (at most simultaneously with) *B*. This principle holds in all possible worlds, and it seems that sequential postulates in developmental psychology can claim strict universality only as far as they can be analysed according to this principle.

Schematic Implications Acts such as dancing a waltz, baking an omelet or playing a free kick involve a general configuration of contextual and behavioural elements which form the schematic structure (the blueprint, recipe, script, prototypical pattern) of the respective actions. This holds especially for actions which involve a *rule* of construction or execution. There may be of course stylistic variations in the execution of such acts, but there are also structural invariants that characterize any realization of the given act type. One can dance a waltz only to a particular type of music, make an omelet only with eggs, as one can play Mozart's Jupiter symphony only according to a specific score. This again seems to hold in all possible worlds, even if there are, have been and presumably will be cultural and historical contexts where no one dances a waltz or plays Mozart. As formal structures, schematic or script-like structures impose restrictions upon the actual as well as on the ontogenetic construction of the corresponding action patterns and competences.

Conceptual Implications Developmental tasks and competences are denoted by concepts the meaning of which partly derives from their relations to other concepts within a semantic network. For instance, achievement-motivated behaviour conceptually implies the distinction between success and failure, which in turn presupposes 'internalization' of certain quality standards; altruistic action conceptually implies the perception of needs of other people and some element of personal sacrifice; and so on. Such relationships are not (and need not be) derived from the observation of developmental contingencies, but rather from an analysis of conceptual structures. Like formal and schematic structures, conceptual or semantic structures impose constraints upon the ontogenetic construction or acquisition of developmental tasks and competences.

In emphasizing the role of structural constraints in development, we have to admit that structures themselves develop (cf. Piaget, 1970). This holds in particular for schematic structures and conceptual structures, which, as historical and conventional entities, are basically open to modification and change (we may leave open the question whether this also applies to formal structures). Creative and innovative processes characteristically involve a more

or less radical departure from established structures; the requirements of successful communication and co-orientation, however,
impose certain limits on the modification of, and deviation from,
such structures.

Ontogenetic Sequences and Conceptual Structures: Emotional Development as a Paradigm Case

The relevance of a 'structural' perspective can be exemplified for a
diversity of research areas such as moral development, language
acquisition, development of attributions and emotional development
(cf. Brandtstädter, 1982, 1984b, 1987). Here, I will consider
emotional development as a paradigm case.

I shall start with the observation that emotion terms, like other
'mental' predicates, are 'cluster concepts' which stand in a network
of relationships to other concepts that we commonly utilize to
describe a person's beliefs, expectations, intentions and action
tendencies. These semantic relationships regulate the use of
emotion terms in everyday as well as in scientific contexts. Let us
consider, for example, the concept of 'fear': we know, among other
things, that fear arises in a particular type of situation (namely, in
'dangerous' situations), and that it is related to specific and typical
behavioural tendencies (such as tendencies of escape or avoidance);
furthermore, we assume that a situation is subjectively dangerous to
the extent that the individual anticipates the loss of something
personally valued and doubts that he can avert the imminent
danger; and so on. Such a semantic structure categorically typifies
episodes to which the term 'fear' (or 'afraid') is applicable; from a
cognitivistic point of view, it may be considered as a schema, script
or production system that controls the processing of information in
the ascriptional use of 'fear' (cf. Anderson, 1983; Schank and
Abelson, 1977; Smith, 1984; Taylor and Crocker, 1981). Generally,
to ascribe some emotional state, we have to scrutinize the
contextual and behavioural evidence for critical features that
correspond to the pertinent conceptual scheme. Thus the application
of emotion terms is a concept- as well as data-driven process (cf.
Lindsay and Norman, 1977).

We can extend this reasoning to other emotion terms. To say
about someone that he or she feels *proud* (for example, with respect
to some achievement) usually implies that this person sees himself
or herself as the originator of an action outcome which is perceived
as success in relation to some personal standard of excellence. If we
ascribe *jealousy*, we imply that the person perceives a specific social
constellation; we associate *envy* with a specific social comparison
process. When we ascribe feelings of *guilt*, we assume that the

person in question believes that he or she has violated some personally accepted standard of conduct. The feeling of *pity*, as we understand it, involves a tendency to help somebody whom we believe to be in a state of distress. It is part of a usually unquestioned structure of thought that relationships of this kind are often understood as causal–empirical hypotheses in need of experimental test (see, for example, attributional research on cognition–emotion links; Weiner, 1982; Weiner, Russell and Lerman, 1978). This, in our view, is a misunderstanding which can lead to serious methodological faults.

Obviously, the ties that relate an emotion term to other emotional, behavioural or mental attributes may differ in strength. Some of these relationships may be open to revision under the impact of new evidence (for example, propositions about physiological correlates of specific emotional states). Others, however, seem to constitute central meaning elements, which cannot be eliminated without radically changing or even destroying the concept. Wittgenstein (1965) refers to these differences when he distinguishes between 'symptoms' and 'criteria' of emotions, that is, between indicators of emotional states that have been established inductively by empirical research, and indicators that are derived from, or are constitutive to, the meaning of the respective emotional term (cf. also Tugendhat, 1979). For example, when we associate 'grief' with the anticipation of some subjectively unpleasant event, or 'surprise' with the perception of some unexpected event, then this is obviously not because we have never witnessed empirical exceptions. Rather, these relationships appear as part of a 'language game', as conceptual yardsticks against which we have to validate our observational methods in the first place, before we can use these methods to establish further empirical contingencies – and which thus are, in a methodological sense, prior to experience. One may conceive of such criterial relationships as a system of rules which delimit the range of admissible combinations between emotional, cognitive and behavioural attributes and thus determine which attributes are, and which are not, 'co-predictable' (cf. Keil, 1979).

While empirical regularities in the ascriptive use of emotional terms are often interpreted as nomic, cause–effect relationships (for example, Weiner, 1982), the current argument leads to a different interpretation. When we ascribe to ourselves, for example, a feeling of gratitude in cases where we relate some positive experience to an intentional action of another person, this is not because this type of emotion is *caused* by this type of perception, but rather because the emotion term, as it is conventionally used, conceptually implies, or refers to, this type of cognition and evaluation. Describing oneself as grateful, but at the same time denying the corresponding criterial cognitions, would not falsify some hypothetical causal law, but violate established rules of language.

As a corollary, we can derive the assumption that the presumedly 'causal' cognition–emotion links unearthed by attributional research, as far as they portray established language games, are valid only for competent language-users. This assumption has been empirically substantiated by Brandtstädter, Krampen and Vesely (1985; cf. also Roos and Brandtstädter, 1988). In these studies, attribution theory propositions on the cognitive 'antecedents' of emotional experiences were translated in a logical format and evaluated by non-parametric prediction analyses (cf. Hildebrand, Laing and Rosenthal, 1977). Generally, the analysed propositions were found to have high predictive efficiency. Of course we also obtained response patterns which deviated from the predictions (the 'error cells' in the predictive scheme were not empty, to put it in technical terms). The point, however, is that these cases are not plainly hypothesis-discrepant or falsifying cases in the usual sense. Further analytical steps clearly showed that the probability of producing a 'deviant' response pattern is inversely related to the subjects' linguistic competence. To obviate possible misunderstandings at this point, it has to be emphasized that propositions about the use of terms in ordinary language, as any other empirical proposition, may fail. But it should be evident that they cannot be disproved by observing the verbal behaviour of individuals who are not, or not yet, familiar with the use of the terms in question.

The *constituent-theoretical* interpretation of emotions delineated here (see also Brandtstädter, 1985a) has obvious implications for the controversial and much discussed question of the relationship between cognitions and emotions (cf. Lazarus, 1982; Zajonc, 1980, 1984). As already intimated, it competes with the view that this relationship is a causal one (whatever the assumed causal priorities may be). For causal relationships, it is traditionally assumed that antecedents and consequents are logically and conceptually independent and thus can be independently assessed. But if the ascription or observation of a specific emotion has to be validated by reference to certain (criterial) cognitions – as, for example, the emotion of envy is assessed with reference to some cognitive process of social comparison – then one can no longer speak of a *causal* relationship. The objection may be raised at this point that it might be sufficient simply to ask the person what he or she feels. But to ascertain the validity of self-ascriptive statements we have again to refer to certain criterial evidence. Parenthetically, these considerations do not imply that *all* emotions involve a complex cognitive elaboration of perceptual inputs. In certain cases there may be no, or only rudimentary, post-perceptual cognitions involved; this may hold for emotions that appear very early in ontogenetic development, and especially for emotional automatisms that have been phylogenetically established to elicit a quick and stereotyped emergency response to specific distal stimuli, independent of what the individual happens to want or believe.

It has to be emphasized that a constituent-theoretical perspective of emotions does not exclude or remove the need for empirical analysis. On the contrary, many interesting questions in emotion theory can *only* be answered by observation and experiment. Clearly, the biophysical (physiological, biochemical, neurological) aspects of emotional processes can only be established experimentally. Furthermore, as a conceptual–structural analysis describes emotion–cognition linkages only in a categorical fashion, it has to be complemented eventually by more 'idiographical' observations to concretize this scheme for different historical, cultural and biographical contexts.

I have argued that the semantic structure of emotion terms imposes specific restrictions upon ontogenetic sequences. In this respect, we have to distinguish carefully between the *ascription* or attribution of an emotion and the *experience* of an emotion. Attributions are conceptually guided; the development of attributional processes is therefore closely linked with aspects of concept acquisition and language development, and reflects the implicational relations within semantic structures. This however does not apply in the same manner to the experience of an emotion. The experience of an emotion does not presuppose self-attributional judgements; this can be seen, for instance, in the fact that, if someone declares that he feels sad, we may eventually say that he is lying or using the concept of sadness incorrectly, but not that he is wrong (cf. Putnam, 1975). This point has been neglected to some extent in cognitivistic and constructivistic accounts of emotion (cf. Averill, 1980; Schachter and Singer, 1962). We certainly do not need a concept of sadness in order to feel sad. But it is nevertheless correct that a certain emotion can only be experienced when the 'criterial' cognitions which are conceptually related to this emotion, and the corresponding cognitive capacities, are developed. Thus we can assume, for example, that feelings of envy presuppose certain cognitive achievements that enable the individual to make certain social comparisons. Likewise, surprise cannot appear before specific expectations can be constructed; feelings of pride, shame or guilt are only possible when actions can be compared with certain standards of conduct. Furthermore, 'mixed' feelings (anger–shame, guilt–embarrassment, sadness–joy and so on) can only be experienced when an episode can be interpreted on different levels of meaning and with respect to different implications, and so on. It is of course possible to document these relationships empirically (see, for example, Heckhausen, 1985). This, however, should not detract from the fact that we are dealing here not with empirical contingencies in the usual sense, but with sequence postulates which reflect the semantic structure of emotion terms.

Again, we can generally state that if a specific developmental outcome O implies or entails – formally or conceptually – a developmental achievement (or set of developmental achievements) O', then the ontogenetic construction of O, too, presupposes the construction of O'. O' may be attained simultaneously with or temporally precede O. Questions about the timing of such a sequence or about conditions which may retard or enhance the involved developmental steps may call for further empirical research. In any case, however, we can strongly exclude that O precedes, or occurs without, O'; O' is a formally necessary but not sufficient condition for the achievement of O, and conversely O is sufficient, but not necessary for O' (the conjunction of all necessary conditions is of course necessary *and* sufficient for O). Relationships of this type can be found in diverse domains of developmental psychology. For example, theories of moral development have postulated that social–cognitive competences are 'necessary but not sufficient' conditions for competent moral judgement. Considerable effort has been invested to subject this assumption to empirical test (cf. Kohlberg, 1973; Lickona, 1976; Selman and Damon, 1975), but obviously it has not been found worthwhile to examine whether this relationship may not already follow from a conceptual analysis of the terms involved in moral judgements. I have defended this latter view elsewhere (Brandtstädter, 1981b, 1985b). While I do not question the potential usefulness of attempts to document structural implications empirically, I would argue that what can be tested in such research are not the structural relationships (even when they are cloaked in the guise of empirical hypotheses), but rather the formal or conceptual validity of the utilized observational procedures and measurement devices.

In which sense now can sequence postulates derived from conceptual structures claim universality, given the undisputed fact that such structures are historical entities that are open to modification and change? How can notions of necessity and universality be reconciled with the fact that language games are culture-bound constructions? To resolve this apparent contradiction, we have to note that concepts cannot be separated from the conceptual structures that constitute their meaning in the first place. All that we can say is: whenever and wherever an X-type emotion or a Y-type competence develops, the developmental sequence will conform to structural constraints that are implied by the concepts which refer to these types of developmental outcomes. It would be inconsistent to argue that the concepts might be used in a *radically* different way in other cultures or historical eras; because 'When language games change, then there is a change in concepts, and with the concepts the meanings of words change' (Wittgenstein, 1967: 65). Of course there may be cultural and historical differences with respect, for example, to concrete circumstances under which emotions of a given type are experienced or expressed. But these different patterns must at least display certain structural homologies (or 'homotypic' equivalences, cf. Kagan, 1971); otherwise there would be no reason to consider them as tokens of the same type.

Developmental Psychology between Apriorism and Empiricism

The preceding arguments may have a strong aprioristic flavour. I have formulated them somewhat pointedly, in order to highlight the inconsistencies of a usually unquestioned methodological stance which often confuses empirical hypotheses and analytic or structural implications (cf. also Smedslund, 1978, 1984). This is the place to add some notes of caution. The extremes of a rigid and closed apriorism and of a free-floating, uncommitted empiricism do not constitute methodological alternatives for psychological research. Rather, we have to look out for a middle position that carries the strengths and avoids the weaknesses of both extremes.

To substantiate this methodological plea, we may consider some basic difficulties of drawing a sharp boundary between empirical relationships and structural implications. In my opinion, these difficulties are not primarily due to the alleged 'fuzzy' nature of concepts in everyday language (for example, Smith and Medin, 1981). Though not a strictly normed system, everyday language is by no means unnormed – successful communication would be impossible in this case. Rather, the use of concepts in everyday language is *partially* normed (cf. Kamlah and Lorenzen, 1967); this norming provides the standards against which diffuse and incoherent forms of language use can be critically evaluated, as we commonly do in contexts of socialization (and also in psychological diagnostics, for example, when assessing the linguistic competences of a person). Everyday concepts such as intelligence, aggression, happiness and so on may change with time (and also under the impact of psychological research), and the conceptual variants may only stand in a remote relationship of 'family resemblance' (Wittgenstein, 1965). Nevertheless, the psychological researcher attempting theoretically to elaborate such concepts cannot completely dismiss their established core meaning: that intelligence has ' to do with competent problem-solving, altruism with helping, happiness with the fulfilment of wants and so on. It would be a sign of conceptual confusion to subject such basic meaning postulates to empirical test, but there is nothing wrong with using them as reference standards for the validation of research procedures and assessment strategies. On the other hand, we should be mindful of the fact that semantic structures are tools that guide our epistemic and actional transactions with the social and material world. To function in this way, they have to be responsive to experience; though different parts of the structure are differently resistant against recalcitrant evidence, the impact of experience may induce changes everywhere in the system (cf. Putnam, 1979; Quine, 1951).

Problems of distinguishing between conceptual implications and empirical hypotheses already arise in the interpretation of theoretical terms. The standard procedure for explicating theoretical terms consists in assembling a list of interpretative propositions or 'reduction statements'. For example, to interpret an emotion term E, such a list would typically specify sufficient conditions from which an emotional state of the E-type can be inferred (for example, certain situational conditions), as well as necessary conditions the absence of which excludes an E-type emotion (for example, certain behavioural correlates). Such lists of reduction statements have an epistemic status which, with respect to the analytic–empirical distinction, seems somewhat hermaphroditic. From the conjunction of sufficient and necessary reduction statements, propositions of the following type may be derived: whenever an individual is in a situation of type S, he or she will display a behavioural tendency of type B. As far as these propositions have empirical content, they have to be evaluated *a posteriori* in light of pertinent research results, which eventually lead us to eliminate these propositions from the list. Thus a system of interpretative propositions that relate a theoretical term with observable conditions cannot be a purely definitional or analytic construction. On the other hand, we would not and could not simultaneously discard all propositions on the list (or even a critical portion of them), because the theoretical term would then be stripped of those elements which constitute its core meaning by relating it to other concepts within a broader semantic network. Obviously, a set of interpretative propositions which combines necessary and sufficient reduction statements, though not a purely analytic construction, is not a purely hypothetical system either. Obviously, analytical and empirical elements are already closely intertwined in the interpretation of theoretical concepts (cf. Lenk, 1987; Stegmüller, 1969). What are the implications for the problem of distinguishing conceptual implications and empirical propositions? In view of the last arguments, one might be tempted to conclude that this distinction is bootless. A more sensible conclusion would be to use this distinction in a methodological sense to differentiate between meaning postulates that we need in order to construct conceptually valid observational procedures, and propositions that we test by using such procedures. The epistemic status of a proposition with regard to this distinction thus should be evaluated by considering its role in a theory or research programme; in any case, we cannot use a proposition simultaneously as a conceptual yardstick for the construction of observational methods *and* as a hypothesis to be tested with these very methods. Confusions to this type loom large in psychological research. The conceptual premises of our research programmes, of course, do not stand above criticism and change. Though it would be a fallacy to assume that conceptual rules can be tested in the same way as hypothetical statements, we have to admit that their *usefulness* may be evaluated with respect to the success of the theoretical structures and research programmes that are built around them.

Note

Thanks are due to Gün Semin for his valuable help in the English translation of this chapter.

References

Anderson, J.R. (1983) *The Architecture of Cognition*. Cambridge, MA: Harvard University Press.

Averill, J.A. (1980) A constructivistic view of emotion. In R. Plutchik and H. Kellerman (eds), *Emotion: Theory, Research and Experience*. Vol 1: *Theories of Emotion*. New York: Academic Press. pp. 305–39.

Bandura, A. (1982) The pyschology of chance encounters and life paths. *American Psychologist*, 37: 122–47.

Berztiss, A.T. (1975) *Data Structures: Theory and Practice* (2nd edn). New York: Academic Press.

Boesch, E.E. (1980) *Kultur und Handlung*. Bern: Huber.

Brandtstädter, J. (1981a) Entwicklung in Handlungskontexten: Aussichten für die entwicklungspsychologische Theorienbildung und Anwendung. *Trierer Psychologische Berichte* 8, Heft 8. (Also in H. Lenk (ed.) (1984) *Handlungstheorien*

104   *The cultural construction of development*

interdisziplinär. Vol. 3, II: *Verhaltenswissenschaftliche und psychologische Handlungstheorien.* Munich: Fink. pp. 848–78.)

Brandtstädter, J. (1981b) Begriffliche Voraussetzungen der Moralpsychologie. In W. Kempf and G. Aschenbach (eds), *Konflikt und Konfliktbewältigung.* Bern: Huber. pp. 231–54.

Brandtstädter, J. (1982) Apiorische Elemente in psychologischen Forschungsprogrammen. *Zeitschrift für Sozialpsychologie,* 13: 267–77.

Brandtstädter, J. (1984a) Personal and social control over development: some implications of an action perspective in life-span developmental psychology. In P.B. Baltes and O.G. Brim Jr (eds), *Life-span development and behavior.* Vol. 6. New York: Academic Press. pp. 1–32.

Brandtstädter, J. (1984b) Apriorische Elemente in psychologischen Forschungsprogrammen: Weiterführende Argumente und Beispiele. *Zeitschrift für Sozialpsychologie,* 15: 151–8.

Brandtstädter, J. (1985a) Emotion, Kognition, Handlung: Konzeptuelle Beziehungen. In L.H. Eckensberger and E.-D. Lantermann (eds), *Emotion und Reflexivität.* Munich: Urban & Schwarzenberg. pp. 252–61.

Brandtstädter, J. (1985b) 'A rose has no teeth' – zum Problem der Unterscheidung zwischen Begriffsverwirrungen und überraschenden empirischen Befunden in der Psychologie. In P. Wapnewski (ed.), *Wissenschaftskolleg – Institute for Advanced Study – zu Berlin, Jahrbuch 1983/84.* Berlin: Siedler. pp. 27–39.

Brandtstädter, J. (1987) On certainty and universality in human development: developmental psychology between empiricism and apriorism. In M. Chapman and R. Dixon (eds), *Meaning and the Growth of Understanding: Wittgenstein's Significance for Developmental Psychology.* Berlin: Springer. pp. 69–84.

Brandtstädter, J. and von Eye, A. (1982) *Psychologische Prävention. Grundlagen, Programme, Methoden.* Bern: Huber.

Brandtstädter, J., Krampen, G. and Vesely, H. (1985) Attribution und sprachliche Kompetenz: zur Bewährung attributionstheoretischer Annahmen bei Grundschülern mit unterschiedlichem sprachlichen Entwicklungsstand. *Sprache und Kognition,* 3: 130–8.

Brim, O.G. Jr and Kagan, J. (1980) Constancy and change: a view of the issues. In O.G. Brim Jr and J. Kagan (eds), *Constancy and Change in Human Development.* Cambridge, MA: Harvard University Press. pp. 1–25.

Bruner, J.S. (1972) The nature and uses of immaturity. *American Psychologist,* 27: 687–708.

Bunge, M. (1967) *Scientific Research I: The Search for System.* Berlin: Springer.

Childe, C.G. (1956) *Man Makes Himself* (3rd edn). London: Watts.

Chiszar, D. (1981) Learning theory, ethological theory, and developmental plasticity. In E.S. Gollin (ed.), *Developmental Plasticity: Behavioral and Biological Aspects of Variations in Development.* New York: Academic Press. pp. 71–100.

Dennett, D. (1971) Intentional systems. *Journal of Philosophy,* 68: 87–106.

Dilthey, W. (1894) Ideen über eine beschreibende und zergliedernde Psychologie. *Sitzungsbericht der Berliner Akademie der Wissenschaften.* pp. 1309–1407. (Reprinted in: W. Dilthey (1968) *Gesammelte Schriften.* Vol. 5. pp. 139–240.)

Frankfurt, H.G. (1971) Freedom of the will and the concept of a person. *Journal of Philosophy,* 68: 5–20.

Geertz, C. (1973) *The Interpretation of Cultures: Selected Essays.* New York: Basic Books.

Gehlen, A. (1971) *Der Mensch. Seine Natur und seine Stellung in der Welt* (9th edn). Bonn: Bouvier.

Gergen, K.J. (1980) The emerging crisis in life-span developmental theory. In P.B. Baltes and O.G. Brim Jr (eds), *Life-span Development and Behavior*. Vol. 3. New York: Academic Press. pp. 31–63.

Gould, S.J. (1977) *Ontogeny and Phylogeny*. Cambridge, MA: Belknap.

Harré, R. (1983) *Personal Being: A Theory for Individual Psychology*. Oxford: Basil Blackwell.

Hayek, F.A. von (1979) Die drei Quellen menschlicher Werte. *Vorträge und Aufsätze*. Vol. 70. Walter Encken Institut. Tübingen: Mohr.

Heckhausen, H. (1985) Emotion im Leistungsverhalten aus ontogenetischer Sicht. In C. Eggers (ed.), *Emotionalität und Motivation im Kindes- und Jugendalter*. Frankfurt am Main: Fachbuchhandlung für Psychologie. pp. 95–132.

Heckhausen, J., Dixon, R.A. and Baltes, P.B. (1989) Gains and losses of development throughout adulthood as perceived by different adult age groups. *Developmental Psychology*, 25: 109–21.

Hempel, C.G. and Oppenheim, P. (1948) Studies on the logic of explanation. *Philosophy of Science*, 15: 135–46, 152–7, 172–4.

Herder, J.G. (1772) *Abhandlung über den Ursprung der Sprache*. Berlin: A. Weichert.

Hildebrand, D.K., Laing, J.D. and Rosenthal, H. (1977) *Prediction Analysis of Cross Classifications*. New York: Wiley.

Hofstätter, P.R. (1977) Einleitung: Psychologie und Gesellschaft. In T. Herrmann, P.R. Hofstätter, H.P. Huber and F.E. Weinert (eds), *Handbuch psychologischer Grundbegriffe*. Munich: Kösel. pp. 7–14.

Kagan, J. (1971) *Change and Continuity in Infancy*. New York: Wiley.

Kagan, J. (1976) Emergent themes in human development. *American Scientist*, 64: 186–96.

Kagan, J. (1980) Perspectives on continuity. In O.G. Brim Jr and J. Kagan (eds), *Constancy and Change in Human Development*. Cambridge, MA: Harvard University Press. pp. 26–74.

Kagan, J. (1981) Universals in human development. In R.H. Munroe, R.L. Munroe and B.B. Whiting (eds), *Handbook of Cross-Cultural Human Development*. New York: Garland STPM Press. pp. 53–63.

Kagan, J. (1983) Developmental categories and the promise of connectivity. In R.M. Lerner (ed.), *Developmental Psychology: Historical and Philosophical Perspectives*. Hillsdale, NJ: Erlbaum. pp. 29–54.

Kamlah, W. and Lorenzen, P. (1967) *Logische Propädeutik oder Vorschule des vernünftigen Redens*. Mannheim: Bibliographisches Institut.

Kant, I. (1969) *Critique of Pure Reason*. London: Dent. (Originally published 1781.)

Keil, F.C. (1979) *Semantic and Conceptual Development: An Ontological Perspective*. Cambridge, MA: Harvard University Press.

Klaus, G. and Buhr, M. (eds) (1971) *Philosophisches Wörterbuch*. Vol. 2. Leipzig: VEB Enzyklopädie.

Klix, F. (1980) *Erwachendes Denken. Eine Entwicklungsgeschichte der menschlichen Intelligenz*. Berlin (DDR): VEB Deutscher Verlag der Wissenschaften.

Kohlberg, L. (1973) Continuities in childhood and adult moral development revisited. In P.B. Baltes and K.W. Schaie (eds), *Life-span Developmental Psychology*. New York: Academic Press. pp. 179–204.

Lazarus, R.S. (1982) Thoughts on the relations between emotion and cognition. *American Psychologist*, 37: 1019–24.

Lenk, H. (1987) Strukturelle und empirische Implikationen: über einige struktur-induzierte Implikationen und deren Umkehrungen in der Soziometrie und

Sozialpsychologie. In J. Brandtstädter (ed.), *Struktur und Erfahrung in der psychologischen Forschung*. Berlin: de Gruyter. pp. 14–34.

Lerner, R.M. (1984) *On the Nature of Human Plasticity*. Cambridge: Cambridge University Press.

Lerner, R.M. and Busch-Rossnagel, N.A. (eds) (1981) *Individuals as Producers of their Development*. New York: Academic Press.

Lerner, R.M. and Kauffman, M.B. (1985) The concept of development in contextualism. *Developmental Review*, 5: 309–33.

Lewontin, R.C. (1982) Organism and environment. In H.C. Plotkin (ed.), *Learning, Development and Culture*. Chichester: Wiley. pp. 151–70.

Lickona, T. (ed.) (1976) *Moral Development and Behavior: Theory, Research and Social Issues*. New York: Holt, Rinehart & Winston.

Lindsay, P.H. and Norman, D.A. (1977) *Human Information Processing* (2nd edn). New York: Academic Press.

Looft, W. (1973) Socialization and personality throughout the life span: an examination of contemporary psychological approaches. In P.B. Baltes and K.W. Schaie (eds), *Life-span Developmental Psychology: Personality and Socialization*. New York: Academic Press.

Lorenzen, P. (1974) *Methodisches Denken*. Frankfurt am Main: Suhrkamp.

Müller, A. (1982) *Praktisches Folgern und Selbstgestaltung nach Aristoteles*. Freiburg: Alber.

Munroe, R.H., Munroe, R.L. and Whiting, B.B. (eds) (1981) *Handbook of Cross-Cultural Human Development*. New York: Columbia University Press.

Nagel, E. (1957) Determinism and development. In D.B. Harris (ed.), *The Concept of Development*. Minneapolis: University of Minnesota Press. pp. 15–24.

Overton, W.F. and Reese, H.W. (1981) Conceptual prerequisites for an understanding of stability–change and continuity–discontinuity. *International Journal of Behavioral Development*, 4: 99–123.

Piaget, J. (1970) *L'Epistémologie génétique*. Paris: Presses Universitaires de France.

Plomin, R. (1986) *Development, Genetics and Psychology*. Hillsdale, NJ: Erlbaum.

Popper, K.R. (1963) *Conjectures and Refutations: The Growth of Scientific Knowledge*. London: Routledge & Kegan Paul.

Putnam, H. (1975) *Mind, Language and Reality: Philosophical Papers*. Vol. 2. Cambridge: Cambridge University Press.

Putnam, H. (1979) Analyticity and apriority: beyond Wittgenstein and Quine. In P.A. French, T.E. Uehling Jr and H.K. Wettstein (eds), *Midwest Studies in Philosophy*. Vol. 4: *Studies in Metaphysics*. Minneapolis: University of Minnesota Press. pp. 423–41.

Quine, W. (1951) Two dogmas of empiricism. *Philosophical Review*, 55: 20–41.

Reese, H.W. and Overton, W.F. (1970) Models of development and theories of development. In L.R. Goulet and P.B. Baltes (eds), *Life-span Developmental Psychology: Research and Theory*. New York: Academic Press. pp. 116–49.

Roos, J. and Brandtstädter, J. (1988) Strukturelle und ontogenetische Bedingungen der Zuschreibung von Peinlichkeitsgefühlen. *Sprache und Kognition*, 7: 84–98.

Rudolph, W. and Tschohl, P. (1977) *Systematische Anthropologie*. Munich: Fink.

Scarr, S. and McCartney, K. (1983) How people make their own environments: a theory of genotype-environment effects. *Child Development*, 54: 424–35.

Scarr-Salapatek, S. (1976) An evolutionary perspective on infant intelligence: species patterns and individual variations. In M. Lewis (ed.), *Origins of Intelligence: Infancy and Early Adulthood*. New York: Plenum. pp. 165–97.

Schachter, S. and Singer, J.E. (1962) Cognitive, social and physiological determinants of emotional state. *Psychological Review*, 69: 379–99.

Schank, R. and Abelson, R.P. (1977) *Scripts, Plans, Goals and Understanding*. Hillsdale, NJ: Erlbaum.

Schopenhauer, A. (1951) *Essays from the Parerga and Paralipomena*, trans. T. Bailey Saunders. London: Allen & Unwin. (Originally published 1851.)

Selman, R. and Damon, W. (1975) The necessity (but insufficiency) of social perspective taking for conceptions of justice at three early levels. In D.J. DePalma and J.M. Foley (eds), *Moral Development: Current Theory and Research*. Hillsdale, NJ: Erlbaum. pp. 57–74.

Simon, H.A. (1957) *Models of Man, Social and Rational: Mathematical Essays on Rational Human Behavior in a Social Setting*. New York: Wiley.

Simon, H.A. (1969) *The Sciences of the Artificial*. Cambridge, MA: MIT Press.

Smedslund, J. (1978) Bandura's theory of self-efficacy: a set of common sense theorems. *Scandinavian Journal of Psychology*, 19: 101–2.

Smedslund, J. (1984) What is necessarily true in psychology? *Annals of Theoretical Psychology*, 2: 241–72.

Smith, E.E. and Medin, D.L. (1981) *Categories and Concepts*. Cambridge, MA: Harvard University Press.

Smith, E.R. (1984) Model of social inference processes. *Psychological Review*, 91: 392–413.

Spranger, E. (1914) *Lebensformen. Geisteswissenschaftliche Psychologie und Ethik der Persönlichkeit*. Tübingen: Niemeyer.

Stegmüller, W. (1969) *Wissenschaftliche Erklärung und Begründung*. Vol. 1: *Probleme und Resultate der Wissenschaftstheorie und Analytischen Philosophie*. Berlin: Springer.

Taylor, S.E. and Crocker, J. (1981) Schematic bases of social information processing. In E.T. Higgins, C.P. Herman and M.P. Zanna (eds), *Social Cognition*. Hillsdale, NJ: Erlbaum. pp. 89–134.

Tugendhat, E. (1979) *Selbstbewußtsein und Selbstbestimmung*. Frankfurt am Main: Suhrkamp.

Van Inwagen, P. (1975) The incompatibility of free will and determinism. *Philosophical Studies*, 27: 185–99.

Waddington, C.H. (1957) *The Strategy of the Genes*. London: Allen & Son.

Warren, N. (1980) Universality and plasticity, ontogeny and phylogeny: the resonance between culture and cognitive development. In J. Sants (ed.), *Developmental Psychology and Society*. London: Macmillan. pp. 290–322.

Weiner, B. (1982) The emotional consequences of causal attributions. In M.S. Clark and S.T. Fiscke (eds), *Affect and cognition*. Hillsdale, NJ: Erlbaum. pp. 185–209.

Weiner, B., Russell, D. and Lerman, D. (1978) Affective consequences of causal ascriptions. In J.H. Harvey, W. Ickes and R.F. Kidd (eds), *New Directions in Attribution Research*. Vol. 2. Hillsdale, NJ: Erlbaum. pp. 59–90.

Wittgenstein, L. (1965) *The Blue and Brown Books*. New York: Harper & Row.

Wittgenstein, L. (1967) *On Certainty*. New York: Harper & Row.

Wollheim, R. (1984) *The Thread of Life*. Cambridge, MA: Harvard University Press.

Zajonc, R.B. (1980) Feeling and thinking: preferences need no inferences. *American Psychologist*, 35: 151–75.

Zajonc, R.B. (1984) On the primacy of affect. *American Psychologist*, 39: 117–23.

6

The Cultural Construction of the Developing Child

Kenneth J. Gergen, Gabriele Gloger-Tippelt and Peter Berkowitz

In recent years developmentalists have paid increasing attention to beliefs about the child in varying cultures and historical periods. What do various cultures believe children possess in the way of psychological abilities, dispositions, capacities and the like? In this context, for example, Borstelman (1983) has carried out a comprehensive survey of beliefs about children in various historical periods and has surveyed various attempts to classify the child over the ages. Attempts have also been made to locate the source of parents' conceptions of children in the present era. As such research has demonstrated, parents' views may be affected by expert opinion (Bronfenbrenner, 1958), socio-economic status (Armendariz, Sameroff and Karter, 1983), self-serving bias (Sigel et al., 1980), generational cohort (Frenkel and Roer-Bernstein, 1982) and other factors (Sigel, 1985; Goodnow, 1988).

Most interesting, such research makes clear that conceptions of the child may depend on a host of factors uncorrelated to the actual nature of the child. Beliefs about the child vary markedly as a result of history, culture and personal disposition; yet the genetic make-up of the actual child seems to remain relatively constant. Perhaps the most radical view within this domain is that of Kessen (1979). As Kessen proposed, 'the child is essentially and eternally a cultural invention and . . . the variety in the child's definition is not the removable error of an incomplete science' (1979: 815). From this perspective the concept of the child is essentially a social construction, and no amount of observation will provide the basis for an unconstructed or interpretation-free account of the child's nature.

These various investigations are important in a variety of respects. At the outset historical research fosters a reflexive self-consciousness of the temporal dependency of the currently taken for granted. That is, we confront pressing tendencies to view today's child as the universal child – an exemplar of human nature. The way we conceptualize our children in the present era, their fears, levels of activity, capacities for thought and the like, we tend to generalize across time and culture. Haven't children always been the same? Yet, as historical inquiry into conceptions of the child reminds us, today's views are just that. And – of equal importance – they could be otherwise. We are free to explore other alternatives to conceptualizing the child.

Beliefs about the child are also significant because of their societal implications. For beliefs about children serve as the grounding rationale for the actions of parents and educational and religious institutions, as well as government policymakers. Within this context research has revealed, for example, systematic relationships between parents' beliefs and their teaching strategies (McGillicuddy-DeLisi, 1980, 1982; Sigel, 1982), beliefs in autonomy and options allowed to children (Skinner, 1985), the characteristics parents and teachers attribute to children and children's mathematical perform-ance (Holloway and Hess, 1985) and beliefs about children's capacities and child competence in a variety of tasks (Schaefer and Edgerton, 1985).

Finally, such exploration is important because of its unsettling implications for the science itself. This concern is based on two contrasting arguments. First, to the extent that conceptions of the child are pegged to actual childhood behaviour, then one must question the extent to which developmental psychology is a cumulative discipline. In the degree to which psychological disposi-tions and/or behavioural patterns of children undergo historical change (cf. van den Berg, 1961; de Mause, 1974; Aries, 1962), then the results of today's carefully controlled studies may constitute tomorrow's history (Gergen, 1982; see also Brandstädter, this volume). We do not learn increasingly more about children with each passing generation. Rather, we are unceasingly chasing after patterns in continuous motion. It is indeed this implication that underlies much of the interest in cohort comparisons in the area of lifespan development (Baltes and Reese, 1984). In the case of adulthood we are more sanguine about the possibility of changing trajectories of development across different eras. We scarcely believe that adolescence or middle age is the same today as it was a century or even thirty years ago. Yet, if we believe adulthood development is historically dependent, then what is to prevent the same conclusions in the case of childhood?

The second challenge to traditional science proceeds on different grounds. In this case, it is argued, the link between conceptions of the child and the actual activities of children is inherently governed by social convention. Whether children are believed to possess 'fear', for example, and what behaviours constitute manifestations of fear are not given through observation of the child. They are not read off the surfaces of the body. Rather, *such categories and their application derive from social negotiation within the culture.* The culture imposes on the child a particular framework of interpretation. As a result, commonsense beliefs about the nature of the child furnish both the context for and the limits over scientific understanding. Because scientific concepts cannot be inductively derived from observation (Hanson, 1958), developmental research must inevitably draw from the compendium of commonsense beliefs within the culture. Further, because developmental research must make sense within the existing frameworks of cultural understanding, such research can scarcely draw conclusions that lie beyond the range of common understanding (Smedslund, 1985). Should the scientist propose, for example, that the zenith of individual development occurs at birth, and thereafter one's capacities only deteriorate with age, virtually no one would take it seriously. Such an account would so violate the commonsense conceptions of development that no data would be convincing otherwise. It is for these and other reasons that proposals have been put forward for a sociology of socialization (Lüscher, 1975). If limits to the conception of the child are principally social in origin, then in what sense can science transcend culture?

The present chapter extends these concerns with beliefs about children in three specific ways. First, the vast share of existing research has focused on specific traits, dispositions or capacities of children, without special regard to conceptions of developmental trajectory. Selected research has been concerned with the kinds of activities parents judge children to be capable of at various ages (Dix and Grusec, 1983). However, very little attention has been given to the implicit theories of developmental change of which such age gradings may be manifestations. Are there prevailing but largely unarticulated theories of childhood development to which parents in contemporary society subscribe? Do parents anticipate a natural course of psychological development and, if so, what kind of trajectory do they anticipate? It is to these questions that the research reported in the present paper is initially oriented. However, to broaden the scope of study, the research will also compare implicit beliefs about child development across national boundaries and age groups. Based on the results of historical study, we might anticipate significant cultural differences in the concept of development. However, within various cultures, the narratives or cultural scripts for describing development may be more homogeneous. Thus, regardless of whether we are concerned with an unmarried youth or a practising mother, development may be described similarly for those who share a common pool of cultural accounts.

Two closely related lines of study will also be reported. After documenting common beliefs about the developing child we shall explore the relationship between such beliefs and the mother's role in child-rearing. As reasoned earlier, parental treatment of the child is largely based on the way in which the child is conceptualized. If this is so, then we should find beliefs about developmental trajectory linked to specific forms of parental activity. In particular we might locate a trajectory in preferred forms of mothering during the early period of development.

After exploring the cultural construction of the child and related approaches to mothering, we shall finally turn our attention to the question of origin and sustenance in such constructions. If there are widely shared assumptions about developmental change, how are we to understand their emergence and continuation within the culture? Within this context we shall attend to the ways in which discourse about the child and associated practices of mothering are enmeshed within a broader network of assumptions about the nature of personal well-being, the social structure and the economic system. In this case we shall explore the possibility that conceptions of development are little related to the actual child, but are embedded in a broad array of cultural belief systems. Let us begin, then, with a consideration of women's beliefs about child development.

Mechanistic versus Organismic Conceptions of Development

Although there are many possible ways of conceptualizing developmental sequences, two are of particular historical interest. The well-known distinction between mechanistic and organismic theories of development, as documented by Overton and Reese (1973) and Reese and Overton (1970), does far more than isolate two localized preferences within the profession. Rather, the distinction calls attention to two longstanding intellectual (and ideological) traditions within western culture. The mechanistic conception, in which humans function much as machines whose actions are the fixed outcomes of environmental inputs, has deep roots in the longstanding empiricist tradition. It essentially echoes a line of thought appearing and reappearing in the writings of Locke, Hume and the Mills, and again within logical empiricists accounts of the present century. From this perspective, the effective functioning of the organism is achieved when it is a pawn to nature's messages; we adapt most adequately when we accurately perceive and record the nature of the world as it is. When extended to the developmental sphere, this is to say that proper development will necessitate an environmental dependency. The view is captured within the present century by a variety of behaviourist and neo-behaviourist theories of child development (Gergen and Benack, 1983).

In contrast, organismic theories of development typically hold that the individual harbours an ontogenetic potential for directed growth. Thus human beings should manifest a predictable unfolding of capacities, with the fully effective functioning of the organism the natural endpoint. This orientation towards development can be traced to the tradition of continental rationalism, with its emphasis on the inherent capacities of persons for logic, reason or functional categorization. The organismic view also has its roots in the broadly shared belief of the nineteenth century in the 'great chain of being', wherein the child's development is towards increasing affinity with God. Similar thoughts later emerged in Haeckel's *recapitulation theory*, or the theory that ontogenetic development of the child recapitulates the phylogenetic movement of the species from lower to higher organisms. Organismic views are expressed today in the theories of Piaget, Erikson, Kohlberg and many others.

With these thoughts in mind an initial study was mounted in which samples of female adults estimated the age at which various psychological capacities and dispositions generally emerge in the developmental course. To the extent that the mechanistic view is commonly shared, we might anticipate little systematic ordering of such beliefs. From this perspective traits or capacities should be subject to environmental moulding; thus psychological tendencies should emerge at whatever time there are effective shaping processes brought to bear. For example, a child should learn to be sociable, altruistic or empathetic when it receives proper training; children will learn to reason when appropriately instructed, and so on. Yet, if the organismic view is more widely shared, we might anticipate a systematic ordering in the kinds of traits or dispositions attributed to children at various ages. Specifically, this ordering should reveal a belief in ordered and possibly progressive change. (It is possible to believe in a systematic ordering of development based on age-graded socialization practices. However, the rationale for such practices would inevitably fall back on beliefs about the nature of the child at various stages, for example, readiness for various socialization experiences, and might thus be considered fundamentally organismic.) To expand on the implications of this initial study the following variations were also added.

Cross-cultural comparison. In the same way that historical injury has demonstrated changes in conceptions of the child across time, so have researchers begun to search for variations in belief across disparate cultures. Ethnographic research has revealed striking variations in the indigenous psychological theories (Heelas and Locke, 1981) to which various peoples are committed. Among these are differences in beliefs about emotion (Lutz, 1982), motivational states (Rosaldo, 1980), and personal traits (Shweder and Miller, 1985). With specific regard to the child, parental conceptions have been explored, for example, among East African tribes (Sameroff, Seifer and Elias, 1982), and differences documented between Mexican and Anglo parents (Armendariz, Sameroff and Karter, 1983), Japanese and American mothers (Hess et al., 1980), and Australian- and Lebanese-born mothers (Goodnow et al., 1984). Harkness and Super (1983; Super and Harkness, 1981) have also explored a variety of cultural dynamics at play in generating specific constructions of the child. To extend such concerns, the present study employed two samples of women, one from the United States and the other from West Germany. Because the roots of the mechanistic view of children are lodged in the soil of British empiricism, along with American pragmatism, it was reasoned that the American sample might demonstrate less pronounced beliefs in a specific developmental trajectory than would the German sample. The commitment to more organismic perspective in the German sample should also be reinforced by the deep historical links between this view and continental rationalism.

Variations in motherhood experience. It is traditional to hold that conceptions of the child vary in their degree of objectivity. If so, one might anticipate that women possessing greatest experience with children should be more accurate in their accounts than those with little experience. It is through ongoing interaction with children, it might be ventured, that one acquires knowledge concerning the nature of the child. Thus within any given culture we might anticipate differences between mothers and non-mothers in prevailing conceptions of the child. And, for scientific purposes, we might be especially sensitized to the views of the experienced group in terms of fashioning scientific accounts. However, if variations between groups are not found, the relativist conclusion is again congenial. Views of children may simply reflect broadly shared conventions of discourse or cultural scripts regarding the nature of child development. Such scripts may determine women's accounts of child development regardless of actual experience (see Knight and Goodnow, 1988).

Gender variations. A considerable body of literature has revealed major variations in the patterns of child-rearing employed with male as opposed to female children (see reviews by Maccoby and Jacklin, 1974; Huston, 1983). Such variations in child-rearing are felt to be particularly important in shaping gender differences in the adult. However, comparatively little attention has been given to the belief systems upon which such child-rearing patterns may rest. This initial study attempted to address the issue by inquiring into beliefs regarding the development of male versus female children. Do women bring to the female child different anticipations regarding patterns of development from those they bring to the male child? In particular, is there a prevalence of male bias, with males viewed as more advanced in their developmental acquisitions than females? Further, if such biases do occur are they general across cultural boundaries? And are their effects reduced by the experience of motherhood itself?

Depictions of Development

The participants in this research phase were 128 women, half from West Germany and the other half from the United States. Within each national group half the sample was made up of mothers (average age thirty-one years) and the remaining half of women who had not had children (average age twenty-three years). A variety of developmental texts and child-rearing manuals were consulted to establish a basic repository of commonly used terms for understanding the psychology of the child. From these sources a pool of twenty-seven characteristics were developed, subsequently reduced for the present study to represent three separate clusters: *emotional tendencies* (feels pain, feels affection, feels fear, feels sad), *social tendencies* (wants to help, feels pride, feels sympathetic, wants understanding) and *reflective tendencies* (thinks logically, makes plans, thinks abstractly). A questionnaire was subsequently developed asking participants to estimate the age at which a child generally begins to exhibit each of the characteristics. Response options for each characteristic began with 'at birth' and proceeded with additional options offered at every six months interval up to the age of six years.

For present purposes let us consider the women's estimates of the child on the aggregated items within each of the three clusters (emotional, social and reflective). The mean number of months at which the participants believed the characteristics in each of these clusters emerged during the course of development is featured in Figure 6.1.

The initial interest of the study is whether there exists a common

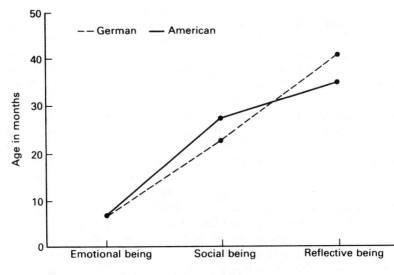

Figure 6.1   *Perceived characteristics of children*

belief in a natural unfolding of the child's psychological tendencies. Are adult women 'organismic' in their views, or do they adopt a mechanistic stance in which any trait may be trained or shaped at any time? And if there is an organismic orientation, what form does the developmental trajectory assume? As an examination of Figure 6.1 makes clear, there is a widely shared belief in orderly psychological development. Regardless of national background, or status of motherhood, the participants demonstrate a belief that the psychological tendencies of the child emerge in a particular developmental order. Specifically, this order is one in which emotional tendencies are said to exist in the child during the first year of life. Pain is said to be present within the first month, affection and anxiety emerge by approximately mid-year, and sadness emerges at approximately twelve months. In sharp contrast, it is held that such social tendencies as sympathy, pride and conscience do not emerge until the child is a little over two years of age (mean number of months = 24.99). Such social proclivities are also believed to precede the capacities for reflection. Abilities for abstract or logical thought are not granted to the child until he/she has reached the third year of life (mean number of months = 37.50).

While differences in the above means proved statistically reliable (all beyond 0.01 level using MANOVA), there is no overall difference between American and German samples in their beliefs about the order in which these psychological characteristics emerge in the child. The belief in orderly development prevails in both cultures. Nor is there an overall tendency to see males versus females manifesting these characteristics at differential rates. Male children do not *generally* enjoy a higher estimate (exceptions to be noted shortly). However, there is a significant tendency ($p < 0.05$) for women with experience at mothering to believe that all the psychological characteristics as a whole emerge earlier than for women without experience at motherhood. Differential accuracy in perception cannot be ruled out. However, this result may also reflect the fact that the presence of children in the lives of the mothers encourage a search for various psychological qualities. With selectivity in search these various characteristics can be 'discovered'. We shall return to this point shortly.

Although we found no evidence of overall gender bias, statistical analyses show that the overall conclusion must be qualified. In particular, the sample of American mothers harbours a significant male bias in their beliefs about development. They believe that male children manifest both social ($X = 23.48$ for males; $X = 29.63$ for females) and reflective tendencies ($X = 28.25$ for males; $X = 32.00$ for females) earlier than females. In contrast, German mothers believe female children generally develop more rapidly than males. In each domain the female is said to demonstrate the psychological characteristic between four and five months earlier than the male. It should also be noted that the differences in gender bias are primarily found in the mother sample; the non-mothers do not demonstrate the biases in significant degree.

The initial concern of the first study was with women's implicit theories of childhood development. As we asked, is there a pervasive belief in the developmental trajectory of the child, and if so what kind of trajectory is envisioned? If mechanistic views of the child are prevalent, we might not anticipate generalized agreement among women in the age grading of various psychological characteristics. As the results of the study indicated, there was overwhelming agreement that development occurs in an orderly way. Across cultures, motherhood status and gender of the child, the women agreed that emotional characteristics generally emerge in the first year of the child's life; social tendencies come into play during the latter part of the second year, and capacities for logical reflection emerge at roughly three years of age. The pervasiveness and uniformity of these beliefs can be more precisely demonstrated in correlation analyses. Specifically, rank-order correlations were conducted in which the ranks (according to mean number of months at which development occurs) of each psychological characteristics judged within each sub-sample were correlated with the rank assignments within every other sub-sample. For example, the ranking of the traits assigned by German mothers to female children was correlated with the ranking of the same traits to female children by German non-mothers. This particular correlation was found to be 0.97 – indicating virtually perfect agreement regarding the relative timetable for which traits precede others in the developmental course ($p < 0.05$). Of the twenty-eight possible correlations among samples, all were both positive and statistically significant. Seven were over 0.90, fourteen were between 0.80 and 0.90, and seven were between 0.67 and 0.80. In effect all samples of women rating both male and female children showed broad agreement about the specific order of development.

Is one to conclude from this univocal view of developmental trajectory that children actually do go through these various stages of growth – that they are born with inherent emotional tendencies, develop social capacities during roughly their second year, and only thereafter manifest abstract conceptual capacities? There is ample reason to be suspicious of such a conclusion. First, on the conceptual level there is the insoluble difficulty of determining, on the basis of overt action, whether or not a child does or does not possess any particular psychological capacity, trait or motive. This is essentially a problem in hermeneutics or interpretation (Gergen, Hepburn and Comer, 1986). How, for example, does one move logically from an infant's facial expression, body movements or vocal sounds to the conclusion that the child possesses 'reason', 'desire', 'insight' or 'compassion'? In differing cultures and historical periods the same overt signals are read in dramatically different ways. Similarly the way a Freud, an Erikson or a Skinner would interpret these notions would differ markedly from that of a Piaget or Vygotsky. And on what grounds is one interpretation to be preferred to another, if there is no means (outside additional conjecture) on which to base judgement?

Certain aspects of the data also lend themselves to the social constructionist conclusion. Most important, we find that German and American women differ (regardless of whether they have experience as mothers) in their perception of male as opposed to female development. American mothers believe males manifest certain capacities earlier than females; German women believe the opposite. If developmental trajectories are in fact organismic, and developmental accounts are accurate descriptors, such differences would not be anticipated. In addition, the high degree of agreement between experienced mothers and the younger non-mothers in the rank ordering of the psychological tendencies suggests that these reports are sampling from shared understandings within the culture rather than close observation.

Developmental Conceptions and Rearing the Child

Thus far we see that across cultures and motherhood status, and regardless of the child's gender, there are widely shared beliefs in the character of psychological development. Earlier we proposed that such conceptions were important, for one, because they furnished the grounds for action. Depending on what one believes about the nature of the developing child, certain forms of child-rearing will be favoured over others. A second line of research attempted to explore this critical assumption more directly (Brauks and Machka, 1986). In particular, the question is raised as to whether the beliefs about children's development are geared to patterns of child-rearing. Do women believe that the nature of the child as he/she develops places specialized demands on them as mothers?

In this study 104 German and 31 American women participated. In each case two forms of questioning took place. First, women in both samples responded to a questionnaire composed of twenty-one psychological characteristics. These traits fell into the same three clusters as those used in the initial study (emotional, social and cognitive). Mothers again indicated the approximate period of a child's development in which they believed the traits were initially evident. In effect, this portion of the study replicated the preceding research, using an expanded number of traits in each of the three categories. The replication was felt to be particularly important, as well, in offsetting the possible criticism that any randomly produced difference in ordering would spuriously produce results favouring an organismic conception of development.

However, the women also completed a second questionnaire. In this case they were asked to indicate the approximate age of the child at which a mother should emphasize each of a series of twenty motherly activities. These activities were again divided into three distinct clusters: *mother as emotional caretaker* (including such activities as being affectionate, comforting, calming and giving sympathy); *mother as social partner* (including playing games, sharing feeling, fostering assertiveness, and giving praise and blame); and *mother as cognitive enhancer* (including such activities as giving explanations, furnishing reasons, solving problems together and explaining rules and their consequences).

If conceptions of psychological development have directive implications for action, then we should anticipate that women's conceptions of their role at various points in the child's development should correspond to their views of the child's development. Is this the case? An indication of the relationship between beliefs about development and characterization of the mother's role is contained in Figure 6.2. Here we have first plotted the average ages that the women assigned to trait development in the three clusters (top

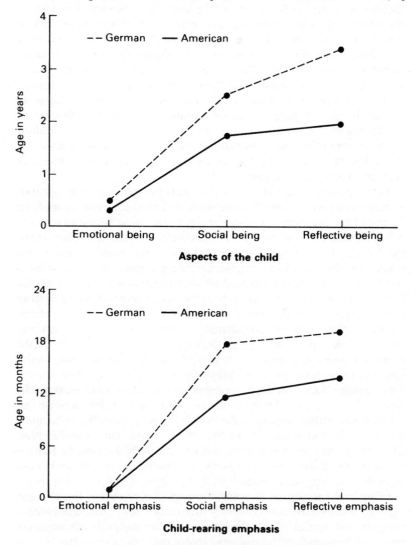

Figure 6.2   *Relationship between perceived characteristics of children and child-rearing emphasis*

graph), and the average ages at which the women believed the three clusters of child-rearing behaviours are most essential (lower graph). As the graphs first indicate, the results of our first study were replicated. In both the German and American samples, an orderly sequence is evidenced. Emotional traits are believed to emerge within the first year of life, social traits towards the end of the second year, followed by cognitive tendencies somewhere toward the third year. The means prove reliably different (MANOVA, $p < 0.1$) in each case. The precise means do differ somewhat from those shown in Figure 6.1. However, it should be recalled that the number of traits in each cluster has been expanded for the second study. It is further noticed that the difference between German and American women in their views of the age at which cognitive tendencies are evidenced is again demonstrated. In the initial study we found that German women tended to believe that cognitive tendencies emerged at a later period than did American women; we again find this a statistically significant discrepancy ($p < 0.05$), in this case more accentuated.

Turning to the question of child-rearing patterns, we again find an orderly trajectory. As the figure demonstrates, the mothering roles favoured by the samples also evidence the same trajectory as the beliefs about the child's nature. Specifically, in the first year of the child's life, the women believe that mothers should be especially tuned to their child's emotions, being affectionate, soothing, comforting, giving sympathy and the like. However, toward the beginning of the second year, the emphasis shifts to social interchange. Here the women emphasize the importance of the mother's playing games, praising and blaming, setting limits and the like. Later in development the emphasis shifts again. Here the mother's major role becomes one of cognitive enhancement. In this case the women see the major tasks of the mother as giving reasons and explanations, solving problems with the child, stimulating fantasy and the like. Differences among mother roles in the three periods also differ significantly (MANOVA, $p < 0.05$). The same trajectory is evidenced in both the German and American samples. Further, paralleling the earlier results, the German women tend to place the requirements for cognitive enhancement significantly later than do the American women.

Of special interest, it is notable in both samples that the average age at which various child-rearing techniques are emphasized *precedes* the age at which the various psychological tendencies are believed to manifest themselves. (Note differing calibration of the axis for the two figures.) Based on these differences, it may be conjectured that women do not typically see their mothering as a response to traits evidenced on the child's part. Rather, they believe that their activities are significant elicitors of the innate tendencies of the child. Much as they might treat a tender plant to daily watering and sunlight to ensure healthy growth, they may view their actions as stimulating the child to reach its inherent potential.

Although this organismic explanation of the patterns is appealing in its consistency with our earlier conjectures, competing explanations are also possible. In particular, it is possible that the causal network is the reverse from that implied in our earlier theorizing. There we suggested that the parents' treatment of the child is based on, or made reasonable by, a forestructure of conceptions of the child's nature. However, one might also argue that the mothers first of all engage in a set of child-rearing procedures, and as a result come to view the child in ways that are consistent. Thus beliefs about the child may be rationalizations for behavioural commitments already made. The present pattern of results would lend credibility to such a conjecture. However, if this view is taken, one is still left to confront the problem of the basis for the child-rearing patterns. It is less than appealing to propose that the preferred patterns of child-rearing are simply accidental emergents, nonsensical to the participants until they can think of reasons for their existence. Rather, one is invited to consider conceptual grounds that would render such actions intelligible. This consideration brings us to our third line of study.

The Child in the Web of Cultural Meaning

A broad array of social constructionist inquiry suggests that theories of human action – on both the lay and scientific level – may fruitfully be viewed as patterns of social discourse (see Gergen's 1985 review; also Potter and Wetherell, 1987). Forms of discourse, it may be ventured, are embedded within broader social patterns – including not only patterns of discourse, but wide-ranging patterns of daily conduct. The regularity in relationship between various patterns (both within and outside discourse) is not causal but conventional. To illustrate, if one employs a subject and a transitive verb within a partially formed sentence, one can predict with some reliability the subsequent use of a direct object as the sentence is completed. The inclusion of the object is not caused by the preceding fragment of the sentence in the sense of lawful determination; rather the inclusion is required by conventional rules of grammar.

From this perspective we may view discourse about children as an arrangement of actions that, figuratively speaking, stand in a grammatical relationship to other patterns of action. What may be said of the child should thus be systematically related to other forms of conduct in which the person is engaged (Kagan, 1983; Reid and Valsiner, 1985). These forms of conduct may include both discourse and other activities. For example, whether one claims that children have strong erotic impulses should typically be related to one's espousal of other psychoanalytic suppositions. To lay claim to the entire psychoanalytic scaffolding and disavow such impulses, while possible in principle, would be problematic by academic conventions of language usage. Similarly, to espouse beliefs in the nurturant and protective care of children would be inconsistent with what is commonly called 'physical punishment' as a parenting technique. In effect, beliefs about child development may have their origins in and be sustained by a substantial array of conventionally related activities.

Earlier research has demonstrated mutually supportive links among various beliefs, values or theories people have about children (McGillicuddy-DeLisi, 1980; Svensson-Garling, Garling and Valsiner, 1985). In this third study, however, we wished to expand the array of cultural beliefs that may be relevant to conceptions of the child. If the nature of the child does not itself demand a particular account of its development, can we trace accounts of the child to other linguistic commitments? Is the account one gives of child development related, for example, to conceptions of the work place, the family and the role of the mother more generally? Can we view these various conceptual arenas as mutually interdependent bodies of discourse?

To pursue these matters more deeply three questionnaires were developed to assess language practices that might have an important relationship with implicit theories of the child.

Competition in the work place. People differ in the extent to which they view the work place as competitive and threatening as opposed to nurturant and dependable. Such differences might reasonably be related to differing beliefs about the character of the developing child. As reasoned in the present study, it would be consistent with a discourse committed to competition in the work place to hold that the child is psychologically independent as opposed to dependent. If one holds that the work place is stressfully competitive, and one values the child's future, it would be appropriate to describe the developing child as independent rather than dependent. Further, those who see the work place as competitive should feel that a mother's attention is required in order to help the child function rationally and as an independent agent. To measure conceptions of the work place, six Likert items were developed that asked respondents the degree to which they agreed (on a seven-point scale from 'disagree' to 'agree') with such statements as 'The working world is a highly competitive one; you must be on your toes to stay ahead,' and 'Most employers care about their employees; they support them when they are down.'

Solidarity of the family. People differ in the extent to which they view the family as an emotionally bonded set of interdependent relationships as opposed to a collection of fundamentally independent agents. Differences in such views may also be related to beliefs about the developing child. Specifically, those who view the ideal family as an emotionally solidary unit might congenially view children as more dependent and as possessing strong social needs. They might also contend that the child's emotional life requires parental attention, but that capacities for rationality and independence are less in need of attention. The measure of family conceptions was composed of twelve items on which respondents indicated on a five-point scale the degree to which they felt each item represented their ideal family. Agreement with such items as 'Each family member strongly needs the other' and disagreement with such items as 'Family members have commitments outside the house' counted as indicators of belief in the emotionally solidary family.

Centrality of motherhood. A variety of studies have demonstrated historical shifts in the conception of motherhood (Badinter, 1980; Dally, 1982; Schütze, 1986). Differences in beliefs about the role of the mother may also play a part in prompting or sustaining beliefs about the child. In particular, mothers may differ in the extent to which they view motherhood as a major commitment as opposed to one among many aspects of their identity. Mothers who believe that child-care is their most important task should tend to see children as more dependent, as having strong social needs and as requiring attention for the development of their rational and emotional capacities, along with their autonomy. To sample discourse about the mothering role a twelve-item scale was developed with scoring similar to that used in the conceptions of family measure. Agreement with such items as 'Gives major attention to her children's needs' and disagreement with 'Tries to develop her own interests' were used to indicate a view of motherhood as central.

We have reasoned above that commitments to these various forms of discourse might be related, by force of common language conventions, to various belief statements about the child. These latter beliefs were assessed in additional questionnaires as follows:

Social needs. On five-point scales respondents indicated the prominence or importance of various characteristics during the child's first six years. Eight characteristics (within a larger pool) reflected social needs (for example, 'need for affection', 'desire for contact').

Independence needs. Within the same measure as above, five items reflected needs of the child for independence (for example, 'need for freedom and independence', 'mastery over environment').

Attention to emotional development. On a separate questionnaire respondents were asked to rate on a five-point scale the amount of parental attention required for the development of various characteristics in children. Four of these characteristics treated the emotional development of the child (for example, 'capacity for affection', 'happiness in being with others').

Attention to cognitive development. On the preceding measure three items were used to tap beliefs in the attention required for cognitive development (for example, 'intellect' and 'creativity').

Attention to autonomy. Four items of the preceding measure tapped beliefs in the attention required for the child's development of autonomy (for example, 'a sense of freedom and independence', 'competitive striving').

To explore how discourse commitments regarding work, family and motherhood are related to these various beliefs about children, an additional sample of forty-five American mothers (with children between one and six years) filled out a battery of questionnaires in which the above instruments were embedded. Scores on each of the measures were then inter-correlated. Resulting correlations (Pearsonian r) between the three societal beliefs (work place, family and motherhood) and the five beliefs about the developing child are contained in Table 6.1.

It was not anticipated that correlations among the various bodies of discourse would be exceedingly high. As pointed out, we are speaking of conventionalized relationships among ways of accounting

Table 6.1 *Work place, family and motherhood discourse as related to conceptions of the child*

	Workplace competition	Family solidarity	Motherhood primacy
Social needs	np	0.33**	ns
Independence needs	0.38***	−0.32**	−0.27*
Attention to emotion	np	0.25*	ns
Attention to cognition	ns	−0.30**	0.35**
Attention to autonomy	0.33**	ns	0.27*

```
  * p < 0.10       np = no prediction
 ** p < 0.05       ns = non-significant
*** p < 0.01
```

for the world. And as we saw in our earlier study, such conventions offer a high degree of latitude in usage (see also Newson and Newson, 1976, and Finch, 1980, for a discussion of multiplicities in cultural messages). However, as Table 6.1 reveals, the instances of moderate relationship are predominant.

If we look first at the way in which views regarding the work place are related to conceptions of the child, we find that two of the three predicted relationships are statistically reliable. Mothers who believe that the work place is competitive are more likely to see the young child as having strong independency needs ($r = 0.38$; $p < 0.01$), and believe that as mothers they must help the child realize his/her potentials for autonomy ($r = 0.33$, $p < 0.05$). Similarly, mothers' ideals of an emotionally solidary family are reliably related to beliefs about children. Those who view the ideal family as one in which there are close emotional ties also believe the young child demonstrates strong social needs ($r = 0.33$, $p < 0.05$) and does not possess strong needs for independence ($r = -0.32$; $p < 0.05$). Although of borderline significance such mothers also tend to see their children's emotional needs as requiring attention ($r = 0.26$; $p < 0.10$), and not their cognitive capacities ($r = -0.30$; $p < 0.05$). The relationship between family solidarity and attention to the child's autonomy proved non-significant.

Although the overall pattern is less powerful, we find similar relationships between mothers' views of their own role and their conceptions of the child. Those who feel their primary commitment is towards their children believe their children's cognitive capacities ($r = 0.35$; $p < 0.05$) along with their potential for autonomy ($r = 0.27$; $p < 0.10$) require more parental attention. The anticipated relationship between conception of motherhood and requirement for emotional development was not found. However, as predicted, there was a tendency ($r = -0.27$; $p < 0.10$) for those who saw motherhood as primary to view children as having low independence needs. Beliefs in the primacy of motherhood failed to predict to a belief in the social needs of the child.

In general, then, the pattern of relationships is supportive of the present orientation towards beliefs about childhood development. Of the thirteen predicted relationships, six were significant at beyond the 0.05 level, and three others at better than 0.10. Four of the thirteen relationships were non-significant, but in the predicted direction. In effect, mothers' beliefs about the work place, the family and their role as mother show a reliable relationship with their conceptions of the child and the extent to which their efforts are required for the child to develop its potential. Beliefs in work, family and motherhood play a complementary and mutually supportive role to beliefs about the nature of the child. To illustrate the real-world implications, such results suggest that if full equality between the sexes is approximated in the work place there will be reverberating effects in other domains of belief. Specifically, changes will occur not only in women's conception of work, but also in conceptions of the family and their task as mothers. Further, such changes will be accompanied by shifts in the prevailing conception of the child's psychological development.

Summary

The present chapter first explored women's conceptions of the developing child. As the inquiry revealed, women in both the United States and Germany implicitly believe in an orderly sequence of child development. In this organismic view, children are viewed as emotional at birth, then manifesting social capabilities in roughly the second year of life, and finally demonstrating capacities for abstract thought in roughly the third year of life. Given the similarities in views between mothers and non-mothers, and cross-national differences in conceptions of male versus female development, the conclusion was favoured that these conceptions were expressions of cultural belief systems rather than the 'true nature of the child'. In the second line of inquiry it was shown how these views of the developing child are tied to various patterns of child-rearing. Women's conceptions of their role as mothers were systematically related to their beliefs about child development. Finally, it was shown how beliefs about the child are linked to other conceptions women have of the world – specifically, the world of work, family structure and the role of the woman. Accounts of the developing child, it was reasoned, are not so much dependent on the actual nature of the child as they are on other forms of culturally shared discourse. Conceptions of the child's development appear as part of a tapestry of interdependent accounts of the world and their associated practices.

References

Aries, P. (1962) *Centuries of Childhood*, trans. R. Baldick. New York: Vintage.
Armendariz, J.M., Sameroff, A.J. and Karter, B. (1983) Effects of Mexican–American acculturation on parents' concepts of development. Unpublished manuscript.
Badinter, E. (1980) *Mother Love: Myth and Reality*. New York: Macmillan.
Baltes, P.B. and Reese, H.W. (1984) The life-span perspective in developmental psychology. In M.H. Bornstein and M.E. Lamb (eds), *Developmental Psychology: An Advanced Textbook*. Hillsdale, NJ: Erlbaum. pp. 493–512.

Borstelman, L.J. (1983) Children before psychology: ideas about children from antiquity to the late 1800's. In P.H. Mussen (ed.), *Handbook of Child Psychology*. Vol. 1: *History, Theory and Methods* (4th edn). New York: Wiley. pp. 3–40.

Brauks, M. and Machka, S.T. (1986) Alltagsvorstellungen über die physische Entwicklung des Kindes und damit korrespondierende mütterliche Tätigkeiten. Unpublished diploma thesis, Psychologisches Institut der Universität Heidelberg.

Bronfenbrenner, U. (1958) Socialization and social class in time and space. In C.C. Maccoby, J.M. Newcomb and E.L. Hartley (eds), *Readings in Social Psychology*. New York: Holt, Rinehart and Winston. pp. 400–25.

Cashmore, J. (1980) Models of intelligence and development: a child's eye view. Paper presented at the Jubilee Congress of ANZAAS, Adelaide, Australia.

Dally, A. (1982) *Inventing Motherhood: The Consequences of an Ideal*. New York: Schocken.

de Mause, L. (1974) *The History of Childhood*. New York: Psychohistory Press.

Dix, T.H. and Grusec, J. (1983) Parent attribution processes in the socialization of children. In I.E. Sigel (ed.), *Parental Belief Systems: The Psychological Consequences for Children*. Hillsdale, NJ: Erlbaum. pp. 201–33.

Feil, L.A. and Sameroff, A.S. (1979) Mother's conception of child development: socioeconomic, crosscultural, and parity comparisons. Paper presented at meetings of the American Psychological Association, New York.

Finch, J. (1980) Devising conventional performances: the case of clergyman's wives. *Sociological Review*, 28: 851–70.

Frenkel, D.O. and Roer-Bernstein, D. (1982) Traditional and modern contributions to changing infant-rearing ideologies of two ethnic communities. *Monographs of the Society for Research in Child Development*, 47 (4, Serial No. 196).

Gergen, K.J. (1982) *Toward the Transformation in Social Knowledge*. New York: Springer.

Gergen, K.J. (1985) The social constructionist movement in modern psychology. *American Psychologist*, 40: 266–75.

Gergen, K.J. and Benack, S. (1983) Metatheoretical influences on conceptions of human development. In M. Lewin (ed.), *In the Shadow of the Past: Psychology Portrays the Sexes*. New York: Columbia University Press. pp. 274–94.

Gergen, K.J., Hepburn, A. and Comer, D. (1986) The hermeneutics of personality description. *Journal of Personality and Social Pyschology*, 6: 1261–70.

Goodnow, J.J. (1988) Parent's ideas, actions, and feelings: models and methods from developmental and social psychology. *Child Psychology*, 59: 286–320.

Goodnow, J.J., Cashmore, J., Cotton, S. and Knight, R. (1984) Mother's developmental timetables in two cultural groups. *International Journal of Psychology*, 19: 193–205.

Hanson, N.R. (1958) *Patterns of Discovery*. Cambridge: Cambridge University Press.

Harkness, S. and Super, C.M. (1983) The cultural construction of child development. *Ethos*, 11 (4): 222–31.

Heelas, P. and Locke, A. (1981) *Indigenous Psychologies*. London: Academic Press.

Hess, R., Kashiwagi, K., Azuma, H., Price, G. and Dickson, W. (1980) Maternal expectations for mastery of developmental tasks in Japan and the United States. *International Journal of Psychology*, 15: 259–71.

Holloway, S.D. and Hess, R.D. (1985) Mothers' and teachers' attributions about children's mathematics performance. In I.E. Sigel (ed.), *Parental Belief Systems*. Hillsdale, NJ: Erlbaum. pp. 177–99.

Huston, A. (1983) Sex typing. In P.H. Mussen and E.M. Hetherington (eds),
    Handbook of Child Psychology. Vol. 4. New York: Wiley. pp. 388–95.
Kagan, J. (1983) Classifications of the child. Epilogue to P.H. Mussen (ed.),
    Handbook of Child Psychology, Vol. 1: *History, Theory and Methods* (4th edn).
    New York: Wiley. pp. 527–60.
Kessen, W. (1979) The American child and other cultural inventions. *American
    Psychologist*, 34: 815–20.
Knight, R.A. and Goodnow, J.J. (1988) Parents' beliefs about influence over
    cognitive and social development. *International Journal of Behavioral Develop-
    ment*, 11 (4): 517–27.
Lüscher, K. (1975) Perspektiven einer Soziologie der Sozialisation – Die Entwicklung
    der Rolle des Kindes. *Zeitschrift für Soziologie*, 4: 359–79.
Lutz, C. (1982) The domain of emotion words on Ifaluk. *American Ethnologist*, 9:
    113–28.
Maccoby, E.E. and Jacklin, C.N. (1974) *The Psychology of Sex Differences*.
    Stanford, CA: Stanford University Press.
McGillicuddy-DeLisi, A.V. (1980) The role of parental beliefs in the family as a
    system of mutual influences. *Family Relations*, 29: 317–23.
McGillicuddy-DeLisi, A.V. (1982) Parental beliefs about developmental processes.
    Human Development, 25: 192–200.
Newson, J. and Newson, E. (1976) *Seven Years Old in the Home Environment*.
    London: Allen & Unwin.
Overton, W.R. and Reese, H.W. (1973) Models of development: methodological
    implications. In J.R. Nesselroade and H.W. Reese (eds), *Life-span Develop-
    mental Psychology: Methodological Issues*. New York: Academic Press. pp. 170–
    91.
Potter, J. and Wetherell, M. (1987) *Discourse and Social Psychology: Beyond
    Attitudes and Behaviour*. London: Sage.
Reese, H.W. and Overton, W.F. (1970) Models of development and theories of
    development. In L.R. Goulet and P.B. Baltes (eds), *Life-span Developmental
    Psychology: Research and Theory*. New York: Academic Press. pp. 106–23.
Reid, B. and Valsiner, J. (1985) Consistency, praise, and love: folk theories of
    American parents. *Ethos*, 4: 1–25.
Rosaldo, M. (1980) *Knowledge and Passion: Ilongot Notions of Self and Social Life*.
    Cambridge: Cambridge University Press.
Sameroff, A.J., Seifer, R. and Elias, P.K. (1982) Socio-cultural variability in infant
    temperament ratings. *Child Development*, 53: 164–73.
Schaefer, E.S. and Edgerton, M. (1985) Parental and child correlates of parental
    modernity. In I.E. Sigel (ed.), *Parental Belief Systems: The Psychological
    Consequences for Children*. Hillsdale, NJ: Erlbaum. pp. 287–318.
Schütze, Y. (1986) *Die gute Mutter. Zur Geschichte das normativen Musters
    'Mutterliebe'*. Bielefeld: Kleine.
Shweder, R.A. and Miller, Joan G. (1985) The social construction of the person:
    how is it possible? In Kenneth J. Gergen and Keith E. Davis (eds), *The Social
    Construction of the Person*. New York: Springer. pp. 41–72.
Sigel, I.E. (1982) The relationship between parental distancing strategies and the
    child's cognitive behavior. In I.M. Laosa and I.E. Sigel (eds), *Families as
    Learning Environments for Children*. New York: Plenum. pp. 47–86.
Sigel, I.E. (ed.) (1985) *Parental Belief Systems: The Psychological Consequences for
    Children*. Hillsdale, NJ: Erlbaum.

Sigel, I.E., McGillicuddy-DeLisi, A.V. and Johnson, J.E. (1980) *Parental Distancing, Beliefs and Children's Representational Competence within the Family Context* (ETS RR-80-21). Princeton, NJ: Educational Testing Service.

Skinner, E.A. (1985) Determinants of mother-sensitive and contingently responsive behavior: the role of child-rearing beliefs and socio-economic status. In I.E. Sigel (ed.), *Parental Belief Systems: The Psychological Consequences for Children*. Hillsdale, NJ: Erlbaum. pp. 51–88.

Smedslund, J. (1985) Necessarily true cultural psychologies. In K.J. Gergen and K.E. Davis (eds), *The Social Construction of the Person*. New York: Springer. pp. 73–84.

Super, C. and Harkness, S. (1981) Figure ground and gestalt: the cultural context of the active individual. In R. Lerner and N. Busch-Rossnagel (eds), *Individuals as Producers of their Development*. New York: Academic Press. pp. 69–86.

Svensson-Garling, A., Garling, T. and Valsiner, J. (1985) Adults' knowledge of children's competence. Unpublished manuscript, University of Umea, Umea, Sweden.

van den Berg, J.H. (1961) *Metabletica. Über die Wandlung des Menschen*. Göttingen: Vadenhoeck & Ruprecht.

7

Everyday Ideas, Theoretical Models and Social Representations: The Case of Intelligence and its Development

Felice F. Carugati

In sociological social psychology, the view is well established that society is an ever present and necessary condition for the psychological realities and activities of both scientists and lay persons. At the same time, society is only possible to the extent that interacting persons share the same underlying symbolic order (Semin, 1987). Consequently, the psychological reality of everyday life must always refer to a corresponding cultural and historical background upon which it is predicated. This background is manifested in practical activities, conventions, rules, norms and particularly in historically and culturally constituted social representations (Moscovici, 1961, 1984).

Following Berger (1966), one could argue that every society contains a number of different representations of salient issues which constitute a part of the 'objective' world for different persons and groups in that society. Such representations are not only taken-for-granted constituents of 'objective reality', but become subjectively appropriated in the process of socialization. This takes place through the social practices by which culture is transmitted from one generation to another.

Much of psychological theory is predicated upon everyday psychological realities, which are objectified in language as a shared symbolic convention (Semin, 1987). If we take Semin's suggestion (1987) seriously that in psychology empirically tested models or theories can only be established by accessing socially constituted social representations then we have to reassess our traditional assumptions about 'social cognition'. Instead of the information-processing metaphor we must consider working with notions such as implicit theories, lay conceptions, everyday ideas and belief systems. What is common to the latter is that (a) they have a collective character; and (b) they are all mixtures of percepts, images and concepts.

A feature which characterizes the types of representations addressed in implicit theories, everyday ideas and so on is that they channel the give-and-take between us and the reality we face. Furthermore, they are shared by a large number of persons, passed on from one generation to the next, and imposed upon each of us without our conscious assent (Moscovici, 1984). In the following we shall consider the particular domain of lay concepts concerning intelligent functioning and its development.

Belief Systems and Social Representations: An Overview

There has been a growing interest in everyday ideas (Goodnow, 1985; 1988), lay concepts or implicit theories (Sternberg et al., 1981; Fry, 1984) and parental belief systems (Sigel, 1985) concerning development and intelligence since Flugel's classical inquiry (1947) and its replication twenty-five years later by Shipstone and Burt (1973). The predominant emphasis of this research was and still remains descriptive: nevertheless, more recent studies show two main ways of approaching these topics.

An original way of approaching this issue of intelligent functioning was introduced by Sigel (cf. 1985). The focus of this work was to identify a missing link in the common assumptions made about socialization. The link is seen as filling the gap between general sociological variables (for example, socio-economic status, educational attainment) or family constellation (for example, the number and spacing of children) and specific cognitive outcomes (such as scores on cognitive tasks). The intervening variable is parents' belief systems about the learning process that shape parents' actions and influence children's development. This work considers the relationships between all the above noted conditions with parental beliefs. It also links parents' ideas to their actions on two teaching tasks, and to outcomes in the form of scores on a number of Piagetian-type tasks.

Some important findings emerge from these results. First, the relationships between parental beliefs and other variables, although at times small, are clearly significant. Some sharp differences appear between mothers and fathers. In particular, the relationship between ideas and actions is higher for fathers than it is for mothers. This finding substantiates an earlier proposal by Stolz (1967). Furthermore, mothers believe that children's knowledge develops through abstraction from experience, whereas fathers believe that knowledge develops as a function of interactions between internal processes and feedback from the environment. More generally, the ETS group is interested in showing the extent to which the parents' informal theories correspond with more formal Piagetian theory.

The most interesting outcome is a clear proposal for a process that could account for the effect of various conditions on parents' ideas. Parents, like their children, are seen as actively building and modifying ideas on the basis of 'information' that is gained from observing their own children, comparing them with others, receiving feedback from school and trying out various strategies and noting the results. This 'construction process' is conceived to be constant. It is possible that mothers and fathers hold different ideas because the information they utilize in their respective construction processes may vary. Similarly one can understand differences between parents with few and with several children; or between parents with more and parents with less formal education. Such an 'information processing' model has some well-established counterparts in psychological theory, particularly with reference to social comparison models, to expectations modified by feedback, to attribution processes and to the psychology of personal constructs. This proposal was developed in terms of 'belief systems' (Sigel, 1985), a notion first introduced by Rokeach (1954, 1980). Sigel stresses a more cognitive approach. In his view, beliefs are based on knowledge and are accepted as truth. Knowledge is used in the sense of an individual knowing that what he/she espouses is true or probably true, and for which evidence may or may not be deemed necessary. If evidence is used, then it forms a basis for the belief but is not the belief itself (Sigel, 1985: 348). Moreover, beliefs are seen generally as arising from social experiences and as defining an individual's psychological reality. They may be organized in domains (such as political, social and religious) with varying degrees of relationships among them. What is worth noting is that beliefs are schemata. They vary in terms of the probabilities by which new information can be assimilated into them. They may also vary on dimensions such as concrete–abstract (for example, children learn through direct instruction versus children learn through self-regulation). Thus creating a hierarchical organization of beliefs, as in the example of the concrete–abstract dimension, may well help solve some of the problems of predicting consequent behaviours (Sigel, 1985). This in Sigel's view permits direct connections to be drawn between certain beliefs and some actions rather than others, as in the example above.

Finally, beliefs are regarded as guides to actions. Actions can be initiated or reactive to particular classes of events. Beliefs guide not only the action, but also the choice of events to which one reacts. While beliefs appear in the context of behaviour, the range of actions is limited since actions are never free of situational constraints. Thus observations of actions may provide only a limited understanding of an individual's beliefs.

In Sigel's approach, a parent, like a 'thinking machine', gains knowledge by processing the information that reaches him/her from the outside world by means of 'schemata'. We explicitly stress the attention on the singular form 'parent' because the belief system approach is actually concerned with individual perception and logical analysis of information held by each parent about his/her child's development. In this sense, Sigel's approach shares a distinctive feature with models in social cognition in that the individual parent is regarded as the seat of psychic reality, while the category of parents is derivative. This position has a number of implications. An average parent is thought of as a thinking machine more or less biased in his/her judgements about others by his/her belief system or implicit theories. A parent is relatively impervious to his/her experience and the beliefs are considered distinct from corresponding scientific theories.

Experience, however, has a contradictory theoretical status in this approach: it is conceived as a source of beliefs. However, when the beliefs are operative the system is quite impervious to new experience. Finally, reality (the source of information) is viewed as neutral, non-social and presumably objective. The source of bias is located in the thinking machine but with additional variation sources as in cases when the thinking machine may be biased by emotional factors, like anxiety (Rokeach, 1954) or affect (Sigel, 1985).

The second way of approaching lay conceptions of intelligent functioning is inspired by Neisser's assumption (1979) that there can be no process-based definition of intelligence since it is not a unitary quality. A number of authors have reported data on adult subjects' perceptions of what intelligence is and the attributes of intelligent functioning (for example, Siegler and Richards, 1981; Sternberg et al., 1981; Fry, 1984; Sternberg, 1985; Wagner and Sternberg, 1985). In these studies the subject sample varied considerably. They employed diverse methods (from open-ended interviews to rating scales). The focus of these descriptive studies is the 'form and content of people's informal theories' (Sternberg et al., 1981: 37–8), namely conceptions of intelligence as held by the lay person. The fascinating conclusion reached by most studies is typified by the following quote: 'Although the experts in our sample all held doctoral degrees in psychology, and were all employed at major colleges or universities, and had all published major research in the field of intelligence, their conceptions of intelligence differed hardly at all from the conceptions of the general adult population' (1981:

11). In the same research, Sternberg et al. (1981) report that people's conceptions of their own intelligence is related to their objective test performance (as indicated by their IQ). More recently, Sternberg contrasted lay theories of intelligence, creativity and wisdom with explicit-theory-based measures. He was able to show that implicit-theory-based measures show both convergent and discriminant validity and that implicit theories of intelligence and wisdom correspond substantially to their explicit counterparts (1985: 619).

We are forced to consider the phenomenon of intelligence as both the origin and result of *social consensus* in view of the considerable overlap between implicit and explicit models of intelligence, and since implicit theories must be considered as the origins of explicit ones (Semin, 1987; Sternberg, 1985). Therefore, intelligence can be adequately conceived only in terms of the more general issue of the symbolic construction of reality.

The first conclusion of this section is that lay concepts predate persons. These concepts constitute a part of the 'objective knowledge' of persons and become the subjective point of departure for thought processes at the individual level. In line with this argument empirical data collected by Sigel and colleagues and by Neisser's disciples over years of research are certainly valuable, but they also provoke a search for a more fundamental understanding of the issues.

Goodnow et al. (1985) suggest that there is a need for a theoretical reorientation within the adult social cognition approach. They claim that the emphasis put upon individual constructions, intrinsic motivation and an inherent push for progression from one level to another in the classical Piagetian tradition may be more appropriate in specific areas of knowledge. In such areas there are few 'vested interests', an absence of conflicting views and a higher feasibility for experimentation. However in the case of 'social cognition' there is infinite potential for written and oral discussion. Within the boundaries of what may be regarded as 'social cognition' one can include a variety of everyday topics for which there are no unambiguous standards or criteria. There are a number of domains with weak cues or guided by stereotypes that are not readily accessible to experimentation, others that evoke an 'evaluative' stance and yet others with strong vested interests. Therefore, approaches to conceptualizing social cognition in both adults and children that are based on an information-processing metaphor and focus only on issues that are amenable to experimentation will inevitably be restricted to specific types of knowledge domains. Inevitably, large domains will be left out as a consequence.

Goodnow (1985) argues that individuals do not employ the same mental and logical laws under all circumstances. Thus differences in judgement and interpretation cannot be attributed to the incorrect application of general logical laws. Rather, they should be regarded as the correct use of principles or rules in different knowledge domains where socially constructed and shared representations constitute the taken-for-granted and 'given data' which serve as the point of departure for inferring, attributing, judging and explaining. Goodnow shows a more profound approach to the investigation of how development and intelligent functioning are socially constructed. She provides a very insightful review of how ideas about childhood and parenting (Goodnow, 1985) have changed, which permits a better understanding of the emergence of interindividual as well as inter-cultural differences in parenthood. The questions that remain unanswered in her work concern the processes by which shared ideas and actual differences are socially constructed. Similar questions arise in the case of Sternberg's work on lay and expert conceptions of intelligent functioning or Sigel's findings on why mothers and fathers differ in constructions of development. These three main sources of empirical data show that different views of intelligent functioning emerge as a function of the types of questions asked and the type of samples used. This results in a naive or a sceptical relativism about the possibilities for elaborating a theoretical position which is more than just the mere 're-representation' of everyday conceptions. However, the point that 'extra-scientific' content (for example, normative expectations, beliefs, values) is essential in developing a consistent perspective on lay conceptions does not simply necessitate a description of what lay conceptions of intelligence are or where lay conceptions are impervious to scientific information. Essentially, these considerations suggest that we can no longer relate everyday ideas and lay conceptions in isolation, but must grasp their properties within the cultural settings in which they are produced, maintained and transformed.

How to Approach Intelligence as Social Representations

In the general framework introduced by Moscovici (1961; 1984), social representations are seen as a set of concepts, statements and explanations originating in daily life in the course of communication. Their functioning is converse to the functioning of scientific thought. Science moves from premises to conclusions with the task of assuring the primacy of the method over the content. The requirement is to falsify theories and to present counter-evidence to their evidence. In contrast, social representations develop in different domains of everyday life where scientific reasoning is neither economical nor necessary. Social representations are concerned with 'consensual' universes, where conventions and agreements prevail over trials and demonstrations, conclusions over premises. Social representations thus play a central role in establishing, at a symbolic level, everyday experiences and in justifying our attitudes and actions. To sum up, social representations are essential for a socio-cognitive adaptation to everyday reality. In that sense, they vary according to the specific social positions and experiences of individuals and groups. Thus the main point is that our emphasis is on *social representations* of intelligence, the world, space and so on, and not *the* social representation as in mainstream cognitive approaches (that is, where one is concerned with *the* representation of some thing). In mainstream social cognition, lay concepts, implicit theories or representations are used to explain observed biases, errors and imperviousness to new information. From the social-representations perspective the issue is not one of biases or imperviousness to information but rather a search for the dynamics of content areas that contribute and shape a symbolic reality. It is a search for the articulation of the collective or social of which the individual is an indivisible part.

Despite their variety in content, social representations may have an interdependent socio-cognitive organization, and in our approach to the representations of intelligence we attempt to illustrate properties that are common to this organization. Our first concern is with the nature of the information available about the actual object of representation. The type of information may be formal or informal. Lay persons, for instance, are not experts on intelligence, their main sources may be personal experience (such as past experiences as a student or a parent, media exposure). The knowledge of lay persons consists of unsystematically collected information obtained through day-to-day exposure. Some people, on the other hand, acquire information through a more systematic process. Teachers, for example, in the course of their professional education, have access to organized information, such as psychological and sociological models of development. Parents can be seen to fall into a category between laymen and teachers. They have specific reasons for constructing and sharing representations of intelligence and development. For people in this category intelligence and development are not simply matters of gathering unsolicited free information. Parents have to cope with the question of interindividual differences about intelligence and the origins of these differences.

The question of interindividual differences concerning intelligence and their origins is a very old one and one which over the centuries has intrigued philosophers, psychologists and every kind of *maîtres à penser*, giving rise to endless controversies. Intelligence emerges as one of the most predominant positive values of western society; no wonder, therefore, that around this kind of *idola tribus* a polysemantic discourse, by both lay people and scientists, is continuously being built and rebuilt. But while scientists are engaged in an endless discourse on this topic (producing increasingly fragmented theoretical models; Sigel, 1986), teachers and lay people (such as parents) have neither the freedom nor the time for such contemplation, nor do they have the time to wait for the ultimate scientific explanation. Teachers and parents are very busy dealing with everyday problems relating to school and the many responsibilities at home that one encounters when children are involved.

Like people confronted with the unfamiliarity and the relative inexplicability of the unconscious, illness and the mentally ill (Moscovici, 1961; Herzlich, 1972; Jodelet, 1981), parents and teachers confronted with interindividual differences may feel a gap between the information at their disposal and the information necessary to account for this phenomenon. In a social and psychological framework, information is not all that matters. Even when the information is equally available, representations may be different; and the very interpretation of the same information may vary according to different experiences. On the other hand, the explanatory value of different sources of information may vary, and denying information which contradicts with factual opinions may be one way of keeping representations stable, thus illustrating the sense in which in social representations conclusions have primacy over proofs.

In more theoretical terms, parents and teachers as social categories are very sensitive to the relevance of questions such as the origins of interindividual differences. While they may lack a complete grasp of the subject, the concrete and everyday problems which they encounter about intelligence and development press them into making inferences and decisions. And, indeed, it is the coupling of a relative lack of information about intelligence and development with the pressure to make inferences and reach decisions which is a principal characteristic of these social categories.

Parental belief systems are generally taken for granted, as a pattern of schemata individually processed, with the consequence that parents and teachers are studied as categories *per se*, and a parental or teachers' psychology is then elaborated as a psychology of individual differences. Our approach to these issues is different, though complementary. We construe parental belief systems as social representations, and our interest is centred on the socio-cognitive origins and functions of social representations. The first set of hypotheses we put forward is inspired by Moscovici's suggestion that social representations tend to turn an unfamiliar thing into something familiar. For testing our hypothesis, we have an object: the existence of interindividual differences in intelligence, and the unfamiliarity may be explored by the degree of weakness attributed to the scientific explanations.

The second set of hypotheses is devoted to the relationships between social representations and social identity: the experience of conflicts of identification is conceived as a factor influencing some transformations in social representations. Concretely speaking, teachers may also be parents. As teachers, they are compelled to try and prevent pupils failing in school; as parents, they are protective towards their children when necessary in school matters. So, in one sense, they are protecting their children against themselves. A second example is the professional working mother. As housewives, mothers may tend to explain intelligence and development as a product of their direct involvement in child-rearing and as a task socially assigned to mothers. However, as working mothers, they may feel guilty about not being solely involved in the upbringing of their children. In both cases – parents who are teachers and parents who are working mothers – specific socio-professional positions may induce identity conflicts which may be resolved by readjusting their representations of intelligence. We do not conceive of these readjustments as biases or errors, as the social cognition approach suggests. On the contrary, our hypotheses suggest that the functions and the transformations of social representations are located at the interface between the individual and society. Transformations of social representations occur when the unfamiliarity and the inex-plicability of interindividual differences in intelligence become salient for particular social groups and when this topic activates a conflict of identification.

Intelligence, then, is not a simple matter of cognition or the processing of information: the construction of social representations of intelligence is a useful instrument for specific groups to locate themselves in the social field. Social representations, therefore, play a central role in building social identity.

Some Methodological Remarks and Empirical Illustrations

It follows from the above considerations that we are interested in understanding how social representations (at least of intelligence) are produced by an interconnected set of social groups for which we can, theoretically, hypothesize differing degrees of salience for the intriguing question about the origins of differences in intelligence. Two main social–psychological processes are proposed: familiarization of the unfamiliar and conflicts of identification. They are, admittedly, only two of several possibilities! (See Di Giacomo, 1981; Flament, 1981.)

In our research (Mugny and Carugati, 1989) we took a broad sampling of products of the 'thinking society', namely those that involved intelligence and development. These included: general opinions about intelligence and development; didactic strategies for coping with failure in maths, language and drawing; sources of information considered to be important; prototypical images of the intelligent child; and the explanatory power of science. This raw material was drawn from groups such as parents, non-parents, teachers, students in various fields of study, housewives and working mothers. Our choice of groups was intended to enable us to identify both the extent of a consensual universe in the discourses about intelligence, and the social logic of why disagreements arise about specific issues. For these various reasons we also decided to use 'closed' methods of investigation rather than more 'open' ones (such as interviews, observations or word associations). This choice was a consequence of our approach to social representations; that is, we wanted not only to describe representations of intelligence, but also to test specific hypotheses by manipulating social–cognitive variables induced in particular social groups.

Having presented the outline of our research methodology we can now briefly review some of the results. The representations of intelligence revolve around a variety of dimensions. First, all the adults wonder about the origins of interindividual differences in intelligence between children. In particular, they are concerned whether this phenomenon is inexplicable or whether science can provide satisfactory answers regarding the apparently 'unequal' distribution of intelligence across individuals. A second dimension concerns intelligence as learning the social rules of modern society. A third sees intelligence as being founded on 'superior' cognitive processes, for which logical abstraction and mathematics are the prototypes and the computer is the symbol. Other dimensions are intelligence as an adaptive capacity to physical and scholastic environments; the role of the family's socio-economic status regarding 'heredity' of intellectual capacities; school, and more specifically teachers, seen as responsible for scholastic success or failure and for the accentuation or even creation of interindividual differences in intelligence. In addition they also draw on some themes of daily life in school: the use of school programmes suitable for the more intelligent child being negatively affected by the presence of the less intelligent one; the role of subjects, like maths, which have a greater scholastic value; and last but not least, explicit reference to intelligence as a 'given' biological fact, as a *gift*.

As we can see, the adult's representations of intelligence are rich in content. If it is true that the logico-mathematical model is valued, intelligence is nonetheless also considered as the interiorization of social norms and values; as a manifestation of social ability; as personality traits linked to discipline, rigour, personal commitment and perseverance.

From the Unfamiliar to the Familiar

In order to test that unfamiliarity is actually an organizing principle of a given social representation, we considered adult subjects' replies to a questionnaire item on intelligence. It stated that 'the existence of differences of intelligence among individuals is a mysterious problem which science has been unable to solve.' This statement was deliberately written to refer to two components of unfamiliarity – that science is considered to be unable to provide a rational explanation of the phenomenon, and that what is unfamiliar is defined by the existence of differences between individuals. For the latter, there is not really any exhaustive explanation, even in scientific circles. On the basis of the replies to this key question, the subjects could be divided into two groups of opinion. The first group was of the opinion that intelligence does not present an insoluble problem (NSTR), whereas the other group thought that differences in intelligence between individuals are strangely problematic and insoluble, even scientifically (STR).

Our results do seem to indicate that the sense of unfamiliarity which inheres in differences of intellectual aptitude does orient the way adults talk about intelligence. The STR group was of the opinion that science (psychology, social, medical and clinical disciplines) was not very useful as far as explaining intelligence was concerned. Moreover, the discourse of these adults about intelligence also appeared to identify two elements in the notion of intelligence. The first element is constructed around the 'theory of natural inequalities' that is set in the context of an ideology of giftedness; the second parallel discourse recognizes the existence of development. This, however, is not intelligence 'properly so-called', but a kind of 'social intelligence' defined in terms of awareness of, and respect for, rules and social norms. This aspect of intelligence is developed through systematic, but not necessarily overwhelming, pressure on the child, pressure which is applied particularly through school experience, where clear responsibilities are attributed to teachers and their competence.

Why though, after all, should these interindividual differences seem so strange? Our hypothesis argues that they seem to be so for those who do not have an alternative explanatory model at their disposal. We can, in fact, assume that in order to put forward such a model, individuals must have access to specific information, particularly to the scientific disciplines concerned with the question. At this level the details of the explanation are unimportant: the only significant factor is a person's belief in the interpretive power of a given model which he/she can adopt if need be, without actually knowing or understanding it.

The main hypothesis is that a lack of information about alternative explanations ought to give greater salience to the question of interindividual differences as the nucleus of a representation of intelligence that is organized around the theory of giftedness. But this information shortage should only have the effect of organizing the representation for those groups which are directly concerned with these differences: that is, for parents and teachers who are more likely to encounter these differences during their parental and/or professional daily experience. It would not have such an effect for students.

We have approached this topic indirectly, on the basis of the adults' 'admission' of their 'ignorance'.[1] Several conclusions can be advanced about the effects of insufficient information. The first is that it does not result in a specifically organized representation among students, but operates simply as a general ignorance, expressed now and then by some sort of refusal to define intelligence. One might surmise that ignorance fails to create a social representation among students as it has no focal point in general, and no focus on intellectual inequalities in particular.

A different situation emerges for parents and teachers. They are confronted with a genuine problem which is more difficult to solve since they do not have a 'rational' explanatory model for the differences of intelligence that they see in their children/pupils. Since not enough information is available for teachers and parents, the result is the absence of a rationale provided by a scientific approach to the question. The place of this impossible rationality is taken by another rationality, that of the 'theory' of giftedness, which is really socio-psychological. As neither science nor educational institutions can explain (from the point of view of our adults) interindividual differences, these differences become naturalized and objectified in the canons of a theory of natural inequalities. In this kind of social thinking, the 'effect' becomes the 'cause' by means of postulating intelligence as a 'gift' unequally distributed among children. Then the dominant model of intelligence – the logico-mathematical model – becomes salient, and as the saying goes, 'you either have a gift for mathematics or you haven't.' However, another form of intelligence, which is in some ways more social and more dynamic, is acknowledged. This form of intelligence can be 'developed' by putting pressure on the child and is defined in terms of conformity to social rules. In the final analysis, this social representation seems to originate from the combination of two sources, both of which are socio-psychological: on the one hand, a focus on the unfamiliarity which is relevant to the individual's relation to the phenomena of intelligence (a focus induced by the actual experience of the unfamiliarity as a result of parental and/or professional experience), and, on the other hand, insufficient models that can be seen as an explanation of this unfamiliarity.

Parental Experience and Parental Identity

In what way is parental experience likely to be able to organize representations of intelligence? Our (tentative) answer is directly related to the conception of social representations as familiarizations of the unfamiliar. The idea is really very simple, although it also has a great many serious consequences: the child constitutes in a sense an element of unfamiliarity within the family. He is unfamiliar because he is unpredictable. Quite apart from the unpredictability of appearance, it is almost impossible to anticipate his personality, character, behaviour patterns or intelligence with any degree of certainty. But, paradoxically, parents must anticipate the person their child will develop into and perhaps also the person they would like their child to become. Nevertheless, parental experience has to be considered as one of the main sources of 'information' about child development. Parental identity seems to rest on characteristics specific to various psychological aspects which are important for the building of representations of intelligence. We have identified several of these aspects.

The socio-cognitive disquiet (a mixture of uncertainty and unpredictability) that surrounds the future of the newborn child not only relates to the 'shock of birth' (for parents and the child), but continues throughout life, or at least until adolescence. Thus the model of giftedness or of natural inequalities provides a particular and fruitful background for parents; this might explain the 'mysteries' of intelligence. Once parents have got over the initial 'shock', they are faced with the necessity of socializing the child, especially in preparation for school. A somewhat conformist view of intellectual and social development is provided by a representation of intelligence defined by success in the important subjects at school (mathematics, language and so on). From the point of view of the psychological significance of parental experience, parents' relationships with their children gradually become more dependent on the child's integration into the school. The degree of success of this integration can also be a major influence on the extent of uncertainty. Finally, parents markedly refuse to acknowledge the importance of the family in the development of intelligence. In this case the representation appears to function as a way of protecting parents' self-image which their own social identity is capable of threatening.

So a parental identity seems to exist with its own mode of sociocognitive functioning. But if it is real, ought it not to be more marked in cases where the parents have more than one child?

The Intensity of Parental Experience
If the unpredictability of the characteristics of the newborn is at the core of parental experience, then having a second child ought to accentuate the dynamic we have so far illustrated. The differences between children are themes that parents talk about more easily and about which they seem to have deep-rooted beliefs. In our hypothesis, the parents with at least two children ought to voice the representations typical of parents but in a more accentuated fashion. To verify this hypothesis, we subdivided the parents into two sub-groups: those with one child and those with at least two children. This comparison shows that parental identity becomes progressively more influential as one moves from groups of non-parent adults to parents with two children, tracing out a real process of 'socialization' during which the experience of becoming parents (subsequently renewed by the presence of a second child) leads the parents to construct for themselves a specific interpretive model. This model is characterized by an increasing recourse to the 'theory of inequalities' among children inspired by a conception of intelligence as a 'gift' present in the child, and which reveals itself (but does not develop) through biological maturation. The influence of environmental factors is excluded and, more particularly, any influence whatsoever of family characteristics. If this is the heart of the matter then it is hardly surprising that parents with two children become even more sceptical about any information from experts, the mass media or science.

An important aspect, which affects the experience of parents with at least two children, is derived directly from the reorganization of family relationships following the birth of the second child (Dunn and Kendrick, 1982). It is therefore no wonder that our 'two-children' parents are more aware than our 'one-child' parents of the importance of the 'psychological climate' and the relative equilibrium for the development of intelligence, both at home and at school. Finally, the presence of a second child does not modify the reference to the school as criteria for a good development in intelligence. From the arrival of the first child, parents seem to develop two complementary conceptions. On the one hand, they share the idea of development as socialization to existing social norms which can be achieved through different sorts of 'pressure' put on the children; on the other hand, the parents stick dutifully to the scholastic model regarding the definition of intelligence. These two concepts merge in underlining success at school as the symbol of intelligence and scholastic failure as the symptom of lack of intelligence.

The Roles of Father and Mother
At this point we can ask whether fathers and mothers have a different understanding of intelligence and its development. Differences associated with gender can be expected here, even though the literature on this seems to point to differences that are less considerable than expected (cf. Goodnow et al., 1985).

Fathers agree that they don't have specific knowledge of the 'children's world', probably because they are less involved than the mothers with their upbringing; they do not feel such a pressing need to read, to keep themselves informed, to listen to programmes about development and so on. Furthermore, fathers, more than mothers, tend to consider intelligence as a 'gift' and consequently to see development as a process that comes about autonomously and that can reap benefits from interaction with peers. Peer relations are also capable, in their opinion, of producing a reciprocal form of teaching, and hence an approach to education that is less 'interventionist'. One could suppose that the typically male norm and ideal of 'autonomy' may have one of its origins (or at least a possible justification) in the specifically male parental experience!

As far as the mothers are concerned, it is the socializing function that takes priority in their assessment of their child's adaptation to school life and its requirements. This implies a major interest in the educational procedures for the child's cognitive activation. The mothers are also more interested than the fathers in acquiring information. (This information is acquired through formal channels – from experts on a specific subject and through the mass media; chatting with friends, neighbours or acquaintances is a more informal means of getting information.) Mothers are more informed about the 'children's world' than fathers are; they consider intelligence as the learning of social rules (again, more so than fathers). This 'social' orientation is enriched by a multiplicity of perspectives linked to the fact that the information sources rarely agree on how to define the problems. Above all, they rarely agree on the ways of dealing with children. It is not surprising, therefore, that the mothers are, on the whole, more sensitive to a relativist conception of intelligence, a relativism which justifies, in a more social way, the interindividual inequalities regarding intelligence.

How can one fail to see in these results the personification, in the fathers and mothers, of the two sides of intelligence: intelligence as a 'gift' whose prototype is the rational thinking of the computer, and intelligence as the capacity of functioning in the social world, as the learning of the rules that govern everyday life? In this way we have shown that, if it is true that parental experience, in the largest sense of the word, plays an important role in the organization of the social representation of intelligence, then it is also true that being a parent seems to orient and modulate certain specific aspects of the representation. The fathers seem to emphasize the maturationist aspect, whereas the mothers underline more the socializing function of intelligence.

Housewives versus Working Mothers

We have argued that, because they go out to work, fathers will be less involved with their children and possess less information about the children's world. Mothers, too, may sometimes be less involved with their children and have limited opportunities of directly interacting with them. They may, in short, possess some of the characteristics we used to describe the fathers: this is obviously the case with working or professional mothers. Are these mothers more similar to fathers or to housewives? What sort of conceptions do they have about intelligence in relation to their status as working mothers? If it is true that identity is an organizing principle of the representations, then we do not expect simple similarities or differences between working mothers and fathers or housewives, but specific effects.

We now present a direct comparison between housewives with children and working mothers (the comparison with the fathers will be qualitative and indirect). Working mothers talk about a maturationist conception of intelligence less than housewives do, but they deny more strongly that intelligence develops over the years. Although this maturationist idea was linked to the idea of intelligence as a 'gift' in the discourse of the fathers, there was no such linkage in the comparison between housewives and working mothers. To think that the child spontaneously manifests its own intellectual capacities would seem to have a justifying function for the working mothers who are less involved (at least as far as they themselves are concerned) with the child. On the other hand, this idea of spontaneous development can facilitate the decision to restart work at the end of their maternity leave (cf. Lamb, Chase-Lansdale and Owen, 1979).

Elaborating a conception of intelligence as the spontaneous manifestation of intellectual capacities enables the working mothers to cope with their fear of not participating personally in the development of their child. In this sense they seem to develop a way of protecting their own social identity, which they would see as 'deviant' when compared to the dominant mother model. These 'defences' seem to be present in the attribution of responsibility for their children's failure or difficulties at school. In fact, the working mothers are much more inclined to think that certain difficulties at school could be avoided if the teachers were more understanding, but they are very sceptical about the professional capabilities of the teachers. The attribution of responsibility is directed at the teachers *ad personam*, that is, at specific and genuine teachers. So it seems that working mothers put their trust fully in the school as an institution (recognizing and accepting its aims) and holding the teachers directly responsible for any eventual failures or difficulties of their pupils. If this is the conclusion that one can draw about the position of working mothers, then even an indirect comparison with the fathers will show how the idea of intelligence and its development 'provokes' the working mothers much more profoundly than the fathers, within the parental model that we described earlier.

For the working mothers, the theme of intelligence is very closely linked with parental and professional identity and with all the ambivalence that such experiences produce in many of them. These two experiences have a 'point of equilibrium' in the social identity of working mothers. It is for this reason that within the dynamic of the representation of children's intelligence the preservation of a relatively positive social identity plays a much more direct role for working mothers than it does for fathers: the way their children develop is much less pertinent for the father's definition of their identity.

Working mothers and fathers have criteria for intelligence which are relatively alike. In this area the housewives differ quite distinctly from the working mothers. We can, therefore, put forward the hypothesis that the woman who works assumes certain judgement criteria that are typical of the male's. These are not, however, merely beliefs and opinions about a theme, important though these may be. The theme of intelligence, particularly in the case of working mothers, disturbs a difficult equilibrium of parental–professional identity which is preserved by means of a complicated strategy which emphasizes certain opinions at a general level and by attributing responsibility for the consequences (or at least those which are feared) of the development of the child's intelligence, both in general and in the case of one's own children.

Being Both Parents and Teachers
Let us now have a look at how parental identity comes into play in the case of teachers. When we compare teachers without children with those who have children it is clear that the teachers with children refute, in a distinctly more decided manner, the direct responsibility of teachers in cases of school failure. An explanation for the refusal to accept responsibility could be that the parent–teacher is confronted with two identities, the role of parent as well as that of teacher. We have seen, however, that parents who are not teachers attribute a specific responsibility to the teacher (an attribution which is even stronger for those parents, such as working mothers, whose identity encompasses conflictual elements). The teachers who are also parents find themselves facing a specific 'conflict of identity': as parents they would blame teachers for their child's negative results, but as teachers they ought to take some of the blame for the outcome. The socio-cognitive solution that our teachers adopt is to deny responsibility contemporaneously as teachers and as parents. This denial of responsibility goes beyond its direct implication: the teachers who are parents also deny the responsibility of the scholastic institution for failures, legitimated at a more abstract level by referring more to intelligence as a 'gift' unequally distributed among children. Teachers, when asked about intelligence, find themselves caught up in a crucial conflict of identity (this is more obvious among parent–teachers), which they resolve by shelving their responsibility both as individuals and as 'agents' of the scholastic institution. A 'scientific' legitimization of this socio-cognitive solution can be found in the interpretation of intelligence and its development as a gift unequally distributed among children.

Final Remarks
The theoretical argument and empirical illustrations reviewed here may be regarded as a tentative consideration of the apparent interface between social-cognition and social-representations approaches to the study of lay conceptions of intelligent functioning. Descriptions gathered by Goodnow, Sigel and Sternberg may be seen as very interesting and useful 'cognitions', and in this respect lay people sometimes seem to agree with experts. However, there are at times disagreements among lay people such as the normal, everyday mother and father. In a sense, we are confronted with a

negotiation between consensual (that is, of lay people) and reified (that is, of science) symbolic universes as well as conflicts within the consensual universe. In fact, when there is a consensual universe, there is not a precise consensus on every element: divergences are necessary for the continuity of everyday life. People seem to agree to disagree, and in a sense patterns are limited towards uniformity by a common inefficient rule. Thus the dynamics between agreement and disagreement may be viewed as a matter neither of a 'wild' relativism nor of the main effect of 'heavy' sociological variables such as gender, SES, age, occupation, nationality and so on. Cognitions are not merely processed, but are worked out in order to build social thought, which is (with respect to classical logic) by no means a site of incoherence, disorder, errors and biases. Social representations may be seen as a product of this social thought: they have a rationality and a coherence which are based on a multiplicity of different orders of discourse and a diversity of socio-cognitive functions. Different discourses and different functions account for the heterogeneity in the way different groups and individuals talk about 'controversial' things (such as intelligence), as well as their variation in response to particular social experiences or significant events.

To summarize: social representations, particularly representations of intelligence, are constructed and evolve according to the 'chances' of everyday experience by a dual socio-cognitive function. It implies the construction of a consensual universe which is mentally intelligible and coherent and the elaboration of a satisfying social and personal identity, one that may be compatible with socially and historically determined systems of norms and values.

Note

1. One of the questionnaires concerned the relative importance of various scientific disciplines for understanding the nature of intelligence, and in order to have some indication of the degree of information shortage experienced by the subjects we purposely included the option of responding 'I don't know' in addition to the usual seven-point scales. On the basis of their use of this option we divided each group of subjects (students, parents and teachers) into two groups: those who selected this option more than twice (and thus demonstrated a greater shortage of information), and those who never selected this option, or did so only once or twice (and who could therefore be regarded as being better acquainted with the various competing models of intelligence).

References

Berger, P.L. (1966) Identity as a problem in the sociology of knowledge. *Archives Européens de Sociologie*, 7: 105–15.

Di Giacomo, J.P. (1981) Aspects méthodologiques de l'analyse des représentations sociales. *Cahiers de Psychologie Cognitive*, 1: 397–422.

Dunn, J. and Kendrick, C. (1982) *Siblings: Love, Envy and Understanding*. Cambridge, MA: Harvard University Press.

Flament, C. (1981) Sur le pluralisme méthodologique dans l'étude des représentations sociales. *Cahiers de Psychologie Cognitive*, 1: 423–7.

Flugel, J.C. (1947) An inquiry as to popular views on intelligence and related topics. *British Journal of Educational Psychology*, 17: 140–52.

Fry, P.S. (ed.) (1984) Changing concepts of intelligence and intellectual functioning: current theory and research. *International Journal of Psychology*, 19 (special issue).

Goodnow, J. (1985) Parent's ideas about parenting and development: a review of issues and recent work. In M. Lamb, A. Brown and B. Rogoff (eds), *Advances in Developmental Psychology*. Hillsdale, NJ: Erlbaum.

Goodnow, J. (1988) Parents' ideas, action and feelings: models and methods from developmental and social psychology. *Child Development*, 59: 286–320.

Goodnow, J., Knight, R. and Cashmore, J. (1985) Adult social cognition: implications of parents' ideas for approaches to development. In M. Perlmutter (ed.), *Social Cognition*. Hillsdale, NJ: Erlbaum.

Heider, F. (1958) *The Psychology of Interpersonal Relations*. New York: Wiley.

Herzlich, C. (1972) *Health and Illness: A Social Psychological Analysis*. London: Academic Press.

Jodelet, D. (1981) Doctoral dissertation. Paris: Ecole Pratique des Hautes Etudes en Sciences Sociales.

Lamb, M.E., Chase-Lansdale, L. and Owen, M.T. (1979) The changing American family and its implications for infant development: the sample case of maternal employment. In M. Lewis and L. Rosenblum (eds), *The Child and its Family*. New York: Plenum.

Moscovici, S. (1961) *La Psychanalyse, son image, et son public*. Paris: Presses Universitaires de France.

Moscovici, S. (1984) The phenomenon of social representations. In R.M. Farr and S. Moscovici (eds), *Social Representations*. Cambridge: Cambridge University Press.

Mugny, G. and Carugati, F. (1989) *Social Representations of Intelligence*. Cambridge: Cambridge University Press.

Neisser, U. (1979) The concept of intelligence. *Intelligence*, 3: 217–28.

Rokeach, M. (1954) The nature and meaning of dogmatism. *Psychological Review*, 61: 194–204.

Rokeach, M. (1980) Some unresolved problems in theories of beliefs, attitudes and values. In H.E. Howe Jr and M.M. Page (eds), *Nebraska Symposium on Motivation*. Lincoln: University of Nebraska Press.

Semin, G.R. (1987) On the relationships between representations of theories in psychology and ordinary language. In W. Doise and S. Moscovici (eds), *Current Issues in European Social Psychology*. Cambridge: Cambridge University Press.

Shipstone, K. and Burt, S.L. (1973) Twenty-five years on: a replication of Flugel's work on 'lay popular views of intelligence and related topics' (1947). *British Journal of Educational Psychology*, 43: 182–7.

Siegler, R.S. and Richards, D.D. (1981) The development of intelligence. In R.J. Sternberg (ed.), *Handbook of Human Intelligence*. New York: Cambridge University Press.

Sigel, I.E. (ed.) (1985) *Parental Beliefs Systems*. Hillsdale, NJ: Erlbaum.
Sigel, I.E. (1986) Mechanism: a metaphor for cognitive development? A review of Sternberg's 'Mechanisms of cognitive development', *Merril Palmer Quarterly*, 32: 93–101.
Sternberg, R.J. (1981) The nature of intelligence. *New York University Education Quarterly*, 12 (3): 10–17.
Sternberg, R.J. (1985) Implicit theories of intelligence, creativity and wisdom. *Journal of Personality and Social Psychology*, 49: 607–27.
Sternberg, R.J., Conway, B.E., Ketron, J.L. and Bernstein, M. (1981) People's conceptions of intelligence. *Journal of Personality and Social Psychology*, 41: 37–55.
Stolz, L.M. (1967) *Influences on Parent Behavior*. Stanford, CA: Stanford University Press.
Wagner, R.K. and Sternberg, R.J. (1985) Practical intelligence in real-world pursuits: the role of tacit knowledge. *Journal of Personality and Social Psychology*, 49: 436–58.

8

Everyday Assumptions, Language and Personality

Gün R. Semin

The social-constructionist orientation consists of a policy statement. It suggests a very specific way of looking at social reality (cf. Gergen, 1985). The important point about this is that a social-constructionist orientation in general does not specify a systematic theoretical framework with a corresponding methodology (cf. Coulter, 1983). These aspects have to be worked out in detail independently. The influence of social constructionism on psychology is in that sense very much in its early stages. That is, there are some new developments and theoretical frameworks that are emerging, but their history is by no means an established or closed order.

Nevertheless, one of the intriguing questions raised by a social-constructionist approach is about the relationship between everyday and scientific conceptions of the person. In our everyday dealings we talk about persons, we describe their actions and characteristics, we use a number of assumptions and theories about different types of persons and their make-ups. These assumptions and theories are part and parcel of our cultural knowledge. Not only do they help us interpret others, but such theories also provide rationales to explain our own actions. Similarly, in scientific discourse about persons, as for instance in personality theory, the aim is to furnish explanations or understandings of people, of their make-up and of the differences between people and the reasons for their actions.

The chief difference between everyday theories and scientific theories is in the representation of knowledge. Both obviously use language as a medium. In the case of personality theorists there is a specialized language that is developed specifically for the purpose of scientific representation. The assumption is that this language is not necessarily available to all members of a language community in part because it is taken for granted that scientific knowledge supersedes everyday knowledge and is thus encoded in a different language. In contrast, everyday theories are contained in a language that is shared by both the personality theorist and people in everyday life. Indeed, in deriving scientific theories about personality the personality theorist relies on everyday language because this provides the medium by which instructions are issued, responses are provided, descriptions are obtained. Therefore, the construction of scientific theories inevitably relies on information gained through everyday communication and language. What happens with this information in the construction of a scientific model? This general quetsion can be unfolded into the following more specific questions.

What is the relationship between the types of theories that are advanced in scientific work about persons and theories that are found in everyday life? In which ways do scientific models of the person rely on everyday conceptions of persons? Is there explicit acknowledgement of everyday theories in scientific models and how, if at all, is the link between scientific and everyday theories of the person acknowledged? Do scientific models of personality supersede everyday models of personality? These are the types of questions that this chapter attempts to cover.

In examining these questions I shall focus on two specific issues. The first will consist in an examination of a problem that emerged in the 1950s and 1960s bringing about a convergence between person perception in social psychology and taxonomic work on personality. The aim of this work was to examine trait terms that are available in language with a view to developing a taxonomy that would be representative of personality. Indeed, there appears to be a relatively stable taxonomy of trait terms, but the controversy in the 1960s was about whether this was a representation of personality, a manifestation of perceptual phenomena displayed by the implicit theories held by people in everyday life or a representation of the linguistic features of trait terms, namely a phenomenon particular to language rather than personality. We shall explore these issues in a brief overview and then give a social-constructionist interpretation to taxonomic models of personality.

The second question that I shall present is a review of research which is more recent in its origin and which has been explicitly conducted from a social-constructionist standpoint. This research focuses on comparisons of scientific statements about, for instance, what characteristics an extravert or an introvert manifests and the characteristics that are ascribed to them in everyday life. The aim of such comparisons is to unfold similarities and differences between scientific and everyday conceptions of persons and personality.

Traits, Biases and Personality

The construction of a personality taxonomy has been one of the focal concerns for personality theories and has a venerable history. One possible way of coming to terms with this problem has been to analyse how personality characteristics have been coded in language. A prominent approach to this question has been the investigation of trait and other personality descriptive terms. There are literally thousands of trait terms to be found in language and a nearly infinite number of ways to describe persons. A number of psychologists have therefore aligned themselves with a view expressed by Cattell:

> The position we shall adopt is a very direct one . . . making only the one assumption that all aspects of human personality which are or have been of importance, interest, or utility have already been recorded in the substance of language. For, throughout history, the most fascinating subject of general discourse, and also that in which it has been most vitally necessary to have adequate, representative symbols, has been human behaviour. Necessity could not possibly have been barren where so little apparatus is required to permit the birth of invention. (1943: 483)

This statement by Cattell, which has also been termed the 'sedimentation' or 'lexical' hypothesis (see Goldberg, 1981), has served as a guiding framework for a substantive area of research in the exploration of the interrelations between trait terms. As Goldberg (1989) points out, it was Galton (1884) who may have been one of the first to point out that the socially significant aspects of individual differences will become coded in language. The modern approaches towards exploring trait terms have aimed at summarizing trait interrelations structurally. The main methodological approach, which is essentially factor-analytic, attempts to represent traits in terms of those dimensions which best summarize the interrelations between these terms. This consists of finding properties common to a variety of trait terms that allow a simpler representation of the enormous variety that one can find in a dictionary. For instance, the earliest investigators in this area, Allport and Odbert (1936), extracted about 18,000 personality descriptive terms from the second edition of Webster's Unabridged Dictionary of the English Language.

Particularly during the 1960s, there was a considerable debate about what the types of taxonomies obtained by factor-analytic studies meant. One view, maintained by those in personality, was that these taxonomies were representative of the *characteristics of actual people*. Another view that was voiced by people working in the implicit personality theory framework in social psychology was that the interrelations discovered by personality theorists were actually reflections of *perceivers' implicit theories*, that is their *cognitive representations* of personality. Finally, there was a third view (Mulaik, 1964) which maintained that the interrelations between trait terms were due to linguistic conventions about the meanings of terms. For instance, kind and good are analogue terms and are therefore semantically overlapping. They will therefore be used similarly and contrastively to terms that are contraries or antonyms, such as brusque or bad. In this view it is the positive and negative semantic relations between terms or *language conventions* which are essentially regarded as giving rise to the relationship between trait terms. Related to this view are also arguments that judgements about persons on person-descriptive terms are subject to a *bias* mediated *by semantic factors* (for example, D'Andrade, 1965; Shweder, 1982).

In the following section on trait taxonomies and everyday conceptions of personality we shall review this literature and then assess it from a social-constructionist perspective, by examining the fundamental role played by ordinary language in the constitution of the relationships between trait terms.

Trait Taxonomies, Biases and Language: Perspectives on Structure

The central question posed by trait taxonomists is how to simplify the vast number of trait terms that are available by examining trait interrelations. This type of examination can proceed by adopting a number of different empirical strategies. One of them is to find out how they are attributed to other people, that is judgements about the applicability of traits to actual persons. Another procedure is the examination of judgements about the interrelations among the trait terms themselves. In a recent paper, Peabody and Goldberg (1989) distinguish between these two types of judgemental approaches as *external* and *internal judgements* respectively.

The early empirical background to this area can be broadly divided into two separate views on what the relations between trait terms meant. One of these is to regard these systematic relationships between traits as an error source or a bias. The other is to regard these systematic relationships as an indicator of the structure of personality. A systematic response tendency was noted early on in a number of studies employing an 'external judgement' approach (for example, Newcomb, 1931; Rugg, 1922; Thorndike, 1920; Wells, 1907). What would appear to be one of the earliest reports of the systematic relationships observed in the use of trait terms is a study by Wells (1907). He found that if a person was seen as very friendly then a host of related adjectives such as sociable, kind, helpful would also be seen as characteristic of this person. These results drew attention to systematic tendencies in the response patterns of raters or observers. Thus the familiar 'halo effect', a term coined by Thorndike (for example, 1920), referred to the influence that the general impression a subject had formed of a target had on his/her ratings of the target. The finding was that the halo effect would result in spuriously high correlations between, for example, adjectives sharing similar meanings. The argument was that if 'experience' were the actual guide to judgements or impressions, then such high correlations should not occur. Thus the halo effect referred to a constant error in psychological rating which came about through 'suffusing ratings of special features with a halo belonging to the individual as a whole' (Thorndike, 1920: 25). This effect, termed the 'packaging of information' by Bruner and Tagiuri (1954: 641), was also noted by others (cf. Symonds, 1925, 1935). A related tendency was commented on by Newcomb (1931) and termed by Guilford (1936) a 'logical error'. Newcomb found that when judges recorded behaviours of others as they took place then the correlations between behaviours referring to the same trait were consistently lower than when these records of behaviour occurrences were noted after the behaviours had taken place (that is, memory-based ratings of behaviours). He argued that the higher correlations could have resulted from 'logical presuppositions in the minds of raters rather than actual behaviour' (Newcomb, 1931: 288).

A study by Levy and Dugan (1960) attempts to resolve some of these issues by linking these findings to the person-perception literature. Referring to the halo effect and the logical error they suggest that 'from an analysis of the nature of constant errors or intercorrelations found in trait ratings, information might be obtained concerning the nature of certain aspects of person perception.' This conclusion is based on the following reasoning: 'the correlations might arise because the traits are not independent from each other from the stand-point of the perceptual processes involved in making the judgments, but rather represent specific instances of a more limited number of dimensions of judgment or social perception' (1960: 21).[1] In their study, Levy and Dugan asked subjects to rate photographs of 225 white males on fifteen bipolar scales, such as 'good–bad', 'kind–cruel', 'warm–cold'. In examining the inter-correlational structure between the bipolar scales they attributed high correlations to 'the existence of certain dimensions of perception which were responsible for the correlations that were obtained' (1960: 22). The factor-analytically obtained dimensions are seen as representations of 'certain major dimensions of social perception'. Interestingly enough though, neither the design of their study nor their data permit such a conclusion. The alternative hypothesis that they entertain and finally reject is the possibility of interpreting the findings as relationships between trait terms that have emerged as a function of 'the synonymity or logical implication or true relationship between the terms obtained' (1960: 22).

There are a number of different studies (for example, Tupes and Christal, 1961; Norman, 1963) employing different procedural paradigms such as asking subjects to rate their peers, while varying the relative acquaintance between the subject and the target (that is, peer) from three days to three years. The questionnaires used in such studies are personality inventories. Originally, the data from these studies, which yielded stable and consistent factorial structures over widely differing samples of subjects, were interpreted as reflecting the organization of these attributes in the targets (cf. Norman, 1963: 581). Tupes and Christal (1961), using a number of ratee samples and experimental conditions, find a consistent structure solution and suggest that this structural consistency may reflect 'five fundamental *meaning* concepts' applying to the person terms they employed in their study. Their report is in fact regarded as the origin of what has more recently been termed the 'big five' (Goldberg, 1981). However, this more recent interpretation is in terms of five robust factors of *personality*, that is as a representation of personality (cf. also Digman and Takemoto-Chock, 1981; Peabody, 1987; *inter alia*).

Mulaik's (1963, 1964) research appears to be the first to suggest a clear link between the so-called structures of personality inventories (that is, source traits or types, traits) which are supposed to represent the 'structure of the personality of individuals' and 'the role of conventional linguistic usage [of these person terms] in determining the correlation between trait rating scales' (1964: 507). Mulaik, in his 1964 study, employed three independent groups of raters to judge a series of traits as they apply to: (a) 'real' persons; (b) stereotypes; and (c) twenty traits' meanings (person terms). He found that the three inter-correlational matrices had over 60 per cent of common variance despite the fact that the types of judgement involved were distinctly different, as were the objects of judgement. From these findings he infers that the obtained structural patterns were imposed through semantic properties that were prevalent in judges, rather than by some properties of the objects of judgement. He concludes that 'being able to show high correlations between factor scores computed from trait ratings of persons and factor scores computed from physiological measures of the same persons will not prove that trait factors are source traits'

(1964: 511). Mulaik's objection is to the type of position represented, for example, by Cattell (1946: 27), who maintains that factors 'promise for us to be the real structural influences underlying personality which it is necessary for us to deal with in developmental problems, psychosomatics, and problems of dynamic integration'. Mulaik concludes that his 'results strongly indicate a reinterpretation of the results of factor analytic studies of personality based upon trait ratings by observers. The traits, heretofore thought to be linked by processes in persons rated, may be linked in reality in the minds of raters by linguistic convention' (1964). Similarly, Passini and Norman (1966) demonstrated that subjects' ratings of peers gave rise to factor solutions which were highly comparable, despite the fact that subjects' acquaintance with the target of judgement varied from considerable to barely any at all. On the basis of their study they inferred that 'all that was available to the raters was whatever they carried in their heads concerning the way and degree to which personality traits are organized in people generally' (1966: 47). Additional studies (for example, Norman and Goldberg, 1966; Kuusinen, 1969a, b) also support the above conclusions and suggest that the degree of invariance in the structure of intertrait correlations is not a function of the objects to be rated; is not affected by temporal variation; and displays considerable interindividual agreement.

A number of researchers have subsequently attempted to draw the more radical implications for personality from the idea that the relations between trait are mediated by 'linguistic convention'. The tenor of these developments is the notion of bias. Of these D'Andrade's (1965) study is the first and probably the most important. This is mainly because of the variation it introduced to the empirical paradigm and consequently to the development of this problem in the 1970s and 1980s. He was able to demonstrate that by asking subjects to rate the semantic similarity (or dissimilarity) in meaning between person-descriptive terms it is possible to reproduce a factorial structure comparable to the one which Norman (1963) obtained from peer ratings. In a short study he further demonstrated that the interscale correlational structure of a personality inventory obtained in a clinical sample (Lorr and McNair, 1962) can be largely accounted for by the semantic similarity judgements between inventory items as provided by a normal adult sample. The conclusions he reaches on the basis of these demonstrations are similar to those reached by Mulaik (1963, 1964).

Shweder (for example, 1982) has drawn out the broader implications of the conclusion that the obtained relations between person-descriptive terms are mediated by language conventions. He argues that 'most personality classifications derived from memory based assessment procedures can be reproduced from conceptual association judgments' (1982: 73). These include a wide array, as Shweder (1982) notes. For example, the factor-analytic classification of personality and interpersonal behaviour (Bales, 1970) and the factor-analytic classification of maternal personality (Sears, Maccoby and Levin, 1957) have both been reproduced by Shweder (1975). The alpha factor of the MMPI has been reproduced by Shweder (1977), *inter alia*. These types of findings, which cover a broad range of domains, appear to suggest that taxonomic models of personality are replicable by asking for judgements of similarity in meaning for terms that appear in inventories. Irrespective of whether the empirical procedures are external or internal judgements, the general argument advanced by Shweder and D'Andrade (for example, 1980) is that when one is using memory-based assessment procedures then subjects will confuse 'what is like what' (semantic similarity) with 'what goes with what' (actual co-occurrences of properties, traits or behaviours). The reception of this so-called 'systematic-distortion hypothesis' has however not been completely unequivocal (cf. for detail: Block, Weiss and Thorne, 1979; Lamiel, Foss and Cavenee, 1980; Romer and Revelle, 1984; Semin and Greenslade, 1985; Weiss and Mendelson, 1986; *inter alia*).

There has been a growing research tradition emerging parallel to and independent of these critical developments and influenced largely by the 'five fundamental meaning concepts' (Tupes and Christal, 1961; Norman, 1963). These developments have pursued the idea that this factorial 'discovery' is a representation of the dimensions of personality. These factors have recently been relabelled extraversion–introversion, friendly compliance–hostile noncompliance, will, neuroticism or anxiety, and openness to experience (Digman and Inouye, 1986).[2] Most of this work is grounded on the premise that natural languages should have evolved the necessary terms for all fundamental differences and that an analysis of language would therefore provide a comprehensive representation of the personality terms, namely traits. This is the guiding idea which initiated the research by Allport and Odbert (1936) and Cattell (1946). Goldberg (1981, 1982) in a rigorous and exhaustive analysis of trait terms obtained results with a striking resemblance to the original Tupes and Christal research. In fact, as Digman and Inouye note, 'If a large number of rating scales are used and if the scope of the scales is very broad, the domain of personality is almost completely accounted for by five robust factors' (1986: 116).

An interesting aspect of these robust findings is that it does not matter whether the empirical procedures involved 'external' or 'internal judgements', or variations in the degree of acquaintance between rater and ratee (for example, Passini and Norman, 1966; Norman and Goldberg, 1966; Digman and Takemoto-Chock, 1981; McCrae and Costa, 1985). Digman and Takemoto-Chock (1981), for example, reanalysed the data from six studies (Cattell, 1946; Norman, 1963; Tupes and Christal, 1961; *inter alia*). They used the same factor-analytic technique and arrived at the same five factors that accounted for the domain across the six studies, despite the possible suggestion that more than five may be necessary to handle the complete data (see also Peabody and Goldberg, 1989).

An interesting feature in the interpretation of these research findings is that the respective proponents entertain distinctly different accounts as *exclusive* possibilities in accounting for the systematic findings that were being repeatedly noted in diverse studies. On the one hand, we observe findings that are regarded as a logical error or halo effect reflecting biasing properties of the mind – for instance, a reflection of certain perceptual properties. Similarly, the systematic-distortion hypothesis points to a confusion between 'what goes with what' and 'what is like what'. Those interpretations that refer to possible properties of language generally regard the influence of language on judgements in the personality domain as essentially a confound. In the earlier work, this was in large part due to the psychological approach which was concerned with establishing principles that are free from any cultural elements such as language or linguistic conventions, since these were regarded as psychologically uninformative. A third possibility was that the relations observed between the person-descriptive terms constitute a representation of personality. The point is that these three possible accounts – bias, language conventions and representation of personality – are treated independently and the only critical work to cast these as alternatives against each other was carried out during the 1960s. Most of the subsequent work, particularly within the 'big five' tradition, disregards these issues.

A Constructionist Resolution

In order to have a clearer conception of how social constructionism would address this controversy it is necessary to understand some of the central features of ordinary language. Language has a fundamental role to play as the medium on which *descriptions* or *characterizations* of persons (and their social behaviour) are configured, as well as a medium of *communication* between people. An important characteristic of ordinary language is that it is a medium that generalizes over different actors and observers who occupy the same place at different times or different places at the same time. This property of language, namely to generalize over specific instances, and over different persons in time and space is referred to as *intersubjectivity* and is integrally linked to social interaction.

> In order to transmit some experience or content of consciousness to another person, there is no other path than to ascribe the content to a known class, a known group of phenomena, and as we know this necessarily requires *generalization*. Thus it turns out that *social interaction necessarily presupposes generalization and the development of word meaning*, i.e., generalization becomes possible with the development of social interaction. Thus, higher, uniquely human forms of psychological social interaction are possible only because human thinking reflects reality in a generalized way. (Vygotski, 1956: 51)

In a sense intersubjectivity refers to what might be termed 'socially invariant information' that mediates between individuals. To illustrate, when I am talking to somebody, I often wish to convey an intention, an idea, a directive or an impression. In order to be able to do so, I have to resort to some medium that is shared, abstracted, 'objective', in short, intersubjective. On the one hand, we have a medium that enables human interaction and permits the communication of subjective intentions. Yet, in the process of interaction and communication, the medium is also reproduced (that is, language as an institution). Thus human communication reproduces the socially invariant structures or properties of language (for example, syntax, semantics) that simultaneously allow us to communicate our subjective intentions. A central insight from this perspective is that *intersubjectivity precedes subjectivity* and that 'self understanding is connected integrally to the understanding of others' (Giddens, 1976: 19).

Language as an institution exists as a 'structure', syntactic and semantic. This is something that is traced or identified as those ruleful aspects or consistencies in what people say in the speech acts they perform. Therefore, when we refer to syntax, as one example of such regularities, what we are referring to is the 'reproduction' of similar elements that are noted over speech acts. Such rules, for example, syntax, in turn generate the totality of speech acts which is the spoken language. Similarly, if one were to think about the concrete case of, for instance, trait terms, then one can regard these terms as idealized semantic abstractions that are both the preconditions and consequences of the use of person terms in everyday communication.

In such a view, the issue of intersubjectivity can be understood and conceptualized with reference to those temporally relatively invariant social products that are reproduced in communication. These socially invariant features of language are neither invented by each individual nor discovered in the individual's independent interaction with 'nature'. Nor are they inherited in the form of instincts or unconditional reflexes. Instead, they are 'tools' by virtue of being part of a socio-cultural milieu, and tools which carry information about our world in general and persons in particular. It is in that sense that knowledge and information about persons is configured in the medium of language. In that sense, one can talk about the idealized meanings of person terms, such as the meaning of traits. These are for instance the types of meanings that one would find in a dictionary.[3] In the abstracted sense, a term embodies an idealized meaning with no reference to a concrete person or for that matter a person-in-context (cf. Semin, 1989; Semin and Chassein, 1985).

Such idealized knowledge structures obviously have no pragmatic reference. In contrast, 'meaning in use' or meaning in pragmatic contexts is situated or 'indexical' (cf. Garfinkel and Sacks, 1970; Mehan and Wood, 1975). 'Pragmatic meaning is defined as meaning that is dependent on context, while the semantic value of a sign [in our case a trait or a person description] is the meaning, or notional core, that it has apart from contextual factors' (Meertz, 1985: 4).

Having presented relevant features of ordinary language from a constructionist point of view we can now turn to an assessment of the research controversy. To recap: the systematic findings that are noted in the relations of person descriptive terms are interpreted either as a systematic bias of the perceptual apparatus; a representation of personality; or the product of language conventions. The critical issue that this excursus on the features of ordinary language points to is that the robust empirical findings must reflect the semantic relations between person descriptive terms. This becomes more evident if one considers the characteristics of the methodological procedure by which these results are obtained. One feature of the statistical methods that are employed throughout this research that we have reviewed is that they decontextualize the meanings of the different terms. This is mainly due to the fact that the statistical methods that are employed are mainly designed to find the common properties of data points rather than idiosyncratic variations. Thus a contention that would be advanced by a social-constructionist perspective is that these regular findings are in fact no more or no less than idealized abstractions capturing decontextualized semantic relationships. The main issue in the research we briefly reviewed along with the three alternative positions that have been furnished to account for the regularities in the representations of person-descriptive terms is an attempt to come to terms with the *relationships* between the terms. This is essentially a representation of the semantic domains. Our reanalysis suggests that this type of structural relationship is a representation of an abstracted semantic space. In fact, if one develops an index of semantic association between person terms (such as adjectives) from a dictionary (Semin, 1989), without utilizing any subjects, then it can be shown that the types of associations one obtains from a dictionary reproduce perfectly the empirical results of tasks obtained by 'internal judgements'. Semin (1989) demonstrates that 60 per cent of the variance of semantic similarity judgements are acounted for by the meaning relationships uncovered by a word-association index he developed to examine dictionary meanings. But the question remains as to whether these semantic relationships are only language properties, or also biasing tendencies or are for that matter representations of personality (cf. Semin, 1989; Semin and Chassein, 1985).

We can proceed to answer this question by considering an argument advanced by Vygotski. He suggests that external activity, namely social processes mediated by, for example, language, provide the key to understanding the emergence of internal functioning. In this view:

> It is necessary that everything internal in higher forms was external, that is, for others it was what it now is for oneself. Any higher mental function necessarily goes through an external stage in its development because it is initially a social function. This is the centre of the whole problem of internal–external behaviour. . . . When we speak of a process, 'external' means social. Any higher function was external because it was social before becoming an internal, truly mental function. (1981a: 162)

That is, the dichotomy between the internal and external in this view becomes an unnecessary one. 'The very mechanism underlying higher social functions is a copy from social interaction; all higher mental functions are internalized social relationships. . . . Even when we turn to mental [internal] processes, their nature remains quasi social, in their private sphere, human beings retain the functions of social interaction' (Vygotski, 1981b: 184). Thus, in this view, the question whether the robust structure that emerges is a property of the mind (implicit personality theory), a property of persons (personality structure) or a property of a social institution (language and language conventions) is in fact a non-issue. These aspects are inseparable from each other in that they are inextricably linked to each other. So far we have considered assessing the types of relationships recovered in analyses of internal and external judgements and the potential meanings that have been ascribed to these along with a social-constructionist interpretation. The conclusion that we have reached is that the relationships recovered by such analyses are representations of semantic domains. The next question that is related to this assessment is what the actual content of these semantic domains correspond to. It is possible to argue that what is being recovered in taxonomic approaches to personality is basically semantic domains. Yet it is possible to argue that the manner in which this content is organized is inaccessible to human consciousness. One could therefore argue that this type of discovery, for instance, the 'big five', represent domains of personality that represent true advancements insofar as they capture features of personality that are inaccessible in everyday life. In the following section, we examine the relationship between representations of persons, for instance the domains of personality described by the 'big five', and lay representations of persons. The question which guides this section is specifically content-focused: what is the relationship between the contents of the types of representation of personality we have discussed so far and theories that are found in everyday life? Do scientific models of personality supersede everyday conceptions?

Trait Taxonomies and Ordinary Language: Perspectives on Content

The question about the similarity and difference between the contents of scientific and everyday theories is predicated on the nature of the relationship between the technical languages in personality work (for example, models of personality) and everyday conceptions of personality (Semin, 1987). Ordinary or natural language is central to meaningful social behaviour, as it is to communication in social interaction. By implication, psychological research in personality is impossible without resorting to ordinary language. Indeed, natural or ordinary language permeates all phases of our activities as psychologists, from the instructions to the presentation of the material, to the nature of most of the material itself, and to its presentation in the form of scientific discourse. Therefore psychologists, regardless of their area of specialization, cannot construct a technical metalanguage which is independent of the categories in ordinary language. Essentially, the execution of any type of psychological research with humans demands communication. In particular cases, such as interviews, questionnaire-based investigations, paper and pencil tests or experimental studies with verbal material only, research takes place as an actual interaction between people and in particular experimenter–investigator and subject–participant. However, such studies of human behaviour depend on a mutuality of perspectives and shared knowledge (Semin and Manstead, 1979).

The problem to be considered in this section is the degree to which models of personality, such as the 'big five' or Eysenck's two-dimensional model, can be regarded as reproducing everyday conceptions of personality. The argument from a social-constructionist perspective is that society is only possible to the extent that interacting selves share the *same underlying symbolic order*. Consequently, the second point is that *psychological realities must always refer to the corresponding cultural and historical background upon which they are predicated*. What are the implications of this for theory and empirical findings in personality work? The major implication of the argument leads to the third point which is that personality work, in order to develop models or theories that are 'empirically' testable can only do so by accessing historically and culturally constituted social representations (Moscovici, 1981, 1984). The data that are collected are at the same time part and parcel of a social world, which is integral in the constitution of the psychological reality of the individuals who share it. It can therefore be assumed that the reality of everyday psychology is constitutively and reflexively involved in the production of scientific models in psychology to the extent that proposed models constitute empirically verifiable social representations. Thus, paradoxically, the appropriateness of scientific models will depend on the degree to which they adequately capture the representations of socially constituted realities.

A considerable body of evidence has been accumulated over the years lending direct or 'indirect' support for the contentions advanced here. The indirect evidence is research that is not explicitly set within the theoretical perspective outlined here, but is concerned with questions such as the fakability of personality inventories (for example, Brown and LaFaro, 1968; Power and MacRae, 1971), examinations of lay conceptions of intelligence (for example, Sternberg et al., 1981; Jaeger and Sitarek, 1985; Wagner and Sternberg, 1985), or attribution-theoretical work in personality (Pawlik and Buse, 1979).

A number of studies addressing these issues directly set out with the following general hypothesis: there is a conceptual overlap between ordinary language and scientific propositions due to the interdependence between culturally given psychological realities and scientific psychological theorizing. To demonstrate this hypothesis the methodological approach that is adopted employs procedures by which the overlap in content between scientific and ordinary language propositions can be established. The type of question would thus be the following: are naive subjects able to generate, discriminate, and/or classify the same phenotypic behaviours, attributes, and so on to a given supercategory or dimension (for example, extraversion) of a trait-type model? There are a number of studies that have examined this question.

If the social-constructionist arguments are correct, then lay persons should be able to discriminate successfully between items of diagnostic instruments (for example, the EPI; Eysenck and Eysenck, 1975), that is they should be able to discriminate items belonging to a given scale category from those which do not, in any personality inventory. Semin, Rosch, Krolage and Chassein (1981) examined two multiphasic personality inventories, one consisting exclusively of behavioural items (Freiburg Personality Inventory – FPI; Fahrenberg, Selg and Hampel, 1973) and the other solely of adjectives (Eigenschafts Woerter Liste – EWL; Janke and Debus, 1978). Four subscales (aggressiveness, excitability, depressiveness and inhibition) were selected from the first inventory and a further four (excitability, anger, anxiety and depressiveness) from the second one. The 200 subjects participating in this study were divided randomly into eight groups of twenty-five, one for each scale category. They received either the complete FPI or the complete EWL and were asked to identify those items in the inventory which belonged to a given scale category. As expected, subjects were able to discriminate systematically and with above-chance probability those items belonging to the supercategories. Further corroboration of the ability of lay subjects accurately to identify items belonging to specific personality domains comes from a study by Furnham (1984), who showed that subjects were able to identify with reasonable accuracy those items in the Eysenck (Eysenck and Eysenck, 1975) measure of neuroticism.

These types of studies proceed by supplying the scale-category label in advance and examine whether subjects can discriminate items, thus providing one possible way of establishing 'identity' relationships between psychological and ordinary language representations of personality. A possible objection is that if subjects were not provided with categories in advance, then they would be less likely to come up with a classificatory system. Indeed, this is similar to the argument that Eysenck advances in favour of 'scientific taxonomies'. He argues that the

> demand for one typology instead of a whole collection of different typologies is, in essence, a demand for a scientific methodology which will enable us to test claims advanced for any specific system; the

essential incompleteness of the typologists' achievements lay in their failure to provide a technique of verification by means of which their claims can be subjected to genuine scientific validation. It is only through the method of factor analysis that such verification can be done. (1970b: 35)

The assertion is that by using psychometric procedures a model of personality can be developed which supersedes 'unsystematic' commonsense or ordinary language descriptions, in terms of its abstraction, generality and validity. If, however, as is assumed from a constructionist perspective, this 'systematic' model is already contained in the normative conventions that are part and parcel of everyday life, subjects should actually be able to generate the structure of an inventory without being provided with the scale-category label. Semin, Chassein, Rosch and Krolage (1984) employed the short form of the FPI (Fahrenberg, Selg and Hampel, 1973). Each of the sixty-seven items belonging to the twelve subscales of the inventory were written on separate index cards and presented to forty subjects. The method employed was a card-sorting task (Miller, 1969). Subjects had to put those cards which they thought were similar in meaning into the same group. There were no restrictions in terms of the number of groups they could construct, nor in terms of items per group. On the basis of this procedure an inter-item proximity matrix was obtained. A second sample of fifty-eight subjects filled out the FPI-K from a self-referent perspective. From this sample the inter-item correlations were obtained. The structure of the inter-item correlations and the proximity matrix obtained by the 'subjective' classifications of participants were compared by means of a multidimensional scaling procedure which showed that the two matrices had 75 per cent common variance. That is, the independent subjective orderings of the items replicated the personality inventory structure. Semin and Chassein (1985), employing a similar methodology, were able to establish a more general case for a generic theoretical taxonomy of personality (see Eysenck, 1970a) showing that such generic models are contained in ordinary language propositions.

Another way of examining the social-constructionist argument consists in asking lay persons to generate statements about the characteristics of specific types in trait-type models. These lay statements can then be examined with respect to their 'identity relation' to the scientific model in question, namely the degree of conceptual overlap. For example, Semin, Rosch and Chassein (1981) asked thirty-nine subjects to describe what they thought were the attributes of a typical extravert and a further thirty-nine subjects what they thought were the attributes of a typical introvert. Based on a content analysis of the items generated by lay people these authors selected the most frequently mentioned descriptions of extraverts and introverts and presented these items to a further sample who had to judge how typical each item was for a typical extravert or introvert. The twelve most typical items respectively for an extravert and introvert were selected and a twenty-four-item scale was constructed. This constituted a lay scale of introversion–extraversion. When this scale was administered to a new sample along with the EPI it was shown that the 'lay scale' was as powerful in discriminating between individuals as was the EPI on extraversion–introversion. Furnham (1984) conducted a study similar to this examining neuroticism. His subjects generated over 400 behaviours/traits which he reduced to 100 on the basis of a content analysis. These items were then rated for their typicality for a neurotic person on seven-point scales. On the basis of a qualitative analysis Furnham concludes that the '10 most typical character-istics appear to fit well with explicit theories of neuroticism' (1984: 100).

It would appear to be the case that in a number of domains lay subjects' representations of specific personality domains (such as extraversion, introversion, neuroticism) overlap considerably with the scientific definition of these domains. Another aspect of trait-type models such as Eysenck's is their dimensionality – for example, extraversion–introversion. It may be the case that subjects have access to specific domains but do they represent these domains in dimensional relations as in the case of extraversion–introversion? Semin and Rosch (1981) explored this issue in a study using items from the extraversion and introversion domains, generated by lay persons. They used an attribute-inference paradigm, which involves giving subjects a stimulus item (such as an item describing introversion) and asking which of a list of items apply – or do not apply – to this person (response items are extraversion–introversion items). Indeed, they found a near-perfect symmetry in inferences. If the stimulus item is an item from the extraversion domain, then all extravert items are endorsed as applying, and vice versa for a stimulus item from the introversion domain. This study demonstrates not only that knowledge about personality is organized in discrete propositions relating specific behaviours and traits peculiar to a specific type, but also that ordinary language contains propositions about implicative relationships. These take the form: if person A is X, then all x's (xi to xn) apply. Contained in this are also relational propositions, namely, if X, then not Y and thus all implicative statements belonging to Y (yi to ym) are seen as not applicable to the person as well. Thus dimensional propositions observed, for example, in extraversion–introversion are also found in ordinary language.

The research we have presented so far has dealt with manifest behaviours (such as likes going to parties) or imputed psychological qualities (such as impulsive). One might reasonably argue that although this type of work is prominent in trait taxonomies there is other work such as Eysenck's that makes assumptions about the genotypic foundations of trait-type models. Thus one can contend that although there might be a conceptual overlap between the content of scientific and everyday theories of personality, this remains restricted to manifest or psychological properties of persons and that it is essentially the biological or genotypic foundations of personality models that sets them apart from lay conceptions of personality. The genotypic level lends scientific models of personality their special status (for example, Eysenck, 1983). Intuitively, this level of analysis not only denies lay conceptions the availability of such higher-order, typically psychogenetic models, but it also denies lay conceptions the possibility of entertaining propositions about what types of genotypic property is associated with which types of content (manifest or psychological properties). Such propositions relate to specific and intricate relationships between differences in cortical arousal for extraverts and introverts which are mediated by the reticular formation, and rely on postulated differences in resting levels of arousal. These differences are demonstrated in a number of experimental studies testing behavioural differences derived from this hypothetical model concerning the relationships between postulated cortical processes and behavioural proclivities. Semin and Krahe (1987) examined the commonsense availability of experimental relationships derived from genotypic propositions and their behavioural (that is, phenotypic) statements within Eysenck's E–I trait-type model in two studies utilizing an attribute-inference paradigm. In the first study typically genotype-based statements about either extraverts or introverts served as the stimulus conditions (for example, 'recalls tasks better some time after learning them rather than immediately' – introvert genotypic item; or 'is a person who can tolerate pain relatively easily' – extravert genotypic item) describing two independently manipulated target persons and phenotypic statements derived from the EPI as dependent variables (for example, 'is a person who stops and thinks things over before doing anything' – phenotypic introvert item; or 'likes going out a lot' – phenotypic extravert item). This order was reversed in the second experiment. Results from both studies show a high degree of accuracy in subjects' inferences, suggesting that lay persons have well-formed conceptions about personality containing 'higher-order' psychogenetic propositions corresponding to Eysenck's trait-type model.

A series of highly interesting studies on lay conceptions of intelligence have been conducted by Sternberg and his colleagues (Sternberg, Conway, Ketron and Bernstein, 1981; Sternberg, 1985; Wagner and Sternberg, 1985). These studies, which are primarily designed as descriptive studies, are concerned with reconstructions of the 'form and content of people's informal theories' (Sternberg et al., 1981: 37–8). In part of this research Sternberg et al. (1981) first of all asked lay persons to generate behaviours characteristic of intelligence, academic intelligence and everyday intelligence or unintelligence. They used the final 250 behaviours extracted from the generated items for a number of purposes, but among other things for self-ratings on intelligence and compared these self-ratings with IQ scores. They found that 'the three kinds of self-rated intelligence were . . . significantly correlated with IQ; People's conceptions of themselves were related to their objective test performance. The highest correlation with IQ was that for rated academic intelligence' (1981: 47).

In a more recent paper Sternberg (1985) contrasts lay theories of intelligence, creativity and wisdom with explicit theory-based measures (see Experiment 3). He concludes:

> Correlations of scores from implicit-theory-based measures with scores from explicit-theory-based measures showed both convergent and discriminant validity. The prototype scores correlated with the psychometric tests with which they were supposed to correlate and did not correlate with the psychometric tests with which they were not supposed to correlate. Thus, implicit theories of intelligence and wisdom *do* correspond substantially to explicit theories. (1985: 619)

Similar results are reported by Jaeger and Sitarek, who examine lay conceptions of ability. They compare the Berlin Intelligence-Structure Model (BIS; Jaeger, 1982, 1984) with lay conceptions of abilities and intelligence. This study shows that the ability structure available to lay conceptions yields concepts of practical and social intelligence above and beyond those provided in the BIS.

Conclusions

While it is usual for science or particular areas of science to incorporate theories, concepts or models that are derived from or rely upon commonsense constructions it is often the case that such reliance is observed in the early stages of the development of sciences. However true this may be in the case of natural sciences, in the case of psychological work there has to be a clear link to commonsense constructions at least at one level of the scientific activity. This is necessitated by the fact that our psychological reality is largely guided by the way we construct the world. Furthermore, in most of our dealings as psychologists, in personality work or otherwise, we rely on everyday constructs for at least our data-collection activities (instructions and so on), and more often than not the data that we collect are themselves products of everyday knowledge. To that extent, we should always be more explicit about the links between our activities of theory-construction, data-collection, hypothesis-testing and so on and their link to ordinary language and the theories and assumptions embedded in ordinary language. The point about scientific activities is that they should in the final instance not merely paraphrase assumptions and propositions that are available in everyday life, but transcend these in some manner or to make some discoveries. This is not to say that taxonomic work in personality has not provided us with new insights. Nevertheless, a social-constructionist approach allows us to put these insights into specific perspectives, emphasizing the language-driven aspects of the taxonomic models as well as the everyday-knowledge-based aspects of the contents of these theories. In that sense, a constructionist approach sharpens the types of questions that may be asked in a further step. There are a number of options that present themselves in this context. One of them is to examine the properties of interpersonal language (for example, Semin and Fiedler, 1988) and explore the situated use of these terms in discourse with a view to uncovering their cognitive implications (for example, Maass et al., 1989; Semin and Fiedler, 1989). What appears to be important from the perspective presented here is a more serious consideration of the role played by language in personality and an invitation to investigate the language of personality, not only in the abstract but also in everyday discourse as the neglected counterpart to much of the research discussed here.

Notes

1. The link between 'logical errors', 'biases' and the question concerning the formation of impressions about personality is made explicitly by Solomon Asch (1946: 260). These issues were thus introduced to an emerging and broader social-psychological tradition which was to form the area of person perception. It is with this link to the impression formation work and, more generally, to implicit personality theory (cf. Bruner and Taguiri, 1954: 641, 649) that the research which developed in the early 1960s engendered a debate between theories based on the so-called 'structures' of personality and theories based on (what may be termed) 'perceptions of personality' in everyday life.

2. The 'precise' labelling of these factors is the object of some debate among the cognizantis. For instance, Goldberg and his colleagues (such as Peabody and Goldberg, 1989) term these factors: I Surgency (bold–timid); II Agreeableness

(warm–cold); III Conscientiousness (thorough–careless); IV Emotional Stability (relaxed–tense); and V Culture (intelligent–unintelligent).

3. Although even the dictionary specifies a number of variations of meaning as a function of different contexts. The simplest instance being warm in the context of a person judgement acquires a different semantic value in contrast to a reference to a cup of milk.

References

Allport, G.W. and Odbert, H.S. (1936) Trait names: a psycho-lexical study. *Psychological Monographs*, 47 (1, Whole No. 211).

Asch, S. (1946) Forming impressions of personality. *Journal of Abnormal and Social Psychology*, 41: 258–90.

Bales, R.F. (1970) *Personality and Interpersonal Behavior*. New York: Holt, Rinehart & Winston.

Block, J., Weiss, D.S. and Thorne, A. (1979) How relevant is a semantic similarity interpretation of personality ratings? *Journal of Personality and Social Psychology*, 37: 1055–74.

Brown, J.R. and LaFaro, F. (1968) Fakability of the Sixteen Personality Factor questionnaire. *Canadian Journal of Psychology*, 68: 3–7.

Bruner, J.S. and Tagiuri, R. (1954) The perception of people. In G. Lindzey (ed.), *Handbook of Social Psychology*. Vol. 2. Reading, MA: Addison-Wesley.

Cattell, R.B. (1943) The description of personality: basic traits revolved into clusters. *Journal of Abnormal and Social Psychology*, 38: 476–506.

Cattell, R.B. (1946) *The Description and Measurement of Personality*. Yonkers, NY: World Books.

Coulter, J. (1983) *Rethinking Cognitive Psychology*. London: Methuen.

D'Andrade, R.G. (1965) Trait psychology and componential analysis. *American Anthropologist*, 67: 215–28.

Digman, J.M. and Inouye, J. (1986) Further specification of the five robust factors of personality. *Journal of Personality and Social Psychology*, 50: 116–23.

Digman, J.M. and Takemoto-Chock, N.K. (1981) Factors in the natural language of personality: re-analysis, comparison, and interpretation of six major studies. *Multivariate Behavioral Research*, 13: 475–82.

Eysenck, H.J. (1970a) *The Structure of Human Personality*. London: Methuen.

Eysenck, H.J. (1970b) Explanation and the concept of personality. In R. Borger and F. Cioffi (eds), *Explanation in the Behavioural Sciences*. Cambridge: Cambridge University Press.

Eysenck, H.J. (1983) Psychophysiology and personality: extraversion, neuroticism and psychotism. In A. Gale and J.A. Edwards (eds), *Physiological Correlates of Human Behavior*. Vol. 3. London: Academic Press.

Eysenck, H.J. and Eysenck, S. (1975) *Manual of the Eysenck Personality Inventory*. Sevenoaks, Kent: Hodder & Stoughton.

Fahrenberg, J., Selg, H. and Hampel, R. (1973) *Das Freiburger Persönlichkeitsinventar*. Göttingen: Hogrefe.

Furnham, A. (1984) Lay theories of neuroticism. *Personality and Individual Differences*, 5: 95–103.

Furnham, A. and Henderson, M. (1983) The mote in my brother's eye, and the beam in thine own: predicting one's own and others' personality test scores. *British Journal of Psychology*, 74: 381–9.

172 Domains of everyday understanding

Galton, F. (1884) Measurement of character. *Fortnightly Review*, 36: 179–85.

Garfinkel, H. and Sacks, H. (1970) The formal properties of practical action. In McKinney, J.C. and Tiryakian, E.A. (eds), *Theoretical Sociology*. New York: Appleton Century Crofts.

Gergen, K.J. (1985) The social constructionist movement in modern psychology. *American Psychologist*, 40: 266–75.

Giddens, A. (1976) *New Rules of Sociological Method*. London: Hutchinson.

Goldberg, L.R. (1981) Language and individual differences: the search for universals in personality lexicons. In L. Wheeler (ed.), *Review of Personality and Social Psychology*. Vol. 2. Beverly Hills, CA: Sage.

Goldberg, L.R. (1982) From Ace to Zombie: some explorations in the language of personality. In C.D. Spielberger and J.N. Butcher (eds), *Advances in Personality Assessment*. Vol. 1. Hillsdale, NJ: Erlbaum.

Goldberg, L.R. (1989) Standard markers of the big-five factor structure. Paper presented at the Workshop on Personality Language. University of Groningen.

Guilford, J.P. (1936) Unitary traits of personality and factor theory. *American Journal of Psychology*, 4: 633–80.

Jaeger, A.O. (1982) Mehrmodale Klassifikation von Intelligenzleistungen. *Diagnostika*, 28: 195–226.

Jaeger, A.O. (1984) Intelligenzstrukturforschung, konkurrierende Modelle, neue Entwicklungen, Perspektiven. *Psychologische Rundschau*, 1: 19–35.

Jaeger, A.O. and Sitarek, E. (1985) Implizite Fähigkeitskonzepte in der Kognition von Leien. Unpublished manuscript. Free University of Berlin, Department of Psychology.

Janke, W. and Debus, G. (1978) *Die Eigenschaftswörterliste EWL. Eine mehrdimensionale Method zur Beschreibung von Aspekten des Befindens*. Göttingen: Hogrefe.

Kuusinen, J. (1969a) Affective and denotative structures of personality ratings. *Journal of Personality and Social Psychology*, 12: 181–8.

Kuusinen, J. (1969b) Factorial invariance of personality ratings. *Scandinavian Journal of Psychology*, 10: 33–44.

Lamiel, J.T., Foss, M.A. and Cavenee, P. (1980) On the relationship between conceptual schemes and behavior reports: a closer look. *Journal of Personality*, 48: 54–73.

Levy, L.H. and Dugan, R.D. (1960) A constant error approach to the study of dimensions of social perception. *Journal of Abnormal and Social Psychology*, 61: 21–4.

Lorr, M. and McNair, D.M. (1962) An interpersonal behaviour circle. *Journal of Abnormal and Social Psychology*, 67: 68–75.

Maass, A., Salvi, D., Arcuri, L. and Semin, G.R. (1989) Language use in intergroup contexts: the linguistic intergroup bias. *Journal of Personality and Social Psychology* 57: 981–93.

McCrae, R.R. and Costa, P.T. Jr (1985) Updating Norman's 'Adequate Taxonomy': intelligence and personality language in natural language and in questionnaires. *Journal of Personality and Social Psychology*, 49: 710–21.

Meertz, E. (1985) Beyond symbolic anthropology: introducing semiotic mediation. In E. Meertz and R.J. Parmentier (eds), *Semiotic Mediation*. New York: Academic Press.

Mehan, H. and Wood, H. (1975) *The Reality of Ethnomethodology*. New York: Wiley.

Miller, G.A. (1969) A psychological method to investigate verbal concepts. *Journal of Mathematical Psychology*, 6: 126–31.

Moscovici, S. (1981) On social representation. In J. Forgas (ed.), *Social Cognition*. London: Academic Press.

Moscovici, S. (1984) The phenomenon of social representations. In R. Farr and S. Moscovici (eds), *Social Representations*. Cambridge: Cambridge University Press.

Mulaik, S.A. (1963) A factor analytic investigation of the equivalence of personality factors with semantic factors. *Dissertation Abstracts*, 24: 247.

Mulaik, S.A. (1964) Are personality factors raters' conceptual factors? *Journal of Consulting Psychology*, 28: 506–11.

Newcomb, T. (1931) An experiment designed to test the validity of a rating technique. *Journal of Educational Psychology*, 22: 277–87.

Nisbett, R. and Ross, L. (1980) *Human Inference: Strategies and Shortcomings of Social Judgment*. New York: Prentice Hall.

Norman, W.T. (1963) Toward an adequate taxonomy of personality attributes: replicated factor structure in peer nomination personality ratings. *Journal of Abnormal and Social Psychology*, 66: 574–83.

Norman, W.T. and Goldberg, L.R. (1966) Raters, ratees, and randomness in personality structure. *Journal of Personality and Social Psychology*, 4: 681–91.

Passini, F.T. and Norman, W.T. (1966) A universal conception of personality structure? *Journal of Personality and Social Psychology*, 4: 44–9.

Pawlik, K. and Buse, L. (1979) Selbst-attribuierung als diffrentiellpsychologische Moderatorvariable. *Zeitschrift für Sozialpsychologie*, 10: 54–69.

Peabody, D. (1987) Selecting representative trait adjectives. *Journal of Personality and Social Psychology*, 52: 59–71.

Peabody, D. and Goldberg, L.R. (1989) Some determinants of factor structures from personality-trait descriptors. *Journal of Personality and Social Psychology*.

Power, R.P. and MacRae, K.D. (1971) Detectability of items in the EPI. *British Journal of Psychology*, 62: 395–401.

Romer, D. and Revelle, W. (1984) Personality traits: fact or fiction? A critique of Shweder and D'Andrade's systematic distortion hypothesis. *Journal of Personality and Social Psychology*, 47: 1028–42.

Rugg, H. (1922) Is the rating of human character practicable? *Journal of Educational Psychology*, 13: 30–42.

Sears, R.R., Maccoby, E.E. and Levin, H. (1957) *Patterns of Child Rearing*. New York: Harper & Row.

Semin, G.R. (1986) The individual, the social and the social individual. *British Journal of Social Psychology*, 25: 177–80.

Semin, G.R. (1987) On the relationship between theories in ordinary language and psychology. In W. Doise and S. Moscovici (eds), *Current Issues in European Social Psychology*. Vol. 2. Cambridge: Cambridge University Press.

Semin, G.R. (1989) Impressions of personality revisited: the contribution of linguistic factors to attribute inferences. *European Journal of Social Psychology*, 19: 85–101.

Semin, G.R. and Chassein, J. (1985) The relationship between higher order models and everyday conceptions of personality. *European Journal of Social Psychology*, 15: 1–15.

Semin, G.R., Chassein, J., Rosch, E. and Krolage, J. (1984) Eine sozialpsychologische Eingrenzung des Aussagegehaltes psychometrischer Persönlichkeitsmodellen. *Schweizerische Zeitschrift für Psychologie und ihre Anwendungen*, 43: 75–90.

Semin, G.R. and Fiedler, K. (1988) The cognitive functions of linguistic categories in describing persons: social cognition and language. *Journal of Personality and Social Psychology*, 54: 558–68.

Semin, G.R. and Fiedler, K. (1989) Relocating attributional phenomena within a language–cognition interface: the case of actors' and observers' perspectives. *European Journal of Social Psychology* 19: 491–508.

Semin, G.R. and Greenslade, L. (1985) Differential contributions of linguistic factors to memory based ratings: systematizing the systematic distortion hypothesis. *Journal of Personality and Social Psychology*, 49: 1713–23.

Semin, G.R. and Krahe, B. (1987) Lay conceptions of personality: eliciting tiers of a scientific conception of personality. *European Journal of Social Psychology*, 17: 199–209.

Semin, G.R. and Manstead, A.S.R. (1979) Social psychology: social or psychological? *British Journal of Social and Clinical Psychology*, 18: 191–202.

Semin, G.R. and Rosch, E. (1981) Activation of bipolar prototypes in attribute inferences. *Journal of Experimental Social Psychology*, 17: 472–84.

Semin, G.R., Rosch, E. and Chassein, J. (1981) A comparison of the common-sense and 'scientific' conceptions of extroversion–introversion. *European Journal of Social Psychology*, 11: 77–86.

Semin, G.R., Rosch, E., Krolage, J. and Chassein, J. (1981) Alltagswissen als implizite Basis für wissenschaftliche Persönlichkeitstheorien. *Zeitschrift für Sozialpsychologie*, 12: 233–42.

Shweder, R.A. (1975) How relevant is an individual difference theory of personality? *Journal of Personality*, 43: 455–84.

Shweder, R.A. (1977) Likeness and likelihood in everyday thought: magical thinking in judgments about personality. *Current Anthropology*, 18: 637–48.

Shweder, R.A. (1982) Fact and artifact in trait perception: the systematic distortion hypothesis. In B.A. Maher and W.B. Maher (eds), *Progress in Experimental Personality Research*. Vol. 2. New York: Academic Press.

Shweder, R.A. and D'Andrade, R.G. (1980) The systematic distortion hypothesis. In R.A. Shweder (ed.), *New Directions for Methodology of Social and Behavioral Science*. Vol. 4: *Fallible Judgment in Behavioral Research*. San Francisco: Jossey Bass.

Sternberg, R.J. (1985) Implicit theories of intelligence: creativity and wisdom. *Journal of Personality and Social Psychology*, 49: 607–27.

Sternberg, R.J., Conway, B.E., Ketron, J.L. and Bernstein, M. (1981) People's conceptions of intelligence. *Journal of Personality and Social Psychology*, 41: 37–55.

Symonds, P.M. (1925) Notes on rating. *Journal of Applied Psychology*, 7: 189–95.

Symonds, P.M. (1935) *Diagnosing Personality and Conduct*. New York: The Century Co.

Thorndike, E.L. (1920) A constant error in psychological ratings. *Journal of Applied Psychology*, 4: 25–9.

Tupes, E.C. and Christal, E.E. (1961) *Recurrent Personality Factors Based on Trait Ratings*. Technical Report ASD–TR–61–97. Lackland Air Force Base, TX: US Air Force.

Vygotski, L.S. (1956) *Selected Psychological Research*. Moscow: Izdatel'tsvo Akademii Pedagocheskikh Nauk.

Vygotski, L.S. (1981a) The genesis of higher mental functions. In J.V. Wertsch (ed.), *The Concept of Activity in Soviet Psychology*. Armonk, NY: Sharpe.

Vygotski, L.S. (1981b) The development of higher forms of attention in childhood. In J.V. Wertsch (ed.), *The Concept of Activity in Soviet Psychology*. Armonk, NY: Sharpe.

Wagner, R.K. and Sternberg, R.J. (1985) Practical intelligence in real-world pursuits: the role of tacit knowledge. *Journal of Personality and Social Psychology*, 49: 436–58.

Weiss, D.S. and Mendelson, G.A. (1986) An empirical demonstration of the implausibility of the semantic similarity explanation of how trait ratings are made and what they mean. *Journal of Personality and Social Psychology*, 50: 595–601.

Wells, F.L. (1907) A statistical study of literary merit. *Archives of Psychology*, 7.

9

Commonsense Theories of Personality

Adrian Furnham

Höchstes Glück der Erdenkinder
Sei nur die Persönlichkeit. (Goethe)
(The highest happiness of earth's children
is nothing but personality.)

Magis quis vereris quam quo interest. (Seneca)
(Personality is more important than surroundings.)

Although the lay person and the psychologist use the term
personality somewhat differently, there exists a rich literature in
fiction and journalism as well as scientific writing speculating on the
nature of personality and individual differences. This chapter will
attempt to examine lay theories of personality and contrast them
with 'scientific' theories. First, however, the issue of common sense
will be considered with respect to individual differences. Secondly,
the differences between implicit, indigenous, everyday lay theories
will be contrasted with explicit, universal, specialist scientific
theories. Thirdly, the literature on lay understanding of individual
differences will be considered by looking at different methods to
elicit or uncover these 'theories of personality' as well as findings
from a variety of experiments.

Common Sense

To what extent are psychologists' theories of personality any
different from laymen's? Are they more than commonsense study
dressed up in impenetrable and obfuscating jargon? Surely people
would not be able to understand each other and predict each other's
behaviour if they did not have a pragmatic but basically commonsensical theory of personality?

To many laymen, the personality theories they come across in a
number of the social sciences – psychology, management, sociology,
criminology – are simply common sense. Theories of findings seem
already well known, and hence expensive research is thought to be a
trivial, time-wasting and pointless exercise describing or proving

what we already know. Being sensitive to this criticism, social scientists often warn readers of the dangers of common sense which lulls people into the false security that they understand others, and some have even provocatively mentioned the term 'uncommon sense' in their papers and titles (Gammack, 1982).

For instance, McKeachie and Doyle (1966) begin their general psychology textbook by quoting antonymous proverbs, some of which refer to individual differences such as 'You are never too old to learn' versus 'You can't teach an old dog new tricks.' It is argued that common sense cannot tell us under which conditions each generalization is true – for that, scientific research is required (Fletcher, 1984). Others have attempted to persuade readers that *common knowledge* provides only inconsistent and misleading suggestions for understanding social behaviour by giving a short test. Baron and Byrne (1981), in their popular textbook on social psychology, ask the various questions each of which has a true-false response format. These include: 'In general, women conform more than men'; 'If you pay someone for doing something they enjoy, they will come to like this task even more'; 'In choosing their romantic partners, most people show a strong preference for extremely attractive persons'; 'If you want to get someone to change his or her views, it is best to offer this person a very large reward for doing so'; 'Most people feel sympathy for the victims of serious accidents or natural disasters and do not hold such persons responsible for the harm they have suffered.'

Readers are assured that research findings suggest that *all* these statements are false. Similarly, in a book on Organizational Behaviour, Baron (1983) offers a similar quiz where again all the answers are false. These include: 'Directive, authoritative leaders are generally best in attaining high levels of productivity from their subordinates'; 'In most cases, individuals act in ways that are consistent with their attitudes about various issues'; 'Top executives are usually extremely competitive, hard-driving types'; 'Most persons are much more concerned with the size of their own salary than with the salary of others'; 'Direct, face-to-face communication usually enhances co-operation between individuals'; 'Most persons prefer challenging jobs with a great deal of freedom and autonomy.' These quizzes are all attempts to fend off the lay objection that psychology, particularly social and occupational psychology, is nothing but common sense. Interestingly textbooks on personality theory, of which there are many, rarely do this, simply ignoring the issue of common sense.

Furnham (1983a) has suggested that the commonsense objection to social science in general or personality theory in particular normally takes three forms. The first is that the findings are well known, intuitive, unsurprising, uninformative, and hence common sense and science are no different. The second is partly the obverse – that is, disciplines which investigate issues which are the stuff of personal experience (personality differences, love and attraction) have tended either by use of excessive jargon or technical language, or the focusing on minute, esoteric, trivial or irrelevant aspects of social behaviour, to debase or corrupt common sense. That is, topics that are amenable to common sense should have explanations in terms of commonsense language and concepts, not jargon. The third, related objection occurs when experimental findings or social-science writings appear to contradict widely held views of human nature. Many studies have demonstrated that people are cruel, uninsightful, self-centred, compliant, anti-social, and hence these studies have raised more of an objection than those that have painted the opposite picture (Milgram, 1974; Zimbardo et al., 1973). That is, where findings are against the consensus or commonsense belief that people are basically good, altruistic, intelligent and so on, objections are made.

Stroebe (1980) has argued that many social-psychological theories are intuitive and therefore not easily abandoned in the face of contradictory evidence. He mentions the complementary-needs hypothesis, which has not been replicated or supported in over two dozen attempts to test it. 'Despite this devastating record, the theory is still presented in most attraction and social psychology textbooks. It just makes too much sense that, for example, somebody who loves to push people around should get along better with a spouse who prefers being pushed than pushing' (1980: 186). Perhaps this observation is even more true of personality theory. Many textbooks reproduce again and again theories of personality that have received almost no empirical support, indeed the opposite, yet appear not to 'die'. For instance Maslow's 'theory' of hierarchical needs is known by nearly everyone who has had barely one lecture in psychology, yet empirical studies have shown it to be at best a poor simplification of human behaviour.

The objection from 'common sense' takes various forms, yet not all academics see this as a problem. Paradoxically, it is the 'hard' scientists who are most convinced that all science is just common sense. Julian Huxley, the Nobel Prize-winning scientist, noted in an essay: 'Science is nothing but trained and organized Common Sense, differing from the latter only as a veteran may differ from a raw recruit: and its methods differ from those of Common Sense only as far as the guardsman's cut and thrust differ from the manner in which a savage wields his club'. Whitehead is reputed to have said that 'Science is rooted in the whole apparatus of Common Sense thought.' This idea of organized, disambiguated common sense is also supported by Rock, who has suggested that all the different academic theories of crime and delinquency are to be found in commonsense formulations:

> Common Sense can neither be wholly incorporated nor wholly abandoned. Rather it is typically subjected to a double form of exploitation. . . . Ideas of anomie, differential association, relative deprivation, functional interdependence, conflict, and labelling theory may all be found in folk wisdom, early tracts, and conventional explanation.
> They represent parts of the common stock of everyday analysis. It is only the tendency of criminological discourse to become independent that renders such formulations academically novel and remarkable. They have to be restructured before they become available to criminology enquiry. Restructuring may resolve contradictions, unearth implications and refine arguments. But it also sets up a barrier to participation in the larger conversation of ideas. The criminologist is at once unusually sophisticated and unusually simple. (1979: 78)

Others have seen the commonsensical nature of scientific theories, particularly in the social sciences, as inevitable because of the 'trickle-down' phenomena. That is, many commonsensical ideas and theories started out as scientific hypotheses but have become familiar as the findings of studies have been 'popularized'. The Type A literature on heart attacks and personality may be seen as an example of this. Thus, as Brickman pointed out, because social science returns its findings to the general culture, they are apt to become more familiar and commonsensical over time.

> A finding in social psychology cannot remain non obvious as people hear it again and again any more than a joke can remain funny to people who hear it again and again. More generally, we may propose that discoveries emerge from a region in which we disbelieve them into a zone in which we find them interesting, and then a zone in which we find them obvious, and eventually perhaps, into a further region in which we are again oblivious to them. (1980: 12)

However, the view of the social scientist as an originator, taxonomist or disambiguator of common sense cannot explain how counter-intuitive theories or ideas occur (Peters, 1960). As Gergen has noted: 'This presents us with a special paradox: if one's understanding inevitably depends on existing interpretative modes, how can one engender interpretation that is alien to the existing modes. If "Common Sense" is employed as the instrument of understanding, how can one absorb an argument that violates "Common Sense"?' (1980: 263).

Furthermore, this position does not explain the very different theoretical and methodological differences between social scientists.

That is, if social science is simply common sense, why do we find so much disagreement among social scientists? Of course, one might reply that the very contradictory nature of psychological theories proves that they are simply common sense because common sense is itself contradictory. Furthermore, it is not clear why some 'scientific' findings become common sense and others do not; nor why some commonsensical theories are completely misguided and incorrect, have no foundation in actual behaviour, yet do not disappear.

Yet some scientists have dismissed common sense as a source of ideas, let alone of testable theories. Skinner wrote: 'What, after all, have we to show for non-scientific or prescientific good judgement, common sense or the insights gained through personal experience? It is science or nothing' (1972: 160). Similarly, Broadbent (1961), Cattell (1965) and others have talked about pre-scientific or moralistic thinking which is to be ignored as wrong, unable to be proven and so on. Eysenck in his celebrated book *Sense and Nonsense in Psychology* states:

> This is only one example of what appears to be an almost universal belief to the effect that anyone is competent to discuss psychological problems, whether he has taken the trouble to study the subject or not and that while everybody's opinion is of equal value, that of the professional psychologist must be excluded at all costs because he might spoil the fun by producing some facts which would completely upset the speculation and the wonderful dreamcastles so laboriously constructed by the layman. (1957: 13)

Thus for these eminent psychologists, common sense is a dangerous area from which to draw ideas as they are often misguided or untestable. Even worse, various 'commonsense' ideas may be based not on simple surmise but on prejudice and political ideology. Moreover one can cite extensive literature that illustrates 'faulty' reasoning: for example, the repeatedly observed failure of lay people to make appropriate use of negative information in problem-solving, and the overwhelming preference for confirmatory strategies in logical reasoning tasks. Finally, as scientific findings trickle down into common sense they get distorted, simplified and corrupted so that they become fundamentally wrong or misleading. A good example of this is lay understanding of handedness and hemispherical differences. Another objection to common sense is that often commonsense notions are unclear, ambiguous, inconsistent and occasionally contradictory. For instance, many proverbs are antonymous. Of course, it could be pointed out that both supposedly contradictory sayings may in fact be compatible, when they are made specific for certain circumstances. Thus it might be that one is 'never too old to learn' certain verbal tasks; however, when it comes to reaction-time skills, 'you can't teach an old dog new tricks'. Similarly, 'out of sight, out of mind' may apply to an acquaintance or distant relative but 'absence makes the heart grow fonder' to a lover or close friends (Furnham, 1987). However, the standard argument advanced is that of McKeachie and Doyle, namely: 'A major weakness of all these pre-scientific modes of explanation – superstition, Common Sense, and intuitive philosophy – is that contradictory predictions and explanations are offered without any means of resolving the differences' (1966: 3).

This discussion begs the question what constitutes common sense, particularly with reference to personality. Indeed it is not sure what the term (common sense) actually refers to (Schwieso, 1984). Although Descartes said that common sense is the best-distributed commodity in the world, because everyone is convinced that they are well supplied with it, it remains quite unclear what it is. Different writers have described it differently: 'the layman's conviction' (Köhler, 1947), 'good sense' (Ryle, 1949), 'intuitive philosophy' (McKeachie and Doyle, 1966), 'prescientific good judgement' (Skinner, 1972). Schwieso (1984) has examined four terms: common sensation, ordinary intelligence, good sense and common opinion, which he argues have subtle different meanings but still offer no clear working definition of common sense. Fletcher (1984) has suggested that three aspects of common sense need to be delineated:

1 Common sense as a set of shared fundamental assumptions about the nature of the social and physical world. These assumptions are thought to be culturally held unanimously; never questioned, justified or even articulated; and the very stuff of philosophy. Examples are, according to Fletcher, that the world exists independently of our perception of it; that other people possess states of conscious awareness, that we are the same person from day to day.

2 Common sense as a set of cultural maxims and shared beliefs about the social and physical world. These assumptions, in the form of proverbs, allegories and fables, are highly invariant across and within cultures as regards whether they are known or believed. Examples include that severe punishment deters criminals, that the unemployed are lazy and that our country needs a powerful army to survive.

3 Common sense as a shared way of thinking about the social and physical world. These are tacitly known mental processes involved in explaining, interpreting and understanding the behaviour of self and others. Essentially this concerns all aspects

of lay social cognition and the ways in which people process information about their world.

But social scientists, originally so dismissive of commonsense beliefs, accounts and explanations primarily on grounds of ambiguity, unfalsifiability and inferential errors, are beginning to examine them in detail. Whereas psychologists seem particularly interested in the *process* of lay people explaining everyday events, sociologists seem more interested in the *content* of lay theories. Further, philosophers have subjected social-science theories to tests of whether they are common sense or not, and found that at heart many of them are perfectly understood by the lay person.

Perhaps the greatest advantage of this current interest in common sense (or its many synonyms – lay epistemology, everyday accounts) is that it has encouraged social scientists to elucidate and systematize *their* theories and do more pre-empirical, logical analysis. In one sense the realization that people are prone to numerous logical and inferential errors has encouraged social scientists to inspect their own theories for the same errors. This is particularly the case because, of late, psychology has become more concerned not with behaviour itself but rather with the accounts of behaviour (Shotter and Burton, 1983).

Lay versus Scientific Theories

Though they do not always acknowledge it, many social scientists have explicit axioms about social behaviour. Economists devise sophisticated models of the economy based upon axiomatic beliefs about lay people's purchasing, saving, investing, gambling and so on. Similarly, health educators construct posters, pamphlets and other material based on what they think lay people believe about their health and the behaviours they exact to ensure it. Politicians occasionally commission surveys and consultants to help present themselves in accordance with the beliefs and expectations of prospective voters.

Furnham (1986b, 1988a, b, c) has suggested that commonsense theories differ from scientific theories on a number of specific dimensions spelt out in Table 9.1. Furnham (1988b) has admitted that this is a somewhat simplified picture and could even be misleading. Thus not all lay theories are implicit, inconsistent, content-oriented and so on, nor are 'scientific' theories always process-oriented, falsifiable and so on. Table 9.1 perhaps presents rather too much on four-legs good (science) versus two-legs bad (lay) simplification, yet it does highlight some of the more important criteria upon which one might evaluate a personality theory.

Table 9.1   *Possible dimensions along which prototypically
'scientific' versus 'commonsense' lay theories differ*

	'Scientific' theories	'Lay' theories
1 Explicit and formal	Frequently explicit	Rarely explicit
2 Coherent and consistent	Frequently consistent	Rarely consistent
3 Verification versus falsification	Falsification, deductivism	Verification, inductivism
4 Cause and consequence	Rarely confuses cause and effect	Often confuses cause and effect
5 Content versus process	Often process-oriented	Often content-oriented
6 Internal versus external	Cognizant of both factors	Underestimates external factors
7 General versus specific	Mostly specific, some general	Mostly general, some specific
8 Strong versus weak	Strong	Weak

Valentine (1982) has listed eight criteria: scope, parsimony, clarity, logical consistency, precision, testability, empirical support and fruitfulness. Not everyone would agree that they are the best or most relevant criteria, and there would probably be little agreement as to the rank order of those criteria. Furthermore, whereas some observers may agree with any criterion, they may not agree with its implied *other* policy. Thus to take Valentine's first criterion of *scope*, she notes: 'Both breadth and completeness of coverage *may* be considered advantageous' (1982: 96), which suggests that some might argue that the greater the scope of the theory (in the style of grand theories) the better, while others would reasonably argue the opposite. This is not to suggest that there is *no* agreement as to the criteria by which one may judge theories but rather to note that agreement about them is far from perfect.

Furnham (1988a) did however spell out some of the more interesting and important questions that one would ask of any lay (or scientific) theory of personality.

1   What is the aetiology or development of the individual differences observed? For instance, what part does heredity versus environment play in the origin of stable individual differences?
2   What is the relationship between different aspects, features or dimensions of personality? For instance, if one comes up with a taxonomy or typology, one would want to know how one type (extraverts, endomorphs, aquarians) are related to or correlated with other types (introverts, mesomorphs, librans)?
3   How do these individual differences or personality factors function? That is, what is the process, mechanism or biology that

determines how individual differences occur? Related to this is the question of the function of holding any particular theory by any one individual.

4   Are individual differences and personality features stable across time and consistent over situations? This question, widely debated in academic circles, is of course crucial to the definition of personality.

5   What are the consequences of being one type/having a trait? That is, what are the characteristics of people with different personalities – what are their strengths and weaknesses?

6   How can one change one's or another person's personality? For instance, can one change personality and, if so, how?

7   How does one particular theory of personality relate to another? That is, what is the overlap between various concepts? For instance, it has been suggested that Eysenck's concept of extraversion, Zuckerman's of sensation-seeking, Mehrabian's of stimulus-screening, Strelau's of temperament and Rosenman's of A-type are all closely linked. To what extent are lay theories essentially the same but using different terms?

8   How useful are the language, analogies and models of the theory? Nearly all theories use analogies to explain or describe phenomena and some of these are more or less useful.

Clearly there are dangers in attempting to compare and contrast lay and scientific theories, but what is most useful is to have a set of agreed dimensions or questions to evaluate any lay theory of personality.

Lay Understanding of Individual Differences

The use of the term 'personality' by the lay person (she has no personality; he has a strong personality) is very different from that of the academic psychologist who uses it in a technical sense. This does not suggest, however, that there is an agreed definition of personality. Furthermore, there are numerous, very different theories of personality in academic psychology. Reviewers and propagandists of these theories appear to fall into three groups; benevolent eclectics, partisan zealots and taxonomic enthusiasts (Furnham, 1988b).

Benevolent eclectics list and describe the theories of the most famous personality theorists: Adler, Cattell, Eysenck, Freud and so on. Although limitations of each theorist are mentioned, they are usually impartially described with no good–bad, correct–incorrect, valid–invalid judgement made. For instance Hall and Lindzey

(1957) in their celebrated textbook compared seventeen personality theorists on eighteen dimensions, including unconscious determinants, organismic emphasis and multiplicity of motives. Similarly Phares (1984), who reviews personality theorists from various approaches, argues that they can be compared on six dimensions: systematic versus unsystematic; operational versus non-operational; content versus process; experience versus heredity; generality versus specificity and internal versus situational. A major problem with this approach is that there is no explicit criterion for inclusion or exclusion of any theory or theorists, perhaps because there is no agreed paradigm in personality research (Eysenck, 1983).

Partisan zealots tend to ignore all theories except a chosen one, denying the relevance, significance or validity of all theories except the one. Thus Cattell (1965) rejects psychoanalytic and phenomenological theories of personality, arguing for multivariate experimental methods to define and measure underlying traits. Similarly, followers of Kelly's (1955) personal-construct theory frequently choose to ignore all other theories of personality in favour of their chosen approach. The main danger of this zealous defence of one theory is the potential blindness to contradictory evidence that may result. On the other hand, it could be argued that there is only one correct description of personality and that is worth pursuing.

Taxonomic enthusiasts attempt to classify all personality theories into groups or categories. This may be done historically in terms of schools, empirically in terms of methods or epistemologically in terms of the sort of data admitted in support of theory. Although there are numerous and dramatic differences between the resultant taxonomies of reviewers there does tend to be agreement. For instance, Cook (1984) describes four types of personality theory: those on the surface (the description of traits and factors) and those below the surface (biological, phenomenal and motivation).

Of course one could split each one of these approaches (schools, lines) into further groups. Thus trait theorists may be split into single-trait theorists who emphasize just one major dimension (such as field independence–dependence, A/B type behaviour patterns, locus of control) or those who favour multi-trait theories (Cattell has sixteen, Eysenck three).

These three approaches, however, share a number of assumptions. Yet as Hampson (1982) has pointed out there are three quite different possible perspectives on personality: the *personality theorists* perspective, which involves studying *other* people and deriving coherent theories about personality types or traits; the *lay* perspective, which concerns everyday theories about other people derived from experience, general knowledge, language and so on that are not 'scientific' or explicit; and the *self* perspective, which concerns our knowledge of and theories about *ourselves*. Personality theorists have the first and third (academic and self-theories); lay people, be they trained scientists or not, have only the second and third (lay and self-theories).

The lay perspective has been investigated extensively by psychologists, who have usually referred to it as *implicit personality theory*. For instance the boxer, Mohammed Ali has made explicit his theory of personality, which is based on fruit. The theory depends on the hardness/softness of the inside and outside of fruit. This allows for the four types of fruit shown in Figure 9.1. The boxer confessed to being a Grape (in his view the most desirable of the various fruit), though usually letting the public see only his Walnut personality.

Lay theories of personality are to be seen in various contexts but perhaps are best observed at work. Managers frequently hold strong beliefs about individual differences and as a result many 'theories' in occupational psychology reflect this bias. McGregor (1960) has argued that managers have two basic theories (called *X* and *Y*) about the personality of their employees which leads them to exercise light levels of control (if a follower of theory *X* and less if a follower of theory *Y*). In essence, theory *X* assumes that human beings inherently dislike work and will, if possible, avoid it; most people must be controlled and threatened with punishment if they are to work towards organizational goals; the average person actually wants to be directed, thereby avoiding responsibility.

Security is more desirable than achievement. Theory *Y* proceeds from a different set of assumptions. These are: work is recognized by people as a natural activity; human beings need not be controlled and threatened. They will exercise self-control and self-direction in the pursuit of organizational goals to which they are committed; commitment is associated with rewards for achievement; people learn, under the right conditions, to seek as well as accept responsibility; many people in society have creative potential, not

| | Outside | |
	Hard	Soft
Hard	Pomegranate	Prune
Soft	Walnut	Grape

Inside

Figure 9.1   *Mohammed Ali's personality theory*

just a few gifted individuals; under most organizational conditions the intellectual potential of people is only partially utilized.

The plethora and diversification of these idiosyncratic lay theories have led cynics to argue that there are basically two types of people in this world – those who believe that there are two types and those who do not!

The Measurement, Assessment or Investigation of Lay Theories

The social sciences offer a plethora of methodologies for studying social behaviour, each with its own distinct advantages and disadvantages. But which method is best at eliciting the subtle and fragile lay theories of personality? To what extent does the method dictate the kind of results obtained?

Essentially three types of methodologies may profitably be used to investigate lay theories of human behaviour: those based on *self-report*; those derived from *test data*; and those actually concerned with observing *behaviour*. These methodologies are by no means mutually exclusive but each has its strength and weaknesses.

Self-Report

An obvious way to 'get at' lay theories of behaviour is through listening to or recording the answers to specific questions. This may be done through questionnaires and surveys as well as interviews. Each may differ according to the amount, type and quality of information available, though of course one may use more than one methodology at the same time. Therefore, as Furnham (1983b) and Forgas et al. (1982) did, one can simply ask, 'What causes people to become rich?' and do a content analysis on these answers, which may or may not reflect the scope and subtlety on lay theories. However, these open-ended questions provide useful examples of statements or explanations which may be given to other groups in the form of a questionnaire.

The use of questionnaires with either open-ended or closed questions has obvious advantages and disadvantages. Some of those have been psychometrically assessed and may be useful for investigating general lay beliefs about human nature (Furnham et al., 1985). Questionnaire measures have been constantly criticized, for four major reasons. The first is the problem of *response sets* – faking good or bad, acquiescing with the perceived demands of the researcher and so on. Though this is a frequent objection aimed particularly at personality inventories, it may well be far less relevant when investigating lay theories. However, it is the extent to which response sets threaten the validity of self-report measures which has been challenged by Furnham (1986a). The second objection is the limitation of self-report data in that people may *tell more than they know* (Nisbett and Wilson, 1977) or simply be unable to report on certain features such as their needs or motives. Once again it is not always clear to what extent this objection applies to studies on lay theories, except perhaps as regards the cognitive processes involved in their maintenance. Thirdly, there are inevitable *sampling problems* when using self-report measures such as questionnaires (but not interviews), which are by definition limited to the literate. Indeed interviews are also biased to the articulate. Thus better-educated, higher socio-economic classes may be over-researched while illiterate or marginally articulate people are neglected. It may well be that the latter group holds qualitatively as well as quantitatively different theories that do not get sufficiently researched. Finally, there is always the problem in standard questionnaires of imposing the researcher's own cognitive constructs on to the respondents, rather than allowing them to reveal the range and content of their *own constructs*. This is a well-known objection, favoured by followers of Kelly (1955) and his personal-construct theory. Once again this is probably no less true of studies in lay theories where open-ended questions are frequently used, in which subjects may respond entirely in their own words.

Interviews and questionnaires have been used fairly extensively to investigate lay theories in economics, education, medicine and psychology (Furnham, 1988b).

Test Data
A number of different types of tests may be used to attempt to ascertain lay theories or knowledge. For instance, studies on schema formation or recall may be profitably used. Many studies have supported the selective-recall hypothesis, which suggests that people remember information better than is congruent with their attitudes, because the attitudes or beliefs act as a type of organizing framework which tends to promote the encoding and retrieval of attitude-support material. This has been demonstrated with religious, political and sexual stimulus material, though not all attempts have supported the hypotheses (Furnham and Singh, 1987). Thus by giving lay people material to process (read, watch, listen to and so on) and then asking them to recall as much as they can of it, various organizing schema may become apparent which may shape their lay theories.

A second test method involves asking people *deliberately to dissimilate* in tests (that is, not necessarily give the correct or preferred answers but the one they expect a particular type of person to give). For instance if a person is asked to respond to a test as he or she believes an accountant might, and his or her resultant profile is that of an obsessive, boring, non-spontaneous person, one may argue that this is the stereotype the respondent has about accountants. Similarly if asked to fake good respondents' answers subjects produce a healthy, adjusted, intelligent and so on profile. One may therefore argue that they have understood the underlying dimension investigated by the researcher (Furnham, 1986a; McCarthy and Furnham, 1986). Similarly if a person can *predict* his or her score accurately on a test (of personality, ability, skill and so on) one may conclude that he or she are familiar with the concept being tested.

Thus if you asked non-alcoholics to 'pretend to be alcoholics' and then interviewed them regarding their drinking habits and motives as well as other features of their social behaviour, one might elicit the full subtlety and complexity of their beliefs and theories about alcoholism. Furthermore if they were required to predict their score on some alcoholism-related test, this too may yield interesting insights into their theories of the manifestations of alcoholism.

There are numerous other ways in which test data might be used to investigate lay theories. These include using selective attention tests as measures of pre-conscious processing. A method which appears to be both attracting more attention and highly relevant in this field is the development of prototypes. Essentially these are metacognitive tasks.

Observing Behaviour
Because of the problems associated with self-report, some researchers have preferred to observe behaviour and infer attitudes, beliefs and theories from it. Thus if a person is known to be attempting to lose weight and substantially reduces his or her intake of carbohydrates, one may infer that he or she believes carbohydrates are fattening. However, one cannot know much more than this, which itself may not be informative. For instance, one cannot know whether the person believes carbohydrates are more or less fattening than proteins or animal fats; indeed one cannot even know whether the person knows what carbohydrates are and is just following instructions from a book on what to or not to stop eating. Simple observation of behaviour may not be very useful at all in researching lay theories for human behaviour, particularly as the relationship between attitudes and behaviour are well known to be weak and mediated by many other factors.

Participant observation on the other hand may be much more useful as one can observe contextual and social determinants of behaviour over time, which may lead to many more clues as to the nature of lay theories. However, as participant observation nearly always involves direct interaction between researcher and respondent, it could be seen to share all the advantages and disadvantages of the self-report methods.

Lay Theories of Extraversion and Neuroticism

Despite the plethora of academic, 'scientific' theories of personality, each with its own terminology, basic dimensions and unique processes, certain dimensions appear to recur in a number of theories. Eysenck (1983) has argued persuasively for there actually being a paradigm in personality research which, naturally, encompasses his three-factor theory. Two of the three basic dimensions underlying personality, according to Eysenck's system, are extraversion and neuroticism, dimensions one can find in many other writers, including Galen and Jung (Eysenck, 1981). Both terms are used frequently in lay language. Hence they provide useful dimensions to compare and contrast lay and academic theories.

Extraversion
The term, or at least the concept of, extraversion has a very long and distinguished history in scientific thinking. Eysenck (1981) traced it through the work of Galen the Greek physician, Immanuel Kant the German philosopher, Wundt the German scientist, Gross the Viennese physician, Heymans the Dutch psychologist, Jung the psychoanalyst, Kretschmer the physician, Spearman and Guilford the statisticians, Teplov the Russian physician, Cattell the psychologist and finally Eysenck himself. As one may imagine, therefore, it is a term widely used and understood by expert and layman alike. Indeed it appears to be a personality description frequently used by lay people in describing others.

Comparatively recently there have been a number of studies that have attempted to investigate lay theories of extraversion. However, the work of Semin and Furnham has been programmatic in the sense that they have done a series of studies (with colleagues) examining lay conceptions of personality.

In a series of studies, Semin has examined what he has called commonsense or everyday conceptions of personality, specifically extraversion. Semin, Rosch and Chassein (1981) were interested in the overlap between naive subjects, compared to psychologists' descriptions of extraversion. The method they employed involved constructing a twenty-four item (twelve for extravert, twelve for introvert) lay scale of extraversion from descriptive statements commonly offered by two lay samples and administering it along with the Eysenck Personality Inventory (Eysenck and Eysenck, 1975) to another sample. The scales correlated at $r = 0.51$, $p < 0.001$ ($N = 33$), which was taken as evidence of good convergent validity. The authors agreed that 'it can be maintained that the everyday usage of person descriptions relevant to the categories extraversion–introversion allows individuals to communicate, with relatively high degrees of accuracy, differential information about perceived behavioural indication of others and self' (1981: 82).

In two further rather different studies, Semin and Chassein (1985) argued that hypothetico-deductive models of personality rely primarily on ordinary-language descriptions of persons and do not constitute higher-order models. In the first study subjects Q-sorted the thirty-one trait labels taken from the famous 'Eysenckogram' describing the few quadrants separated by the two factors. As predicted, the subjects' classification was not unlike that of the formal model, so demonstrating again the conceptual overlap between higher-order representations of personality and everyday social representation. A second study concentrated on individual and cultural variations in lay subjects pair-comparing the thirty-five traits used earlier. As predicted there was very high conceptual overlap between subjects' trait-comparison, once again supporting the original theory.

More recently Semin and Krahé (1987) have done two studies which required students who were presented with genotypic (or phenotypic) characterizations of either extravert or introvert to infer corresponding phenotypic (or genotypic) processes. Both studies provided evidence to support the contention that lay conceptions of personality contain genotypic and phenotypic propositions about extraversion which allow correct inferences back and forth.

From the various studies, Semin has concluded that there is very little difference between lay and scientific theories of extraversion. Furnham has reached the same conclusion, but through a rather different set of studies. In a series of studies – Furnham and Henderson, 1983; Furnham and Varian, 1988 – the ability of subjects to predict their own extraversion score has been examined. Furnham and Henderson found a correlation of $r = 0.31$ ($N = 63$) ($p < 0.01$) between estimated score and actual score (derived from the Eysenck and Eysenck, 1975, EPQ), while Furnham and Varian (1988) found a correlation of $r = 0.68$ ($N = 159$) $p < 0.001$. These results are in accordance with others in the field and are not dissimilar from those of Semin mentioned above.

However, a number of important caveats need to be mentioned with regard to the interpretation of these findings. First, although correlations between estimated and test-derived scores are significantly positive, they account for well under half the variance. Secondly, the above studies showed that subjects were less accurate at predicting other personality dimensions such as neuroticism and psychoticism than they were at predicting extraversion, though there is no obvious reason for this. Thirdly, people are considerably less successful at predicting the scores of others compared to themselves.

More importantly Furnham and Henderson have suggested:

> Instead of arguing that people's own personality estimations do/do not accurately reflect the assessment of psychological instruments, it may be just as meaningful to argue it the other way around, concluding that it is the assessment devices of psychologists that do not seem to be able to judge any more accurately. It is possible that only bias and the self-serving interest of psychologists cause them to continue to call their judgments 'true' and 'accurate' and the judgments of those they study as 'mistaken' and 'inaccurate' or 'false'. Thus, this study may be more accurately described as a comparison of two types of personality assessment – a formal test versus an intuitive judgment. Indeed, it may well be that it is the professional psychologist who has the beam in his/her own eye while continually exposing the mote that is in his/her brother subject's eye. (1983: 38)

A second source of information on lay theories of extraversion comes from studies on dissimulating or faking. It could be argued that if lay people can fake a positive, desirable profile, they understand the concept or dimension that the psychologist is attempting to measure and, furthermore, they understand which is the most or least socially desirable score. A plethora of studies looking at faking on the EPQ have shown that people who fake good have inflated extraversion scores but deflated neuroticism scores. Furnham and Henderson (1982) found substantial differences in the extraversion score (range 0–23) between four groups: controls who responded honestly ($X = 12.00$); a group who faked good ($X = 16.15$); a group who faked bad ($X = 5.90$) and a group who faked mad ($X = 10.01$). In other words, subjects asked to present themselves in a favourable light were much more likely to present themselves as extraverts because extraversion is considered much more socially desirable than introversion.

Further evidence for this comes from a study looking at successful and non-successful applicants to the police force. Burbeck and Furnham (1985) found that successful candidates were more extraverted (and less neurotic) than non-successful candidates, but that, comparing applicants' scores with norms, all candidates 'faked good', displaying unusually high extraversion scores.

Thus these studies on extraversion have shown that subjects can describe, predict, recognize and fake extraversion traits and scores with fairly considerable accuracy. This suggests that when lay people and experts use the term extraversion they are doing so similarly. However, that is not to say that subjects recognize or subscribe to academic theories (such as arousal theory) for the origin of these differences!

Neuroticism
Though the term neuroticism is most often used pejoratively, some people have suggested that there can be benefits in being neurotic. For instance Proust is said to have remarked: 'Everything great in the world is done by neurotics, they alone founded our religions and created our masterpieces.' The idea that unhappiness and/or neurosis is related to artistic creativity is relatively widespread among lay people but has little or no empirical support.

Etymologically the term means 'weakness of the nerves' and is derived from the Greek word for nerves. In fact, until the nineteenth century all forms of mental illness were included in the class neurotica, so much that the diagnosis was abandoned as too general until the end of the nineteenth century (Kisker, 1964). Beard (1880) introduced the term neurasthenia, whose symptoms included lack of energy, fatigue, physical complaints and general disability. Kraepelin (1915), however, distinguished between neurasthenia, psychasthenia and hysteria, which remained the basis for the description of the neurotic conditions from the 1890s until the appearance of the American Psychiatric Association's publication of their *Diagnostic and Statistical Manual* in 1952. However, the latest edition (1980) has no reference to neurosis at all.

Most textbooks have difficulty in arriving at a clear definition of neuroticism, though most are agreed on categorizing neurotic symptoms into various groups – anxiety, phobic, obsessive–compulsive, conversion, dissociative and depressing reactions (Buss, 1966; Kisker, 1964). Although he admits a number of ambiguities in the concept of neurosis, Eysenck offered a simple definition for his lay readers: 'Neurosis is a term we often use for behaviour which is associated with strong emotion, which is maladaptive, and which the person giving rise to it realises is nonsensical, absurd or irrelevant, but which he is powerless to change' (1978: 15).

Similarly, in their *EPQ Manual*, Eysenck and Eysenck define a typical neurotic as an anxious, worrying individual, moody and frequently depressed. He is likely to sleep badly, and to suffer from various psychosomatic disorders. He is overly emotional, reacting too strongly to all sorts of stimuli, and finds it difficult to get back on an even keel after each emotionally arousing experience. His strong emotional reactions interfere with his proper adjustment, making him react in irrational, sometimes rigid ways. . . . If the highly neurotic individual has to be described in one word, one might say that he was a *worrier*; his main characteristic is a constant preoccupation with things that might go wrong, and a strong emotional reaction of anxiety to these thoughts. (1975: 9–10)

Psychologists have been fascinated by the *neurotic paradox* – the self-defeating strategies of neurotics whereby they continue behaviour or thought patterns that are maladaptive and bring distress and unhappiness.

Predictably there exists a number of theories which cover aetiology and cure of neurosis: *dynamic* theories which suggest that neurotic behaviour is an external manifestation of an underlying emotional disturbance; *learning* theories which see neurotic behaviour as the product of inappropriate contingency of behaviour learning or conditioning; and *cognitive* theories which suggest that the neurotic condition is characterized by particular patterns of selective information-processing (Young and Martin, 1981). There are, however, other academic theories of neurosis. For instance, followers of *personal-construct theory* have argued that neurotics have tight inflexible construct systems; an anxiety occurs because so many daily occurrences are unable to be interpreted within the construct system. Rogerian *phenomenologists*, on the other hand, believe that the tension and anxiety in neurosis is caused by people's realization that there is a lack of congruity between their experiences and their self-concept, because they falsify their own experiences to perceive them only in terms of values of others (Mackay, 1975).

However, very few theories attempt to explain neurosis, in general preferring to divide neurotics into various categories such as anxiety neurosis, phobias, obsessive–compulsive neurosis, neurotic depression, hysterical conversion-type neurosis and hysterical disassociation-type neurosis (Mackay, 1975).

To some extent researchers have advocated slightly different forms of treatment depending on the precise type of neurosis that they are considering: desensitization, modelling, psychotherapy, electroconvulsion therapy and so on. Suffice to say that most researchers are agreed that neurosis takes different forms but they are not agreed on either the cause or the cure of these different types of neurosis.

A number of issues concerning lay theories of neurosis have been investigated. First, to what extent can people predict their neuroticism score derived from valid measures? A number of studies have looked at normal people's ability to predict their score derived from the Eysenck (EPI or EPQ) measures. Correlations have been modest, positive and significant between the subject's estimate and the actual score: Harrison and McLaughlin (1969), 0.56; Gray (1972), 0.21; Furnham and Henderson (1983), 0.47; and Furnham (1984), 0.40. While the actual/estimated correlations are significant, the data do not provide very strong support for the convergence of ordinary people's estimates and standardized test scores.

Another way of looking at people's conception is to get them to *fake neurotic*. Thus Salas administered the EPI twice to soldiers – once under normal conditions, and then they were asked to respond 'in a manner you would expect of a neurotic, badly adjusted soldier' (1968: 56). As predicted, under the latter conditions their scores rose significantly. There are many other studies which support this conclusion, namely that when asked to fake bad (or mad), neuroticism scores go up, while when asked to fake good, neuroticism scores go down (Power and MacRae, 1977; Furnham and Henderson, 1983). Though the scores change, they do not do so perfectly! In other words, though subjects know which direction to move on a neuroticism score from high to low, they do not (or cannot) move to the extremes.

Interestingly, the evidence suggests that it is not only 'normal' non-neurotic people who can simulate or fake neurotic, but neurotics can fake normal (Gendreau, Irvine and Knight, 1973). McCarthy and Furnham (1986) asked two groups of psychiatric patients – anxiety state, depressed – and a normal group to fill in two questionnaires twice: first responding honestly and then as they believed a 'normal person' might. The results showed that whereas 'normal' people tend to see other normals as much the same if not slightly less well adjusted than themselves, patients see themselves as less well adjusted than the normal person. The controls were significantly more able to predict the normal response to these measures than the patient groups were. However, the depressed and anxiety groups differed in the accuracy of their estimates and in their conceptions of normal functioning. The two patient groups did differ in their levels of accuracy; the depressed patients were generally fairly accurate in their estimate although holding a somewhat negative view of ordinary adjustment. The anxious patients' estimates were always further from the scale norms than those of the depressed patients and they substantially overestimated the adjustment of the ordinary personality and underestimated the adjustment of ordinary social behaviour. Overall, the anxious patients' estimates deviated from scale norms in the same direction as the controls', but this deviation was usually more *extreme*.

Thus it seems that it is not possible to generalize about abnormal groups' perceptions of normality: psychiatrically disturbed patients are *not necessarily* less able than undisturbed normal people to perceive normality accurately. It is anxiety but not depression that appears to impair this ability.

It appears then that both normal and neurotic people have some idea of what normality and neuroses are, even though this is by no means perfect. One reason for them not being able to fake perfectly is that they may not realize the various dimensions of neuroticism. That is, they may recognize that say anxiety and obsessionality are neurotic, but not phobias or hysteria responses.

The second important case for investigating lay theories of neuroticism is to attempt to identify lay people's understanding of the dimensions of neuroticism. One way of going about this is to see which items in a neuroticism inventory people can identify. Furnham (1984) gave subjects the ninety-item EPQ and told them that twenty-three items measured neuroticism. Their task was to identify those twenty-three. Table 9.2 shows the results.

The mean number of items selected by the subjects was 21.3 ($SD = 3.41$), and correct identification for the twenty-three 'neurotic' items ranged from under 10 per cent to over 90 per cent, the mean correct identifications being 53.9 per cent. Six items were identified by over 70 per cent and they related primarily to worrying, while six items were identified by less than 30 per cent of the lay people and they related primarily to feeling bored and listless.

They seemed best able to detect items concerning anxiety, but less sensitive to items about depression. This finding was confirmed when another group of lay people were asked to rate 100 characteristics of people for how characteristic each was of neuroticism. The three most highly characteristic were 'tends often to be very anxious', 'tends to be highly strung', and 'finds it hard to relax'. When these ratings were factor-analysed, four quite clear factors emerged. These were labelled *communication problems* (shy, anti-social, erratic), *unstable* (emotionally labile, unable to concentrate), *obsessional* (ritualized, superstitious) and *phobic* (panics, repetitive). Although people may not be able to taxonomize types of neuroticism or even recognize items from all categories, their rating of traits tends to show a clear underlying structure. Once again, therefore, people are moderately good at perceiving the different types of neuroticism.

Thirdly, there is the issue of beliefs about the *occurrence of neurotic traits* in others as opposed to self. Furnham (1984) and others have demonstrated that people have a tendency to believe themselves to be significantly less neurotic, disturbed, depressed and generally 'mad' and more happy and stable than the average

Table 9.2 *Percentage of subjects correctly identifying the items in the Eysenck Personality Questionnaire (EPQ) which supposedly measure neuroticism*

Items from the EPQ	%
3 Does your mood often go up and down?	45.8
7 Do you ever feel 'just miserable' for no reason?	41.6
12 Do you often worry about things you should not have done or said?	87.5
15 Are you an irritable person?	25.0
19 Are your feelings easily hurt?	41.6
23 Do you often feel 'fed-up'?	25.0
27 Are you often troubled about feelings of guilt?	75.0
31 Would you call yourself a nervous person?	58.3
34 Are you a worrier?	62.5
38 Do you worry about awful things that might happen?	91.6
41 Would you call yourself tense or 'highly strung'?	79.1
47 Do you worry about your health?	79.1
54 Do you suffer from sleeplessness?	66.6
58 Have you often felt listless and tired for no reason?	16.6
62 Do you often feel life is very dull?	8.3
66 Do you worry a lot about your looks?	54.1
68 Have you ever wished that you were dead?	33.3
72 Do you worry too long after an embarrassing experience?	79.1
75 Do you suffer from nerves?	54.1
77 Do you often feel lonely?	20.8
80 Are you sometimes bubbling over with energy and sometimes very sluggish?	54.1
84 Are you easily hurt when people find fault with you or the work you do?	4.1
88 Are you touchy about some things?	37.5
Mean	53.9

person. This appears to be a common adaptive feature of 'normal' people that is not found in psychiatric patients, which may help to account for their problems.

There remains a great deal of work to be done on lay theories of neurosis. Researchers have concentrated far more on the perceived characteristics of neuroticism than on its cause, occurrence or cure. Furthermore, little is known about the perception of people differing in neurotic symptoms about neurosis itself (McCarthy and Furnham, 1986). In view of the current research it would appear that neurotics have a different view of the level and extent of their own neurosis as well as that of non-neurotic people. Furthermore, the manifestations of neurosis may be culture- and time-specific in that, in certain cultures at specific times, it may be more or less acceptable to display forms of neurotic behaviour. Indeed these trends may themselves be a function of the dominant lay theories prevailing at the time.

Other Related Dimensions

Semin, in his various studies on lay conceptions of extraversion (Semin and Chassein, 1985; Semin, Rosch and Chassein 1981), supported a social-constructionist position which stresses the dialectical relationship between social constructions of the world and psychological realities. 'It is argued that hypothetico-deductive models of personality rely primarily on ordinary language description of persons and do not constitute higher order models' (Semin and Chassein, 1985: 1). While the evidence they have accumulated *may* in fact support that position, what of other dimensions of personality? That is, are lay theories of all personality and individual difference measures equally good, and if not why not?

The first point worth mentioning is that not all personality dimensions are well understood by the layman. For instance one of the most extensively researched individual difference measures, namely locus of control, is not well understood. Furnham and Henderson (1982) found no significant difference between groups of subjects either faking good *or* bad on the Rotter scale. Similarly, Furnham and Henderson (1983) found a non-significant negative correlation between subjects' actual and estimated locus-of-control scale scores. On the other hand, research by Semin and Hatfield (1988) suggests that, if lay people are given descriptions of prototypical internal or external people, they can with considerable accuracy identify items from a standard questionnaire that measures this construct. This suggests that the methods whereby lay theories are investigated can have dramatic effects on the apparent results. Thus whereas it seems that people do not recognize the dimension or concept of locus of control, once it is explained to them they appear immediately able to use it in faking studies. To a large extent this inability to predict or fake is also true of Snyder's (1979) self-monitoring construct (Furnham and Henderson, 1982, 1983).

Secondly, it seems that certain well-used constructs, concepts or traits that are frequently discussed in everyday language are those where the differences between laymen and scientists are least great. That is, where the term, concept or dimension is well known to the layman, the difference between lay and expert descriptions is least great. That is perhaps a truism. However, it is not the case that lay and expert *theories* for the causes of these differences are apparent. For instance, Eysenck's (1981) arousal theory of extraversion, with the idea that extraverts are under-aroused and introverts are over-aroused, is perhaps counter-intuitive for most lay people. Similarly the neurotic paradox is equally non-commonsensical. That is to say that, although there might be instances where lay and expert/scientific theories are descriptively very similar, at a theoretical/explanatory level they may have nothing in common.

Conclusion

This chapter has considered the nature of common sense and everyday theories of personality. An underlying theme of this chapter, and the book in general, is the importance of common sense and the similarities rather than the differences between lay and academic conceptualizations of personality processes. At the heart of much of this research is the dichotomy between those researchers who stress the difference between science and common sense, and those who stress the similarities.

Textbooks in many of the social sciences continue to contrast science and common sense in a somewhat simplistic strawman way. Compare the way Kerlinger contrasts the two along five dimensions.

1 While the man in the street uses 'theories' and concepts, he ordinarily does so in a loose fashion. . . . The scientist, on the other hand, systematically builds his theoretical structures, tests them for internal consistency, and subjects aspects of them to empirical test. . . .

2 The scientist systematically and empirically tests his theories and hypotheses. The man in the street tests his 'hypotheses' too, but he tests them in what might be a selective fashion. . . . The sophisticated social scientist, knowing this 'selection tendency' to be a common psychological phenomenon, carefully guards his research against his own preconceptions and predictions and against selective support of his hypotheses. . . .

3 The scientist tries systematically to rule out variables that are possible 'causes' of the effects he is studying other than the variables that he has hypothesized to the 'causes'. The layman seldom bothers to control his explanations of observed phenomena in a systematic manner. . . .

4 The scientist consciously and systematically pursues relations. The layman's preoccupation with relations is loose, unsystematic, uncontrolled. He often seizes, for example, on the fortuitous occurrence of two phenomena and immediately links them indissolubly as cause and effect. . . .

5 The scientist, when attempting to explain the relations among observed phenomena, carefully rules out what have been called 'metaphysical explanations'. (1973: 3–5)

Despite this vision of the heroic scientist versus the muddled layman, Kerlinger attempts to dispel erroneous stereotypes of science! However, his later definition of scientific research is

'systematic, controlled, empirical and critical investigation of hypothetical propositions about the presumed relations among natural
phenomena' (1973: 11). Clearly not all psychologists or social
scientists are as dismissive of common sense in favour of disinterested
empiricism.

Within the academic scientific community there is frequently
antipathy towards disciplines which investigate common sense, or
which by ignoring common sense rediscover it. Giddens (1987), who
considered sociological research, argued that at the heart of
objections to the discipline is the idea that sociologists state the
obvious but with an air of discovery. Worse still, in that it offers
explanations that do not ring true, sociology is doubly redundant
because it not only tells us what we already know, but it parades the
familiar in a garb which conceals its proper nature.

Giddens attempts to rebut these arguments thus: first, common
knowledge (Britain is particularly strike-prone; there has been a
sharp increase in one-parent families) is frequently wrong and may
lead to prejudice, intolerance and discrimination; secondly, correct
knowledge may be the consequence of sociological research;
thirdly, common knowledge about behaviour differs from one
group/milieu to another; fourthly, people are normally able
discursively to identify only a little of the complex conventional
framework of their activities; fifth, behaviour may have unintended
as well as intended consequences, and ways of acting, thinking and
feeling may exist outside the consciousness of individuals; sixth,
ordinary language is too ambiguous for dispassionate analytic
scientific description.

A major problem in the social as opposed to the natural sciences
is that the theories and concepts invented by social scientists
circulate in and out of the social worlds they are coined to analyse.
But while lay concepts obstinately intrude into the technical
discourse of social science, the opposite is also true. Hence the most
interesting and innovative ideas in the social sciences risk becoming
banal:

> the achievements of the social sciences tend to become submerged from
> view by their very success. On the other hand, exactly because of this we
> can in all seriousness make the claim that the social sciences have
> influenced 'their' world – the universe of human social activity – much
> more strongly than the natural sciences have influenced 'theirs'. The
> social sciences have been reflexively involved in a most basic way with
> those transformations of modernity which give them their main subject-
> matter. (Giddens, 1987: 21)

Despite the acknowledgement of the important role common
sense or lay beliefs have in both the determining of social behaviour

and the formulation of academic theories, it is not being suggested that they do not differ. As has been outlined for various reasons and on various criteria, lay theories of personality are different from those proposed by psychologists.

References

Baron, R. (1983) *Behaviour in Organizations: Understanding and Managing the Human Side of Work*. Boston: Allyn & Bacon.

Baron, R. and Byrne, D. (1981) *Social Psychology: Understanding Human Interaction*. Boston: Allyn & Bacon.

Beard, G. (1880) *A Practical Treatment on Nervous Exhaustion (Neurasthenia): Its Symptoms, Nature, Sequences and Treatment*. New York: Wood.

Brickman, P. (1980) A social psychology of human concerns. In R. Gilmour and S. Duck (eds), *The Development of Social Psychology*. London: Academic Press.

Broadbent, D. (1961) *Behaviour*. London: Eyre & Spottiswoode.

Burbeck, E. and Furnham, A. (1985) Police officer selection: a critical review of the literature. *Journal of Police Science and Administration*, 13: 58–69.

Buss, A. (1966) *Psychopathology*. New York: Wiley.

Cattell, R. (1965) *The Scientific Analysis of Personality*. London: Penguin.

Cook, M. (ed.) (1984) *Issues in Personal Perception*. London: Methuen.

Eysenck, H. (1957) *Sense and Nonsense in Psychology*. London: Penguin.

Eysenck, H.J. (1978) *You and Neurosis*. Glasgow: Fontana.

Eysenck, H. (ed.) (1981) *A Model for Personality*. Berlin: Springer.

Eysenck, H.J. (1983) Is there a paradigm in personality research? *Journal of Research in Personality*, 17: 369–97.

Eysenck, H. and Eysenck, S. (1975) *Eysenck Personality Questionnaire Manual*. London: Hodder & Stoughton.

Fletcher, G. (1984) Psychology and common sense. *American Psychologist*, 39: 203–13.

Forgas, J., Morris, S. and Furnham, A. (1982) Lay explanations of wealth: attribution for economic success. *Journal of Applied Social Psychology*, 12: 381–97.

Furnham, A. (1983a) Social psychology and common sense. *Bulletin of the British Psychological Society*, 36: 105–9.

Furnham, A. (1983b) Attributions for affluence. *Personality and Individual Differences*, 4: 31–40.

Furnham, A. (1984) Lay theories of neuroticism. *Personality and Individual Differences*, 5: 95–103.

Furnham, A. (1986a) Response bias, social desirability and dissimulation. *Personality and Individual Differences*, 7: 385–400.

Furnham, A. (1986b) Popular interest in psychological findings: the *Times* correspondence over the Burt scandal. *American Psychologist*, 87: 922–4.

Furnham, A. (1987) The proverbial truth: contextually reconciling the truthfulness of antonymous proverbs. *Journal of Language and Social Psychology*, 6: 49–55.

Furnham, A. (1988a) *Lay Theories: Everyday Understandings of Problems in the Social Sciences*. Oxford: Pergamon.

Furnham, A. (1988b) The geography versus geometry of the mind: central questions in research about 'common sense'. Unpublished manuscript.

Furnham, A. (1988c) Values and vocational choice: a study of value differences in medical, nursing and psychology students. *Social Science and Medicine*, 26: 613–18.

Furnham, A. and Henderson, M. (1982) The good, the bad and the mad: response bias in self-report inventories. *Personality and Individual Differences*, 3: 311–20.

Furnham, A. and Henderson, M. (1983) The mote in my brother's eye, and the beam in thine own: predicting one's own and others' personality test scores. *British Journal of Psychology*, 74: 381–9.

Furnham, A., Johnson, C. and Rawles, R. (1985) The determinants of beliefs in human nature. *Personality and Individual Differences*, 6: 675–84.

Furnham, A and Singh, A. (1987) Memory for informaton about sex differences. *Sex Roles*, 15: 479–86.

Furnham, A. and Varian, C. (1988) Predicting and accepting personality test scores. *Personality and Individual Differences*, 9: 735–48.

Gammack, G. (1982) Social work as uncommon sense. *British Journal of Social Work*, 12: 3–22.

Gendreau, P., Irvine, M. and Knight, S. (1973) Evaluating response set styles on the MMPI with prisoners: faking good adjustment and maladjustment. *Canadian Journal of Behavioural Science*, 5: 183–94.

Gergen, K. (1980) Toward intellectual audacity in social psychology. In R. Gilmour and S. Duck (eds), *The Development of Social Psychology*. London: Academic Press.

Giddens, A. (1987) *Social Theory and Modern Sociology*. Worcester: Polity Press.

Gray, J. (1972) Self-rating and Eysenck personality inventory estimates of neuroticism and extraversion. *Psychological Reports*, 30: 213–14.

Hall, C. and Lindzey, G. (1957) *Theories of Personality*. New York: Wiley.

Hampson, S. (1982) *The Construction of Personality: An Introduction*. London: Routledge & Kegan Paul.

Harrison, N. and McLaughlin, R. (1969) Self-rating validation of Eysenck Personality Inventory. *British Journal of Social and Clinical Psychology*, 8: 315–30.

Kelly, G. (1955) *A Theory of Personality: The Psychology of Personal Constructs*. New York: Norton.

Kerlinger, F. (1973) *Foundations of Behavioral Research*. New York: Holt, Rinehart & Winston.

Kisker, G. (1964) *The Disorganized Personality*. New York: McGraw-Hill.

Köhler, W. (1947) *Gestalt Psychology*. New York: Liverlight.

Kraepelin, E. (1915) *Psychiatrie: Ein Lehrbuch für Studierende und Arzte*. Leipzig: Barth.

Mackay, D. (1975) *Clinical Psychology: Theory and Therapy*. London: Methuen.

McCarthy, B. and Furnham, A. (1986) Patient's conception of psychological adjustment in the normal population. *British Journal of Clinical Psychology*, 25: 43–50.

McGregor, D. (1960) *The Human Side of Enterprises*. New York: McGraw-Hill.

McKeachie, W. and Doyle, C. (1966) *Psychology*. Reading, MA: Addison-Wesley.

Milgram, S. (1974) *Obedience to Authority*. London: Tavistock.

Nisbett, R. and Wilson, T. (1977) Telling more than we can know: verbal reports on mental processes. *Psychological Review*, 84: 231–59.

Peters, R. (1960) *The Concept of Motivation*. London: Routledge & Kegan Paul.

Phares, E. (1984) *Introduction to Personality*. Colombus, Ohio: Charles Merrill.

Power, R. and MacRae, K. (1977) Characteristics of items in the Eysenck

Personality Inventory which affect responses when students simulate. *British Journal of Psychology*, 68: 491–8.

Rock, P. (1979) Another common sense conception of deviancy. *Sociology*, 13: 75–8.

Ryle, G. (1949) *The Concept of Mind*. London: Hutchinson.

Salas, R. (1968) Fakability of responses on the Eysenck Personality Inventory. *Journal of Psychology*, 20: 55–7.

Schwieso, J. (1984) What is common sense? *Bulletin of the British Psychological Society*, 37: 43–5.

Semin, G. and Chassein, J. (1985) The relationship between higher order models and everyday conceptions of personality. *European Journal of Social Psychology*, 15: 1–15.

Semin, G. and Hatfield, J. (1988) Common sense conceptions of locus of control. University of Sussex. Unpublished manuscript.

Semin, G. and Krahé, B. (1987) Lay concepts of personality: eliciting tiers of a scientific conception of personality. *European Journal of Social Psychology*, 2, 239–52.

Semin, G., Rosch, E. and Chassein, J. (1981) A comparison of the common-sense and 'scientific' conceptions of extraversion–introversion. *European Journal of Social Psychology*, 11: 77–86.

Shotter, J. and Burton, A. (1983) Common sense accounts of human action: the descriptive formulation of Heider, Smedslund and Ossorio. In L.L. Wheeler and P. Shaver (eds), *Review of Personality and Social Psychology*. Vol. 4. London: Sage.

Skinner, B. (1972) *Beyond Freedom and Dignity*. London: Jonathan Cape.

Snyder, M. (1979) Self-monitoring processes. In L. Berkowitz (ed.), *Advances in Experimental Social Psychology*. Vol. 12. New York: Academic Press.

Stroebe, W. (1980) Process loss in social psychology: failure to exploit? In R. Gilmour and S. Duck (eds), *The Development of Social Psychology*. London: Academic Press.

Valentine, E. (1982) *Conceptual Issues in Psychology*. London: Allen & Unwin.

Young, G. and Martin, M. (1981) Processing of information about self by neurotics. *British Journal of Clinical Psychology*, 20: 205–12.

Zimbardo, P., Haney, C., Barks, W. and Jaffe, P. (1973) Pirandellian poison: the mind is a formidable jailer. *New York Times Magazine*, April: 38–60.

10

Morality, Domination and Understandings of 'Justifiable Anger' among the Ifaluk

Catherine Lutz

The 'everyday understandings' of health, human development and psychological structure that are described in this volume are learned and most often culturally variable understandings. Learning clearly structures the field of commonsense or orthodox 'knowledge' no less than that of heterodox 'belief'. Anthropological concern with these issues came early in the field's development because the discipline's primary method, cross-cultural fieldwork, places the ethnographer in a social setting in which his or her own implicit understanding system often fails to work in interpreting others' actions and results in bungled social interaction. Otherwise implicit everyday understandings are made explicit, and demonstrate their critical importance for the entire range of social practices. Natural understandings are revealed to be cultural. The denaturalization of knowledge has proceeded in anthropology in many domains from economics (Gudeman, 1986), to gender (MacCormack and Strathern, 1980), to psychiatry (Gaines, 1982). Much work has also been done on cultural understandings of the person and personal processes such as emotion (for example, Abu-Lughod, 1986; M. Rosaldo, 1980; White and Kirkpatrick, 1985; see also Holland and Quinn, 1987).

This chapter considers an aspect of the emotional theories of the Ifaluk people of Micronesia, and focuses on the question of how those cultural understandings of an emotion related to 'anger' are evident, realized in and shaped by their everyday social practices. More particularly, the understandings of 'justifiable anger' shared by most Ifaluk are shown to have both moral and ideological force in social life. In other words, the everyday understanding of this emotion does not simply occur as a form of reflection on experience, but emerges as people justify and negotiate both cultural values and the prerogatives of power that some members of this society currently hold. The more general argument I make is that everyday understanding is a cultural and social process involving negotiation, interpersonal evaluation and power struggles.

The 430 people of Ifaluk live on a half-square-mile atoll in the Western Pacific. Theirs is mainly a subsistence economy of fishing and taro gardening, and social relations are characterized by a hierarchical ranking of individuals and lineages as well as by a strong taboo on interpersonal violence or disrespect. While a group of hereditary chiefs enforce an informal code of law, most conflicts are handled within the household or lineage. A number of the features of life on Ifaluk condition the everyday understanding of emotion, including the island's high population density, precarious position in a typhoon belt which has often meant destruction of their food supply, the frequent adoption of children between living parents, and the strength of women's position in the economy and matrilineal inheritance system (for example, they control horticultural produce and are the owners of household land). These factors have been described elsewhere (Lutz, 1988), and can only be referred to rather than explained below as they relate to understandings of anger.

One of the most central concepts people on Ifaluk use is that of *song*, or 'justifiable anger', an idea that pervades everyday life on the atoll. The term can be heard daily in homes, canoe houses and taro gardens, and can be understood as an expression of the speaker's moral judgement. In lieu of describing the malicious gossipmonger or the aggressive child as bad, someone will often say, 'I am [or someone else is] "justifiably angry" [*song*] at that person.' When this emotional term is used, an assessment is being made; the speaker is saying, 'Something immoral or taboo has happened here, and it ought not to have happened.' As we will see, the moralizing uses to which the concept of *song* is put can also be characterized as ideological in nature; talk about *song* often reinforces the prerogatives of the more powerful members of Ifaluk society, as it is they who have most appropriated the right to be described, or to describe themselves, as 'justifiably angry'.

Whether the concept of *song* is approached as a moral or an ideological construct, we will also see that the term is not simply used to refer to an event (whether that event is seen as internal or external). The use of the word *song* most frequently involves an attempt on the part of the speaker to portray events *before others* in a particular way. Claims to 'justifiable anger' involve a characterization of the world that must be *negotiated* with the audience for those claims. Involving, as the term 'justifiable anger' does, such weighty matters of right and wrong, and of dominance and submission, things could hardly be otherwise.

To understand what people on Ifaluk meant when they said that they or someone they knew was *song*, I did what the reader will do here, which is to move back and forth between my understandings of the concept of 'anger' as it is used in my own society and the concept of *song*. Approaching an adequate translation of the concept involved a process of comparison and contrast – at times unconscious – between my own emotional world and theirs. What immediately drew the world of 'anger' and the world of *song* together for me as an apt comparison is the sense that each of the two concepts is used to say, 'I hate what just happened. I want to move towards that thing or person, and stop it.' Like 'anger', *song* is considered an unpleasant emotion that is experienced in a situation of perceived injury to the self or to another.

The differences between the two concepts would also soon strike me. They were many and went to the root of the differences in our social experience, including our experience of self. Unlike 'anger', 'justifiable anger' is not used to talk about frustrating events that are simply unpleasant, rather than socially condemned. While the uses to which 'anger' is put may often involve the kind of moral appeal that *song* does, for many middle-class Americans 'anger' occurs as much or more in response to the restraint of one's desires or actions as to the violation of moral precept. Moreover, the Ifaluk emphasize, in the concept of *song*, the prosocial aspects of anger;[1] to become 'justifiably angry' is to advance the possibilities for peace and well-being on the island, for it is to identify instances of behaviour that threaten the moral order. This view contrasts with the prevalent view in the west that anger is primarily an anti-social emotion.

Moral Anger and Ifaluk Values

The Ifaluk speak about many types of anger. There is the irritability that often accompanies sickness (*tipmochmoch*), the anger that builds up slowly in the face of a succession of minor but unwanted happenings (*lingeringer*), the annoyance that occurs when relatives have failed to live up to their obligations (*nguch*), and, finally, there is the frustrated anger that occurs in the face of personal misfortunes and slights which one is helpless to overturn (*tang*). But each of these emotions is sharply distinguished from the anger which is righteous indignation, or justifiable anger (*song*), and it is only this anger which is morally approved. While the other forms of anger are attributed both to the self and to others, the person who experiences them does not gain – and often loses – moral force.[2] These amoral forms of anger, if they occur frequently enough, leave one's character open to question or even severe critique. The claim to be 'justifiably angry', on the other hand, is taken seriously as a moral assertion; by identifying *song* in oneself or in others, the speaker advertises himself or herself as someone with a finely tuned and mature sense of island values.

Each word in a language evokes, for the native speaker, an elaborate 'scene' replete with actors, props and event sequences (Fillmore, 1977). The scene that the term *song*, or 'justifiable anger', paints is one in which (1) there is a rule or value violation; (2) it is pointed out by someone, (3) who simultaneously calls for the condemnation of the act, and (4) the perpetrator reacts in fear to that anger, (5) amending his or her ways. Almost all of the hundreds of uses of the term 'justifiable anger' that I recorded evoked this scene, making reference to the violation of some aspect of the widely shared Ifaluk value system. By examining the contexts in which 'justifiable anger' is used, therefore, it is possible to draw the outlines of the Ifaluk worldview; essentially, the term marks the existence of specific cultural values, and serves as an agent for their reproduction.

Chiefly Anger, the Taboo and the Law

It was an evening after the sun had set, and most men had left the drinking circles where they gather on a regular basis with kin and neighbours to drink the fermented coconut toddy collected from their trees each late afternoon. Some younger men of Mai village, however, had continued to drink into the night, and then decided to cross the channel to visit Bwaibwai.[3] Once there, they walked along the village paths speaking in loud voices and occasionally shouting out.

This event was much in discussion the following day. Comment centred around the young men's violation of several standard Ifaluk expectations about how people ought to behave. In their interactions with each other, the Ifaluk value calm, quiet talk, so much so that my first impression of Ifaluk conversations was that of whispered exchanges. Shouting is considered not only a serious disturbance of this otherwise peaceable style, but is also seen as intensely frightening. In addition, people commented, these men were from Mai. They had crossed village boundaries in their escapades, and in so doing threatened inter-village harmony. This is something that the Ifaluk see as potentially more disruptive than misbehaviour whose negative consequences reverberate solely within the bounds of one of the four named communities on the island.

Although several people discussed their panicked fright (*rus*) on hearing the shouting the evening before, most emotional talk centred around the certainty that 'the chiefs will be "justifiably angry" (*song*)' at the young men. Indeed, the chiefs, it turned out, were 'justifiably angry' (*song*), as evidenced by the fact that they soon met and decided to levy a fine (*gariya*) of 200 yards of rope on the men. The rope was to be given to the canoe house in Bwaibwai, where the shouting had taken place. This amount of rope, which represents hundreds of hours of work for the men, who make it from coconut-husk fibre, was a measure of the *song* of the chiefs.

This episode epitomizes one of the most common ways in which the concept of 'justifiable anger' is used; a taboo is violated, a traditional law is disobeyed, and people point not directly to the law but to the *song* of the chiefs. The traditional leaders of Ifaluk, who currently number one woman and three men, each represent the oldest appropriate member of the highest-ranked matrilineage of each of four of the island's seven clans. Their responsibilities are conceptualized as those of 'taking care of' (*gamwela*) the island and its people.[4] Their role as moral leaders of the island is evidenced in the periodic island-wide meetings (*toi*) at which they frequently exhort people to behave properly – to take nothing from the taro gardens of others, to avoid gossip and all 'bad talk', and to work hard, particularly at community-level tasks such as village weeding.

The chiefs are seen as the primary stewards of the island's taboos (*taub*). These taboos forbid traffic in certain areas of the island; uttering certain words in mixed company, including particularly a set with sexual connotations; taking of turtle which belongs to the chief of Kovalu clan, or the taking of marine and other resources out of the season which it is the chiefs' prerogative to declare; walking on the land of the highest-ranked chief at Welipi (who is the leader of Kovalu clan, and is currently a woman) without good purpose and without deep waist-bent posture (*gabarog*); women entering the canoe houses, or riding in the large canoes (*waterog*) during fishing trips, or men entering the birth houses; women working in the taro gardens during their menstrual periods; and men, women or children eating the particular foods that are forbidden to each of them. Although violations of taboos appeared to occur rarely, the idiom of *song* (justifiable anger) was used to explain the consequences when they did occur.

On one such occasion, Ifaluk received a rare visit from a private yacht, whose passengers included several European men and a woman. When the yachters asked to be taken for a sail on one of the island's impressive ocean-going canoes, some men agreed to accommodate them. This event, which had occurred several years before my arrival on the island, was still being discussed. The narrative of this event invariably included, as its the central point, the fact that the chiefs were 'justifiably angry' at the local men when they heard that they had violated the taboo against taking women out (for anything but necessary inter-island travel) on the ocean canoes. While it may have been the case that the men who took the Europeans on the canoe had decided that a non-Ifaluk woman's presence would not constitute an instance to which the taboo would apply, the chiefs' 'justifiable anger' served as notice of the leaders' interpretation of the meaning of the taboos in these new social circumstances. The presence or absence of the chiefs' *song* was looked to in other encounters with new social phenomena (such as events at the island school, or new customs and attitudes brought back by young men who had been off-island); the emotional response of the chiefs could be used as an indication of how the rest of the island ought to feel about, and simultaneously morally react to, such social changes.

The emotion of 'justifiable anger' is strongly associated with Ifaluk's chiefs because it is they who stand as the final moral arbiters on the island, and it is *song* which symbolizes the perception of moral transgression. It is the traditional leaders 'justifiable anger' that marks the violation of those aspects of the moral code which are seen as most crucial for both the harmony and the survival of the island as a whole. Although their authority is sometimes covertly challenged, the near universal concern with the *song* of the chiefs is an index both of the legitimacy that the latter enjoy and of the widespread sharing of values, at least on the explicit level, that obtains on Ifaluk. The intertwining of the political and the moral is seen on Ifaluk in the use of the moral emotion of *song* by the chiefs to maintain traditional value-orientations. Political and moral leadership are thus here, as in many other social systems, closely linked with emotional leadership. As we will see in a moment, the concept of *song* can also be seen as an ideological practice engaged in by the chiefs and others in positions of relative power on Ifaluk to control the behaviour of their subordinates and to bolster their claims to moral suzerainty.

Everyday Interaction and the Marking of Value

The chiefs are certainly not the only individuals on Ifaluk who may claim to be 'justifiably angry'. In an important sense, every person on Ifaluk from the oldest matriarch to the socially emergent toddler not only can be, but is *expected* to be, *song* at appropriate junctures. Since *song* is literally treated as the moral sensibility of a person, the total absence of *song* in an individual could be condemned by others. Let us look now at exactly how this moral sense operates in everyday interaction on Ifaluk.

One of the most frequent contexts in which people spoke about their 'justifiable anger' was when someone had failed to live up to their obligation to share with others. People are expected to share everything, from their cigarettes, food and labour to their children. These expectations are reinforced by the daily sharing that does occur. A woman who smoked a cigarette by herself without sending it on complete rounds among the others with whom she is chatting or working would be considered incalculably thoughtless; a family eating outdoors and within sight of a village path is expected to call out 'Come and eat!' to anyone, kin or relative stranger, who passes by; a group of five people sitting down to eat after an unlucky day of fishing will break the few ounces of their single reef fish into five parts; certain household tasks, such as special food preparation, taro-garden weeding, or the periodic rethatching of a roof, will be done with the contribution of the extra-household labour of up to forty or fifty people; and, finally, the adoption of children from their living parents after about the age of three is valued as a sign of generosity in both adopter and adoptee, and has resulted in an adoption rate of 40 per cent for all children over the age of five. Both the sharing behaviour that occurs every day and the daily conflicts over such co-operation are an index of the extent to which sharing is an entrenched aspect of people's value-orientation on the island. Another index is the fact that the person whose behaviour earns him or her the label of 'stingy' (*farog*) is perhaps the most disliked type of person on Ifaluk, with the sole exception of the 'hot-tempered' (*sigsig*) individual.

What can be termed 'typhoon stories' are frequently told on Ifaluk, and their telling overflows with messages about most of the central emotions and values that occupy people on the island, including particularly the value of sharing. People tell of the entire village gathering together to eat whatever food items can be caught or salvaged after the storm's devastation. The stories draw an image of one coconut being split open by the chief and divided into equal but miniscule portions for the survivors. They also tell of the punishment meted out by the chiefs, again as a measure of their *song* (justifiable anger), for those caught eating alone (and hence not sharing what food they have found); a circle is drawn in the earth out in the direct sun, and the culprit is made to sit there for an extended period, a sanction that is notably harsh by comparison with those for other infractions of law and morality.

The anticipation of the 'justifiable anger' of others is often the explicit motivation for sharing. The consumption of pork and of sea turtle, which are relatively scarce and highly valued resources, is surrounded by careful attention to equity in the distribution of portions to neighbours and relatives. A representative of each of the families who is to receive a basket of turtle or pork pieces is usually asked to assist in its preparation. Hence, I was sent one afternoon to help in the cooking of a large pig belonging to Lemangemar, the clan sister of Tamalekar (the man who was my 'adoptive father'). As we sat around the work area, it was clear that there were many more hands than tasks that required them. Most of those invited were implicitly there in order that each family might directly observe the equity of the division (*gamaku*) of the food, thereby preventing *song* at Lemangemar's household. After small baskets had been woven and set out, and as her daughter dropped pieces into each, Lemangemar supervised by calling out, 'Put more pork in that basket, or the people of [that household to whom the basket belongs] will be "justifiably angry".' The daily anticipation of the 'justifiable anger' of others is a fundamental regulator of the behaviour of individuals and a basic factor in the maintenance of the value of sharing.

What happens when the value of sharing is contravened? 'Justifiable anger' is declared, usually by the party or parties most directly injured by the failure to share; in some cases, an entire village may be 'justifiably angry'. In one such case, the women of two households attempted to circumvent the mandate that each household bring their traditional and clearly identified allotment of food (in this case, one bowl of taro or pot of breadfruit) to communal feasts or to households where there is a serious illness or recent death. These particular women came to a village feast with one pot of food which they had collected and cooked together, and so brought less than the amount expected. As soon as the feast was over and the women in question had left, people declared their 'justifiable anger' and reviewed the offenders' misbehaviour. As is often the case in emotion-attribution on Ifaluk, people spoke in the first person plural; 'We are *song* [justifiably angry]', one woman said, 'because those women did not bring their full allotment [*tub*] of food. Those people are bad.'

What was also typical about this incident was that confrontation between the angry parties and the offender was avoided. Gossip rather than head-to-head discussion is the usual means by which the fact of someone's 'justifiable anger' is communicated to the culprit, and this indirect communication is crucial for the prevention of future violations. The damage gossip can do to one's standing in the eyes of others is done by the accusation of wrongdoing that is central to the meaning of *song*.

Each time a person declares 'I am *song* [justifiably angry]' is an opening gambit or bid in an effort to install a particular interpretation of events as the definition of that situation to be accepted by others. In the above case, as in many others, the opening bid is accepted and the force of public opinion sides with the person who first asserts that the situation is one of rule-violation, and hence one of 'justifiable anger'. In other instances, however, the violation of cultural norms is ambiguous or contested by others, and a more extended negotiation process must occur. This negotiation occurs over the aptness of, or justification for, someone's 'justifiable anger', in other words over the meaning to be assigned to an event. The process of negotiation may take a few moments, or it may continue over the course of many months.

Social Change and the Reconstruction of Emotional Understanding

Negotiation of emotional meaning often occurs where recent social changes have produced or exacerbated cleavages within the body politic or unsettled longstanding cultural agreements on the value or deviance of a particular behaviour. Attitudes towards aspects of particular social changes, and regulation of them, are constantly in process of formulation. The consequences for emotional understanding are intrapersonal ambivalence and interpersonal disagreement on how to reason about social events. Values in flux thus mean emotions in flux – emotions in process of cultural *re*construction.

This general principle can be illustrated by looking at several examples of extended interpersonal negotiation over the ascription of 'justifiable anger'. At the root of the negotiation in these cases is conflict over resources or ideas that have been relatively recently introduced to Ifaluk. Many of these changes stem from the American colonial administration of the island and the rest of Micronesia since the Second World War. Direct US government subsidies of a variety of social programmes have meant a sudden influx of cash to the island. This cash has, moreover, entered the island economy in a highly inequitable way; where money was once primarily acquired through each household's ability to prepare and sell small quantities of copra, most income is now channelled into the island via the small number of individuals who receive government salaries, including the teachers and health aides. Unlike Ifaluk's primary valuables, such as taro, fish and canoes, cash is both readily hidden and hoarded, and people have not yet decided how its sharing ought to be handled. Emotional ambiguity and conflict are the result.

Take the case of a young woman and her husband, whose government job gave him a salary and often kept him near his assignment on Yap. When the woman became pregnant, it was decided that she would give birth in the hospital on the distant island of Yap, and she was accompanied on her ship journey from

Ifaluk by her mother's sister and the latter's husband, who had business (which provided him with some cash) on Yap. During their several months' stay, the elder man made several requests of the young husband for cash for cigarettes and food items. After a point, the requests were ignored, and both parties privately declared their 'justifiable anger'. The young man and woman appealed to the notion that the elder couple had much cash of their own and, hence, should have used that rather than asking for the others' money. In explaining their *song*, the older couple spoke of how they had 'taken care of' the young woman through her travels and birth and of their *gashigshig* (state of being indebted to by others; literally, tiredness) on account of the young woman.

To some extent, each party to the conflict had appealed to a principle of proper behaviour to which other Ifaluk subscribe. On the one hand, this includes the idea that one should not ask for something which one already has in abundance, and, on the other, the expectation that there be reciprocity in relations with others such that one party to an exchange should not feel exploited or 'tired' in their efforts. Were cash not involved (nor, perhaps, the changes in attitude in the younger men whose deference to authority is tempered by their new power in the outside world), the issue would have been clear. The younger couple would have been expected to share any apparent abundance with the elder, and the elder would have had sole claim to 'justifiable anger' were such sharing not to take place.

A more dramatic example of the destruction of emotional meaning that has accompanied the social changes of the most recent colonial period was provided by the return of a 'prodigal son' to the island. I had heard Tamalekar speak often of his sister's son, Palemai, who had gone to school in Oregon many years prior, and not returned. Quite suddenly, however, Palemai appeared as a passenger on the field ship that connects the island with Yap. His family was overjoyed to see him alive and to think that he might have returned to stay. Their joy was quickly tempered by consternation, however, as Palemai, who had arrived drunk, proceeded to sing boisterously – as he careened between his relatives' homes – the *bwarug* (love songs) that should never be sung in the company of both men and women. Between his arrival and departure with the ship a day later, he remained very drunk and displayed the kinds of boastful and disrespectful behaviours which cause 'justifiable anger' in others, behaviours which I had never observed in such profusion in one person at one time. In talking with others, he declared that he needed to return to school to get a degree, and that he would return and get a 'high' (important, top-ranking) job which would greatly help Ifaluk. The frequent repetition of these assertions came on an island where a very high value is placed on modesty and self-effacement.

In the evening, Palemai came to visit Tamalekar, to whom, as his mother's brother, he owed the greatest respect. Tamalekar, though nonplussed by his nephew's behaviour, began quietly to talk to him in the style that is used when someone is attempting to *garepiy* (instruct; cause to become intelligent) his or her social subordinate. Rather than taking the usual quiet listening stance that is expected in these contexts, however, Palemai would periodically interrupt him by breaking into 'love songs'. To Tamalekar's query as to why he had stayed away from the island for so long, he responded with the taunt, 'You [Tamalekar] are the one who gave me permission to go to school.' Palemai went so far at one point as 'playfully' to slap his uncle on the back, a move that is only appropriate between peers and then only when they are drinking together.

Tamalekar's pain at his nephew's disrespect, or more accurately his 'craziness', was palpable, and as the night wore on he looked more and more at the ground in front of him, his shoulders slumping. The tears that he began to shed marked his confusion, his inability to become 'justifiably angry' (or perhaps to feel anything with a name and an accompanying and effective behavioural script) in the face of inexplicably affronting behaviour in a man whom he loved and who ought to respect him. Palemai's horrendous response to his awkward position between two worlds was certainly idiosyncratic, but it was set up by the historical changes of the American colonial period. And so long as an individual's emotional experience in its fullest sense is a social achievement, reached only through some basic agreement between people on the terms in which life's problematic moments are to be defined, such dramatic social disjunctures can only result in emotional ambiguity or even chaos.

Renato Rosaldo (1984) points out that people often emotionally 'muddle through' traumatic life events – that each affecting event, such as a death, is a somewhat unique experience for which cultural scripts cannot completely prepare people, and that each emotional experience reflects the particularities of individual lives. Tamalekar's 'dark night' with his nephew reveals one source – historical social change – for both the rich diversity and the ambiguity of emotional understandings that appears here.

The Place of 'Justifiable Anger' in Moral Socialization
The explicitly moral purpose to which the concept of 'justifiable anger' is put gives it a particularly important role in the socialization of children. The prominent place of the Ought in all aspects of

Ifaluk everyday life is replicated in their approach to children, and contrasts dramatically with the view of socialization as a form of reprehensible coercion that occurs in several more radically egalitarian societies such as the Ilongot of the Philippines (M. Rosaldo, 1980). People told me on many different occasions that a parent *must* at times become 'justifiably angry' with his or her child, 'or the child will not know the difference between right and wrong'. All of the most undesirable characteristics that a child or an adult can display – laziness, loudness, disrespect, disobedience or badness – are explained as the result of the parents' failure to be 'justifiably angry' when those behaviours were first exhibited by the child. The adult's 'justifiable anger' is seen as *telling* the child that a value has been contravened; in one sense, *song* is seen as a clear and natural signal to the child about the nature of value and the characteristics of bad behaviour.

How children learn the uses to which *song* can be put is illustrated by an episode involving a five-year-old boy, Tachimangemar, who lived in the household where I stayed. The two of us had had some difficulty in adjusting to each other. In Tachimangemar's eyes, I was no doubt somewhat unpredictable, while the boy's aggressive style and attention-seeking seemed to me regressive. Although it was similar to the style of many island children between the ages of two and five, it was all the more difficult for me to deal with when contrasted with the soft-spoken co-operativeness of most children over the age of six. Children of Tachimangemar's years are considered by adults to be too old for solicitousness and not yet old enough to have developed the 'social intelligence' (*repiy*) that prevents unsocialized behaviour.

I was feeling charitably inclined as he entered on this particular afternoon, however. Noticing that he wore a flower wreath on his head of the sort that women often affectionately weave for their kin, I asked, with what I meant as a pleasant show of interest, whether the wreath were his. He replied, 'Ilefagomar [his mother] is not *song* [justifiably angry],' puffed out his chest and strode out into the coral-covered yard. Earlier in my stay on the island, this response would have mystified and perhaps depressed me. After six months on Ifaluk, I could make some sense of it. I remained alien enough, and committed enough to another way of seeing children, anger and authority, to need to be *reminded* of what was to the boy obvious, and to find the terms he used striking, both then and now, some years later.

Tachimangemar had drawn several inferences from my question, including the idea that I believed the wreath to belong to someone else. I also understood that, in stating that his mother was not *song*, or justifiably angry, he was telling me that he had done nothing wrong in wearing the wreath, that only Ilefagomar and not I had the authority to make moral judgement of his behaviour, and that he would continue to wear the wreath as long as he pleased. Tachimangemar's statement takes much of its sense and rhetorical force from the fact that the Ifaluk elaborate and emphasize a distinction between moral and immoral anger and from the articulation of the concept of moral anger with the atoll's social hierarchy. It also indexed his knowledge that his mother would have communicated her 'justifiable anger' to him had he been doing something wrong in wearing the headpiece.

Time and again, children were reminded – most often by children a bit older than themselves – that some adult would be 'justifiably angry' if they continued to misbehave, or failed to do something they ought to have done. A girl tells her younger sibling to stop being uncooperative with the teacher at school, or their father will be *song*. A boy who uses a taboo word is warned by his older brother that his parents will be 'justifiably angry'. Sent on an errand by our 'mother', the teenaged foster daughter of my household and I go to the taro garden to gather leaves for soup. In response to my question as to how many taro leaves to collect, she tells me, 'Ilefagomar didn't say how much to take, but we'll fill up the basket so she will not be *song* [justifiably angry].'

The role of *song* in the generation of valued behaviour is thought to stem from the fact that 'justifiable anger' causes fear (*metagu*) in the person at whom it is directed (Lutz, 1983, 1987). *Song*, in fact, would not have its effect on the moral life of the community were fear not to be evoked by it. It is in this regard that the concept of *ker* (happiness/excitement) plays what is, from an American perspective, a paradoxical role. 'Happiness/excitement' is an emotion which people see as pleasant but amoral. It is often, in fact, *im*moral, insofar as someone who is 'happy/excited' is more likely to be unafraid of other people. While this lack of fear may make them laugh and talk with people, it may also make them misbehave or walk around 'showing off', or 'acting like a big shot' (*gabos fetal*). As 'happiness/excitement' (*ker*) dispels the individual's fearfulness, it disrupts the normal functioning of *song*, and with it the moral compass of this society. While American approaches to child-rearing and emotion elevate 'happiness' to an important position, setting it out as an absolute necessity for the good or healthy child (and adult), the Ifaluk view 'happiness/excitement' (*ker*) as something that must be carefully monitored and sometimes halted in children.

The concept of 'justifiable anger' marks the boundary between acceptable and unacceptable behaviour, for both child and adult. Learning to become attuned to both explicit declarations and more subtle non-verbal demonstrations of that emotion is crucial to acquiring an Ifaluk soul and a favoured place in society.

Domination and the Ideological Role of the Concept of 'Justifiable Anger'

The moral ideas that prevail in any particular time and place come into being in the context of the configuration of power relationships existing in that society. In case after case, it has been observed that the unequal distribution of power in society carries with it the risk that the ideas of the dominant sectors will take precedence over other possible perspectives, and, moreover, that those ideas will be presented as the ideas of the entire group, and as natural rather than contrived or self-interested ideas. The power of some members of society to reinforce their prerogatives will include the power to 'sell' their ideas and their morality to the rest of the group.

By some definitions, the 'ideological' realm is not a purely mental one, but encompasses consciousness as it is used in everyday interactions between individuals. The concept is fruitfully used to describe processes rather than static structures; ideologies are consequently seen as in a constant state of production and reproduction through the actions of individuals (for example, Therborn, 1980). The ideological is not simply a rigid structure of domination, but is the arena of thought and practice in which groups and individuals struggle to assert control or to avoid subordination (for example, Corrigan and Willis, 1980; Myers, 1982; Taussig, 1980). We can thus expect to find in cultural understandings – including those aspects which can be termed emotional – both the outline of relations of dominance as well as the attempted appropriation or alteration of those meanings by the subordinate members of society in furtherance of their own interests.

In everything that has been said thus far about the notion of 'justifiable anger' on Ifaluk, it is clear that the concept, while explicitly moral, also has a role to play in the domination of one person by another. To the extent that an individual's claims to 'justifiable anger' are accepted by the community, that person exerts his or her will over others. The 'fear' that must result from 'justifiable anger' stops others in the pursuit of their immediate goals; 'justifiable anger' thereby controls them. In addition, the aura of moral superiority that inheres in the notion of 'justifiable anger' makes the concept a symbol of legitimate power which can further bolster the position of the person who claims to experience the emotion. The claim to moral sense and rectitude which the 'justifiably angry' make is also, then, a claim to power and a crucial part of the ideological process.

As may already be apparent, the social hierarchy on Ifaluk is outlined, to an important extent, by the source of most assertions of 'justifiable anger' and by the direction in which that anger usually flows. It is much more often the case that persons of higher rank or status are 'justifiably angry' towards those of lower station than is the reverse the case. The chiefs are 'justifiably angry' at community members, adults are 'justifiably angry' at children, older women are 'justifiably angry' at younger women, and brothers are 'justifiably angry' at their younger sisters. The direction in which 'justifiable anger' flows is predominantly *down* the social scale.

Resistance to the structure of domination also occurs every day on Ifaluk, and the concept of *song* is used in attempts to alter that balance of power. Teenaged women sometimes resist their elders' attempts to marry them off, women attempt to push back the boundaries of the work men expect them to do, and people malign the actions of the Yapese and through them the whole colonial system. In each of these types of instances, the idea of 'justifiable anger' is marshalled as a source of legitimacy and a method for condemnation of the system as it exists.

The sites at which the regular exercise of power and power struggles occur on Ifaluk are revealed in uses of the term 'justifiable anger'. By looking carefully at the cases in which *song* is used, it is possible to observe the network of power relations on the island and to gain insight into political processes. The daily negotiations which occur over who is 'justifiably angry' and over the proper reasons for that anger lie at the heart of the politics of everyday life.

We can begin with the one most important area in which power relations are, however, *non*-negotiable. No one, in my observation, ever openly declared their 'justifiable anger' at the chiefs in their capacity as traditional leaders. As the ultimate seat of authority on Ifaluk, the chiefs are, in a fundamental sense, infallible; while their edicts and laws are not always obeyed, their judgement is never explicitly called into question. When the chiefs speak at all-island assemblies, their words are seen as having a fundamental importance. The secure place of the chiefs at the head of the Ifaluk social structure is both evidenced and further ensured by the failure of any of their subjects to direct 'justifiable anger' at them.

The relationship between a brother and sister is a central aspect of Carolinean social structure. Although brothers will marry out to another household, exchanges between them and their sisters will continue throughout their lifetimes and constitute the most important source of inter-household exchange. Sisters send their brothers the fruit of their gardens, and adopt their children. Brothers take an important interest in their sisters' children (natural and adopted), having in theory the ultimate responsibility for their proper upbringing and protection. The emotional tone of the relationship between brothers and sisters is often one of extraordinary affection, but it is also one in which the authority to make decisions about each other's lives rests much more heavily with the brother than the sister. Although this authority is generally only fully exercised by a man who is older than his sister, it forms a fundamental source of power in Ifaluk society.

An important index of how solid the authority charter of men over their sisters is can be found in the great extent to which women are at pains to avoid the 'justifiable anger' of their brothers. A woman who has done something improper or about whom a piece of gossip is started will as often worry out loud that 'my brother will be *song* [justifiably angry]' as she will worry about the anger of her parents or of other elders. These concerns are realistic ones; some of the most dramatic demonstrations of *song* were in fact carried out or threatened by brothers of women who had violated some code of conduct. In one such instance, a young woman got on the inter-island steamer with her husband to go to their Woleai household without asking permission of her Ifaluk classificatory brothers. When they heard that she had left, they were 'justifiably angry' and threatened, in a traditional gesture of extreme anger, to burn down her house.[5]

The relations between the generations on Ifaluk generally run smoothly. This is particularly the case when one looks at generations of women. Post-marital residence is matrilocal, so many women live with their mothers and grandmothers, and later their daughters, from birth to death, creating strong and deep bonds between them. The household hierarchy is clear, with the eldest women making the most fundamental decisions and delegating work and authority to the middle-aged women, who in turn direct teenaged and younger girls in work. It is the elder women who determine how to dispose of some of the most basic forms of household wealth. They decide the occasions for giving away the elaborately designed skirts woven by women in the household; they direct the sending of pots of taro and breadfruit to other households; they primarily decide when children are to be sent out as temporary help to another household or when more permanent adoptions are to occur; and they play what is sometimes a major role in arranging marriages for the sons and daughters of the household. And it is these powerful women who become 'justifiably angry' if their charges in the household disobey their instructions, fail to play their role in the household's productive activities or behave in such a way as to become the object of well-founded gossip in the village.

Younger women more often than not anticipate the 'justifiable anger' of their elders in deciding how to behave. The fear that properly results from the anticipation of *song* usually acts to create obedient and deferential younger women.[6] Young women, and particularly unmarried women in their teens and twenties, however, sometimes fly directly in the face of the expressed wishes of the dominant women of their household or wider kinship group. While the 'justifiable anger' of older women is assured by this defiance, it is also occasionally the case that a younger woman will attempt to ignore that anger by failing to become 'fearful' (*metagu*) or will even declare her own 'justifiable anger'.

One such case was that of Lesepemang. A sixteen-year-old girl, she was being temporarily fostered by Ilefagomar, the woman who headed the household in which I lived. She had been sent from her household primarily to help Ilefagomar through the later stages of a pregnancy, birth and confinement. While she was living in the household, a marriage was arranged between her and a young man from another island who was staying on Ifaluk. She did not want to marry, however, fearing the loss of her freedom and the increased likelihood of pregnancy. Her protest against this arranged marriage took many forms; she would be told to prepare a meal for her husband by one of the elder women, but would either silently refuse, giggle or take an inordinately long time to bring it to him. When no one but I was with her and her new husband, she would tease and 'speak badly' (or brusquely and impolitely) to him. The protest soon escalated to a general refusal to perform any and all assigned tasks except under heavy pressure.

All of the adults around her explained her behaviour as due to the fact that she, like all new spouses, was 'ashamed and embarrassed' (*ma*). In attempting to change her attitude and behaviour, she was frequently lectured, with one older woman expressing a common theme in telling her, 'What woman isn't ashamed and embarrassed [*ma*] around her new husband? But we [women] listen to our mothers and so take care of that man.' In private conversations with me and other young women, however, Lesepemang portrayed herself, not as 'ashamed and embarrassed' (*ma*), but as 'justifiably angry' (*song*) at her family (and especially her mother's brothers) for making her marry. In negotiating over the emotion term to be used, Lesepemang was not only denying the older women's definition of the situation, but was also saying that this was *not* a normal or usual marriage (one that produces *ma*) but rather one that should not have occurred (one that produces *song*). Her choice of emotion terminology constituted a strategy of using this fundamental concept in the Ifaluk ideological system against that system.

A final and central arena within which the notion of 'justifiable anger' plays an ideological role is that of gender relations. With the important exception of their roles as brothers, mothers' brothers or chiefs, men did not declare 'justifiable anger' at women appreciably more often than did women at men. This is consistent with the fact that the classes of women and men are not seen as sharply distinguishable on the basis of their moral sense. The *reasons for* 'justifiable anger' did differ in men and women, however, and reflect the particular expectations which are held of each gender. The women frequently complain, for example, of 'justifiable anger' at men for failing to show up in great numbers or to put out much effort at the weekly (and theoretically coed) village weeding sessions. Women also say they are 'justifiably angry' when men become drunk and fail to fulfil their household obligations. Men's 'justifiable anger' at women is generated by what they see as a female propensity to gossip. Men also sometimes become 'justifiably angry' when they are hungry and the women of their household have not prepared food.

The context of women's use of the concept of 'justifiable anger' reveals the nature of what they expect from men. Take the example of Lemalesep, a woman in her late thirties, who answered my question as to when she had recently been 'justifiably angry' in the following way:

> I was *song* when they were re-roofing the canoe house last week and [my husband] got drunk and didn't tell me beforehand [that he was going to drink]. [My adoptive son] came and told me. We had no more food [prepared at the household] and I had planned to give my husband our baby [to take care of so that I could make food]. I was really furious [*sig*] and ran away to my relative's house. Then he went over there to me and I was also still *song*. I didn't want him to come over there.

Lemalesep appeals here to the expectation that a woman with a small baby ought to be aided by other members of the household, including the husband, and most especially when she has an important task to perform, such as food-making. Her statement also draws on the common assumption that a man's drinking may be cause for 'justifiable anger' when it results in his irresponsible or uncooperative behaviour. Women in fact are seen as reasonable if they tell their husbands to stop drinking after they have had a baby, so that he will be better able to help tend the infant in the evenings.

While men dominate women as brothers and mothers' brothers and as the main holders of traditional office, they are not clearly dominant over women in their capacities as wives or as females in general. The ideological struggle on the field of 'justifiable anger' reflects this relative gender balance. We have seen that only one party to a conflict may appropriately characterize themselves as 'justifiably angry', as only one general value system is accepted in most cases and thus only one party is absolutely in the right. While negotiation over the right to use the concept of *song* is absent or rare where one individual is of much higher rank than the other, it is more likely the more equally ranked two parties to a conflict are. In relations between men and women, and particularly between husbands and wives, there are frequent struggles over the use of the emotion term to describe the self and the situation.

The accusations and counter-accusations between men and women that their mutual 'justifiable anger' represents are not generally taken as seriously as are the other cases of 'justifiable anger' we have been looking at so far. Several women told me, for example, that the men are always 'justifiably angry' at the women when the inter-island steamer comes because the women don't make food. But, they said, the women do not listen to the men and just continue in their 'happiness/excitement' (*ker*), visiting with the new arrivals and gathering the news from other atolls.

This brief tour through some of the configurations of power in Ifaluk society has demonstrated that the concept of 'justifiable anger' can be seen as more than a central moral construct of this people, reflecting and constraining their structures of value. *Song* is simultaneously an emotional sign used by individuals and groups in the pursuit of power and legitimacy. As a powerful symbol of both dominance and morality, the appropriation of the right to use the concept can constitute both an ideological ploy and a subversive move. The uttering of the word *song* in everyday life rises like a red flag, marking the form of, and fissures in, Ifaluk socio-political structures.

The Scene that Constitutes 'Justifiable Anger'

Thus far, we have been looking at the contexts in which the concept of *song* is used, or the events that precipitate or are structured by it. This constitutes, however, only a part of the more elaborate 'scene' that is evoked for the Ifaluk listener by the concept of 'justifiable anger'. Equally important are the scripts for subsequent action that are invoked by the concept. Central to these scripts are strategies for communicating one's view of the situation (as violating accepted community values), and for doing this as indirectly and non-violently as possible. The scene that follows 'justifiable anger' involves, first and foremost, moral condemnation of one person by another. This condemnation is accomplished through one or several of the following manoeuvres, including a refusal to speak or, more dramatically, eat with the offending party; dropping of the markers of polite and 'calm' speech; running away from the household or refusing to eat at all; facial expressions associated with disapproval, including pouting or a 'locked' mouth, 'lit-up' or 'lantern' eyes; gestures, particularly brusque movements; declarations of *song* and the reasons for it to one's kin and neighbours; throwing or hitting material objects; and, in some cases, a failure to eat or the threat of suicide or other personal harm. In discussions with each other, people commonly use such behavioural cues in speculating about the emotional position of an individual. When people were asked explicitly by me what the indicators of 'justifiable anger' were, they mentioned most of the above factors, as well as the idea that the 'justifiably angry' person sometimes 'thinks of swatting' the person at whom he or she is *song*.

The expected scenario continues beyond this immediate communication of emotional position. The target of the 'justifiable anger' is subsequently expected to become *metagu*, or 'fearful/anxious', as we have already noted. This occurs when word reaches him or her through the gossip network that the other is 'justifiably angry'. It is sometimes expected that there will be a later 'reciprocal payback' for the offence that caused the 'justifiable anger'. When a woman, Ilefagomar, was not invited to the birth hut of another woman as she ought to have been, she later 'paid back' this woman by not calling her to her own labour and birth celebration several months later. An apology, the payment of a fine or the more informal sending of valued objects to the 'justifiably angry' person or family is also expected to occur on some occasions. It is said that the objects that are sent, such as cloth or tobacco, cause the recipients to become *ker* (happy/excited) and so forget their 'justifiable anger'.

Another important aspect of the scene that is implicit in the concept of 'justifiable anger' is the performance of a kind of semi-formal 'emotional counselling' by someone close to the 'angry' person. Individuals are said to vary in their ability to assist those who are 'justifiably angry', but there are some who take special pains and pride in their abilities in this regard. These people, who might be characterized as 'emotional advisers', are said to be those who are not 'hot-tempered' and who do not allow themselves also to be provoked into a parallel 'justifiable anger' by the counsellee's account of the event.

The most important thing that a person can do to help the

'justifiably angry' person is to calm down the other by speaking gently to her or him. This style of speech involves marked politeness and low volume. A solution to the problem which began the 'justifiable anger' may be suggested – if, for example, a theft has occurred, the adviser might offer to go to the household of the thief and ask for the return of the object (although it is likely that such a promise will not be carried out so as to avoid the confrontation it would possibly involve).

More commonly, however, the 'justifiably angry' person will be advised to 'forget it'. This counsel comes not out of the assumption that the 'justifiable anger' is not just, but rather from the sense that the offending person was at fault in the matter, and is not reasonable. This inference is drawn by the listener from the advisers' frequent statements that the person at whom the 'justifiable anger' is directed is in fact 'crazy and confused'.

When someone is 'justifiably angry', others often anticipate and fear the possibility of aggression against the violator of cultural values. On the other hand, it is expected that people who are 'justifiably angry' will *not* physically aggress against another. And in fact interpersonal violence is virtually non-existent on the island. The dual expectation of both violence and reflective self-control is evident in the kinds of advice that are typically given to those who are 'justifiably angry', as in the following, which represents a reconstruction of the stylized speech that the counsellor will make to a 'justifiably angry' person, in this case a man.

> Sweetheart, you shouldn't fight because you are a man. If you fight people will laugh at you. Throw out your 'thoughts/feelings' about that person [at whom you are angry] because s/he is crazy and confused. We men divide our heads [separate the good from the bad] and then throw out the bad. We don't 'think/feel' so much so we won't be sick. You should *fago* [feel compassion/love/sadness for] me and follow my 'thoughts/feelings' and not be *song*. If you fight, your sister's children will be 'panicked/frightened' [*rus*].

Although the two expectations – of violence and of the lack of it – may appear contradictory, this approach to the angry person can instead be interpreted as the means by which the Ifaluk both remind each other of the possibility of violence while fully expecting that it will be prevented by the individual's maturity (including mature masculinity), and by feelings of *fago* (compassion/love/sadness) for others, of *ma* (shame/embarrassment) over the prospect of being violent before others, and of *metagu* (fear/anxiety) of the person who arrives to calm one down.

The various expectations for behaviours that are to follow the occurrence of *song* constitute emotional or interactional strategies or scripts that are learned by the Ifaluk as they encounter their language in the course of growing up. The theory of 'justifiable anger' and the social course it follows is thus a script, creatively used, for use in achieving individual goals. The concept of *song* is particularly useful for organizing the control of social deviance and for protecting one's interests as they are damaged by such deviance. Simultaneously, the concept's behavioural entailments promote the reproduction of the gentle interpersonal relations that characterize the island. The various scripts that are encoded in the concept of 'justifiable anger' are also guides for predicting and interpreting the behaviour of others.

Conclusion

The concept of 'justifiable anger' plays both a moral and an ideological role in Ifaluk everyday life. The person who declares *song* is making, on the one hand, a moral assertion, a statement about how things ought to be otherwise. The concept is used to mark the violation of any of the number of values that people subscribe to, including the expectation that others will be co-operative, non-aggressive and respectful. As the primary concept in moral discourse, *song* links the person's sensibilities with the wider obligatory order, and thereby mediates between the two.

'Justifiable anger' is also an ideological mask for power and its exercise. With the more powerful factions in Ifaluk society – the chiefs, the brothers, the older women of a household – making more extensive use of the concept, their legitimacy and influence are enhanced. The more powerful are continually reinvested, through their manipulation of 'justifiable anger', with the moral superiority which is at once the source and the symptom of their power. Power is also subverted and appropriated, however, through this same concept when it is used in protest by the less powerful. The use of the term *song* in everyday discourse, then, both reinforces and undermines domination. Having both moral and ideological force, 'justifiable anger' maintains a vital position in the centre of Ifaluk social life. Like all everyday understandings, it responds to cultural values and power relations and helps to structure social practices.

Notes

1 Where the term anger is used without quotation marks, I am referring to both the American–English concept of 'anger' and the Ifaluk concept of *song* (justifiable anger). For a more extended discussion of the similarities and differences between 'anger' and *song*, see Lutz, 1988.

2 The emotion concept of *nguch* (sick and tired/bored/annoyed) may carry an implicit but mild criticism of someone else's behaviour, but it does not have the explicit moral weight of *song* (justifiable anger).

3 This name, as well as those used in all subsequent references to villages and people, is a pseudonym.

4 This turn of phrase is used to describe the responsibility of all people towards those who are more 'needy' than themselves, or, in other words, their subordinates.

5 This threat has not recently been carried out, to my knowledge.

6 Other factors also go into the deference younger women show to their elders, including cultural stress on respect for age and on the value of responding positively to the expressed desires of others, regardless of age.

References

Abu-Lughod, L. (1986) *Veiled Sentiments*. Berkeley: University of California Press.

Corrigan, P. and Willis, P. (1980) Cultural forms and class mediations. *Media, Culture and Society*, 2: 297–312.

Fillmore, C.J. (1977) Topics in lexical semantics. In R.W. Cole (ed.), *Current Issues in Linguistic Theory*. Bloomington: Indiana University Press.

Gaines, A.D. (1982) Cultural definitions, behavior and person in American psychiatry. In G. White and A. Marsella (eds), *Cultural Conceptions of Mental Health and Therapy*. Dordrecht: Reidel.

Gudeman, S. (1986) *Economics as Culture: Models and Metaphors of Livelihood*. Boston: Routledge & Kegan Paul.

Holland, D. and Quinn, N. (eds) (1987) *Cultural Models in Language and Thought*. Cambridge: Cambridge University Press.

Lutz, C. (1983) Parental goals, ethnopsychology, and the development of emotional meaning. *Ethos*, 11: 246–63.

Lutz, C. (1987) Goals, events and understanding in Ifaluk emotion theory. In D. Holland and N. Quinn (eds), *Cultural Models in Language and Thought*. Cambridge: Cambridge University Press.

Lutz, C. (1988) *Unnatural Emotions: Everyday Sentiments on a Micronesian Atoll and their Challenge to Western Theory*. Chicago: University of Chicago Press.

MacCormack, C. and Strathern, M. (eds) (1980) *Nature, Culture and Gender*. Cambridge: Cambridge University Press.

Myers, F.R. (1982) Ideology and experience: the cultural basis of politics in Pintupi life. In M. Howard (ed.), *Aboriginal Power in Australian Society*. Honolulu: University of Hawaii Press.

Rosaldo, M.Z. (1980) *Knowledge and Passion: Ilongot Notions of Self and Social Life*. Cambridge: Cambridge University Press.

Rosaldo, R.I. (1984) Grief and a headhunter's rage: on the cultural force of emotions. In E. Bruner (ed.), *Play, Text, and Story. Proceedings of the 1983 Meeting of the American Ethnological Society*. Washington DC.

Taussig, M.T. (1980) *The Devil and Commodity Fetishism in South America*. Chapel Hill: University of North Carolina Press.

Therborn, G. (1980) *The Ideology of Power and the Power of Ideology*. London: Verso.

White, G. and Kirkpatrick, J. (1985) *Person, Self, and Experience: Exploring Pacific Ethnopsychologies*. Berkeley: University of California Press.

11

Subjective Theories: A New Approach to Psychological Research and Educational Practice

Hanns-Dietrich Dann

Teachers' cognitions and thought processes have become a main topic of research since the middle of the 1970s (for example, Bromme and Brophy, 1986; Calderhead, 1987; Clark and Peterson, 1986; Hofer, 1986). As Hunt (1976: 210) has suggested: 'Teachers are psychologists, too. . . . In their day-to-day teaching, teachers "apply" their own ideas about students, teaching approaches, and learning outcomes.' Hunt has been convinced that we must try to understand the psychology of teachers and that this would improve the application of psychology to educational practice. The present contribution is an attempt to show that this is indeed a promising approach.

Teachers' Aggression-Related Subjective Theories

The research project 'Aggression at School' reported here has been conducted at the University of Konstanz over the past nine years.[1] The final goal of the project was to develop a strategy to improve the social competence of teachers in dealing with aggressive and disruptive students. Since we adopted a cognitive approach our main question was: what are the cognitive representations and processes used by teachers in their conflict-management with students during instruction? Therefore, the project's starting point was the cognitive representations and processes teachers have concerning aggressive and disruptive student actions and their own actions regarding these students. Knowing more about the structure and functioning of teachers' everyday understanding of aggressive interactions is assumed to provide a framework to improve their problem-solving capacities in this respect.

Much of the research on 'teachers' cognitions' or 'teachers' thinking' has been subsumed under the heading of everyday psychology, implicit or 'subjective' theories (for example, Dann et al., 1984; Füglister et al., 1983; Groeben, 1981; Thommen, 1985; Wahl, 1981a). Sometimes the terms naive or lay theories have also been used. However, considering that teachers are experts in their field and acquire a body of expert knowledge (Bromme, 1987; Calderhead, 1987) we prefer to term the knowledge that this kind of professional everyday understanding rests on 'professional theories' (Dann and Krause, 1979), since they constitute a special case of subjective theories. Hence, we are interested in teachers' aggression-related subjective theories.

Similar to the conception of Groeben and Scheele (1984; see also Groeben, this volume Chapter 2) our central assumptions concerning such subjective theories are as follows (Dann, 1983):

1   We conceptualize subjective theories as relatively stable cognitive (or mental) representations, which nonetheless may be altered through experience. As such they are part of the individual's knowledge structure.

2   Subjective theories are often implicit, yet in part they may be accessible to the actor's consciousness at least under some specific conditions (for example, if they are concerned with salient events and were recently activated during intentional behaviour).

3   We conceive of subjective theories as having similar structural qualities as scientific theories; that is, they can be adequately represented as having an argumentative structure (for example, if–then statements).

4   Analogous to 'objective theories' in science, subjective theories fulfil the functions of (a) defining situations, that is, constituting 'reality'; (b) explaining (and often justifying) past events; (c) predicting or merely expecting further events; and (d) generating suggestions for further action.

5   Moreover, subjective theories are important factors in shaping action processes; in fact they constitute part of the knowledge basis of actions. Together with other factors they influence observable behaviour of their producers, especially within the context of goal-directed action.

This latter statement is especially important. Much of the theoretical attractiveness of the concept 'subjective theory' is due to this basic assumption. It is also of considerable relevance for teacher-training programmes, which are substantially based on cognitive functioning. Subjective theories are certainly not the only factors in action processes. Instead, we conceive of actions as complex processes, in which momentary and enduring features of the person and the situation are interwoven, including for example emotions as action-regulating factors (Dann et al., 1982; Krause, 1984).

Considering subjective theories as important co-determinants of actions the following questions have to be answered. How is it possible to assess teachers' aggression-related subjective theories? Is such subjective-theoretical knowledge normally used in the regulation of actions during conflict situations in classroom? If so, under which conditions do these theories lose their action-regulating function? Finally, how can subjective theories and related actions be modified in order to improve the teachers' conflict-management?

Assessing Action-Regulating Subjective Theories

In an endeavour to identify those aspects of teachers' aggression-related subjective theories which have an action-regulating function, we developed a set of assessment methods. These methods include more traditional questionnaire techniques as well as innovative tests and reconstruction strategies.

Psychological Explanations of Students' Aggression
One of our first ideas was that teachers might hold explanations for their students' aggressive behaviour similar to those held by professional psychologists; that is, they would probably adhere either to a type of drive or instinct model, or a frustration model, or an instrumental- and imitation-learning model. Thus we collected a number of statements that we considered representative for these models: for example, 'There are children, who have an inborn tendency to react aggressively', or 'The more success students have with aggressive behaviour the more aggressive they will become.'

These statements could be rejected or accepted by a sample of 400 secondary-school teachers on a four-point scale. Our attempts to establish Likert scales according to these or similar models have been only partially successful. After an item analysis only a small proportion of the statements could be incorporated into the final explanatory dimensions. By factor analysis (main components, varimax rotation) only 20.2 per cent of the total variance was explained. Moreover, these dimensions turned out to be weakly related to overt behaviour in aggressive classroom situations. Obviously, subjective explanations are not identical to professional explanations.

General Explanations of Students' Aggression
During interviews and group discussions we realized that teachers,

in explaining their students' aggressive acts, refer to a substantial number of concrete single factors, for instance the weather, the class composition, the teacher–student relationship and so on. Therefore, we collected a pool of concrete causes or factors to which aggressive behaviour could possibly be attributed. Our sample of 400 secondary-school teachers indicated how important they considered each factor for the occurrence of student aggression to be. A five-point scale ranging from 'rather unimportant' to 'extremely important' was used. According to Weiner's matrix for causal attributions the pool of factors was grouped into four classes (see Table 11.1). For each of the four classes of causal explanations it was possible to establish a scale with satisfactory scaling properties, the internal consistency (Cronbach alpha) ranging from 0.65 to 0.76. This demonstrates that teachers seem to hold a rich and rather concrete explanatory repertory for students' aggression which is not reducible to a few theoretical principles (such as 'drive', 'frustration' or 'learning') but is linked to general attributional tendencies.

Is there any relationship between the teachers' explanatory dimensions and their conflict-related actions during instruction? To answer this question we systematically observed twenty-one secondary-school teachers during classroom hours for a period of two weeks. For this purpose a special event-sampling category system was developed (Humpert and Dann, 1988). Altogether, about 300 lessons were observed and 600 aggressive interactions followed by the teachers' reactions were recorded. Table 11.2 shows the categories of teachers' actions on students' aggressive behaviour. Now, one possibility is to compute correlations between the frequency of the types of reactions and the four subjective theory-variables explained above.

As can be seen from Table 11.3, in particular external variable explanations are linked to overt behaviour, that is classwork

Table 11.1   *Teachers' explanation of their students' aggressive behaviour*

	External (to student)	Internal (of student)
Stable (unchangeable)	Family situation	Character
	Weather	Genes
	Weekday	Temperament
Variable (changeable)	Classwork organization	Bad mood
	Educational climate	Tiredness
	Teacher–student relationship	Frustration tolerance

Table 11.2 *Categories of teachers' actions on students' aggressive behaviour*

	Observed frequencies (%)
Neutral actions	
Inconspicuous observation	40.2
Interruption	4.8
Admonition	30.3
Punitive actions	
Threat	6.5
Punishment	4.2
Disparagement	2.8
Social-integrative actions	
Suggestion of compromise	1.3
Integration	0.9
Encouragement	1.1
Empathy	2.4
Miscellaneous	5.5

organization, educational climate, teacher–student relationship and so on, factors which substantially depend on the teachers' own influence. The more a teacher considers these factors as important causes of students' aggression, the more he reacts with neutral behaviour and the less he relies on punitive reactions.

Moreover, we found that teachers who adhere to these external-variable explanations were also more successful in conflict-management during classroom hours (Spearman's rho = 0.57). For this purpose three factor scores of successful teaching in this respect were generated from data of systematic observation, expert ratings and teachers' self-statements (69.7 per cent explained total variance) (Dann, Tennstädt, Humpert and Krause, 1987).[2]

Table 11.3 *Relationship between teachers' explanations of aggression and their actions on students' aggressive behaviour (Pearson's r)*

Explanations of aggression	Observed actions on aggression		
	Neutral	Punitive	Social–integrative
External variable	0.58**	−0.67**	0.06
External stable	0.40*	−0.40*	−0.16
Internal variable	0.13	−0.17	−0.08
Internal stable	0.18	−0.13	−0.08

N = 21. ** $p < 0.01$. * $p < 0.10$ (two-tailed test)

Finally, it could be demonstrated that teachers who are high on the external-variable scale have a better educational climate in their classroom. They perceive their students as being less aggressive, more co-operative and more emotionally involved (Kohler, 1987). High external-variable explanations for aggressive student behaviour include in all likelihood two aspects, namely teachers (1) feel more responsible for their students and do not shift responsibility to other factors; and (2) see themselves as having more influence on their students and do not feel powerless. In line with this interpretation teacher training which proved to be effective for conflict-management techniques gave rise to an increase in external-variable explanations and teachers' perceived influence on aggressive students (Tennstädt and Dann, 1987).

Instructions for Handling Aggressive Students
Our attempts at measuring subjective theories outlined above are concerned with *functional knowledge*, that is knowledge about the possible causes of behaviour. Another kind of knowledge could be called *action knowledge*, that is knowledge about what to do in certain situations in order to obtain a specific goal. The study reported below addresses this issue.

Based on interviews and intensive field-studies we formulated fifteen short stories about aggressive student behaviour, each story representing one of several aggression categories. For each story we asked teachers which reaction they considered most reasonable provided that they wanted to continue with the classroom routine. They were also asked which reaction they found most appropriate provided that they wanted to exert educational influence, and assuming that they wanted to reduce aggressive student behaviour in the long run. The teachers were furnished with short descriptions of the category system which we developed for systematic behavioural observation in the classroom (Humpert and Dann, 1988; see Table 11.2). Their task then was to give an instruction by choosing one of the ten categories for each goal in each situation.

Subsequently, index scales were constructed. Since there were three types of instructions with three possible goals for each type we ended with nine instruction scales. Each scale represented the frequency with which instructions of a certain type (neutral, punitive, social-integrative) were recommended to attain a certain goal.

Table 11.4 shows the relations between teachers' instructions and their observed classroom behaviour. Confronted with aggressive student behaviour and provided the teacher wants to exert educational influence we find that, the more likely a teacher is to

Table 11.4 *Relationship between teachers' recommendations for actions and their real actions on students' aggressive behaviour (Pearson's r)*

Recommendations for actions	Observed actions on aggression		
	Neutral	Punitive	Social-integrative
To continue classwork			
Neutral	0.29	−0.28	0.01
Punitive	−0.28	0.12	0.12
Social-integrative	0.16	−0.12	−0.20
To exert educational influence			
Neutral	−0.11	0.04	−0.17
Punitive	−0.59**	0.53*	−0.12
Social-integrative	0.51*	−0.52*	0.06
To reduce aggressive behaviour			
Neutral	0.06	−0.07	0.03
Punitive	−0.27	0.50*	−0.32
Social-integrative	0.42†	−0.53*	0.03

$N = 21$. ** $p < 0.01$. * $p < 0.05$. † $p < 0.10$ (two-tailed test)

recommend punitive measures, the more likely he is to use punitive measures and the less likely he is to rely on neutral reactions. In contrast, a teacher who recommends social-integrative measures is less likely to show punitive behaviour and more likely to react in a neutral manner. Roughly the same pattern of results holds for the teachers' instructions if they wanted a long-term reduction of aggressive student behaviour. If instead the teachers' goal is to continue with the classwork routine, then no correlations between instructions and actual classroom behaviour are found. However, for this latter goal the relationship between the teachers' total pattern of instructions (across the ten action categories) and their total pattern of actions (again across the ten action categories) turned out to be significant, the average of the individual rank-order correlations between the two patterns being 0.57 ($p < 0.01$) (Dann and Humpert, 1987).

A relationship between the instruction scores and successful conflict-management could not be established. Similarly, the relationship to educational climate is not very pronounced. However, after taking part in a training programme, teachers recommend less punitive and more integrative measures and they also behave in this manner (Tennstädt and Dann, 1987).

Most of the results reported so far rely on correlational evidence. Of course, they don't allow any statement about the direction of influence between cognitions and behaviour. Is interactive behaviour at least partially dependent on subjective theories? Or are subjective theories only justifications of otherwise guided behaviour? On the other hand, these results show that there are substantial relationships, and it therefore seems promising to go a step further and to develop more elaborate assessment methods which might help in throwing more light on the problem.

Reconstructing Subjective Theories in Dialogue Consensus

From a more rigorous point of view we could ask: do subjective theories assessed by paper-and-pencil tests really represent the perspective of the teachers themselves? Even though these instruments have been carefully developed in close contact with school practice, the single teacher in answering the final questionnaire has no chance of expressing his individual perspective independently from the categories provided in the questionnaire. Such an aim can only be realized through a dialogue between interviewer and interviewee. This type of data would have to be subjected to 'communicative validation'; the ultimate criterion for a correct reconstruction of the subjective theory being the 'consensus in dialogue' between the two interview partners (see Groeben, this volume, Chapter 2).

Another point seems to be important. To enhance the probability that reconstructed subjective theories are those which are normally used for the regulation of actions, the dialogue should be based on real-life episodes evidenced during class hours. Thus, instead of written short stories, real everyday teaching episodes should be used as the reference for reconstructions (Wahl, 1981b).

In line with these arguments Krause and Dann (1986) have developed a post-actional interview and graphic-representation technique. It is based on similar methods proposed by several authors (Feldmann, 1979; Scheele and Groeben, 1984; Wagner et al., 1981; Wahl et al., 1983). The main features of the procedure are as follows.

The reconstruction process is realized in three steps. In the first step, aggressive interactions are observed during classwork. In the second step, immediately after the lesson an interview is carried out focusing on a specific episode which, in the teacher's opinion, contained aggressive student behaviour. Finally, by an intensive dialogue between interviewer and teacher the interview data are arranged in a graphic display.

More specifically, interviews on different episodes are repeated over three to five days. To ensure a clear identification of the

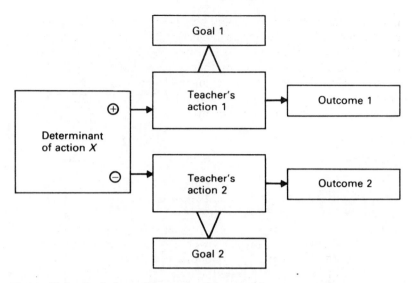

Figure 11.1 *Basic formal structure of the graphic representation of teachers' action knowledge*

episode in question and to stimulate the reactualization of what really went on in the teacher's mind during the original event, a tape or video recording is played back before each interview (stimulated recall). The interview procedure is directed by an interview framework with questions becoming increasingly more specific. Basically, the teacher is encouraged to explicate thoughts and feelings which he had experienced at that very moment, as well as assumptions which have been important to him.

The real construction of subjective theories is carried out through a graphic representation. In this last step variants of the original situations considered important by the teacher are also included. The basic formal structure of the graphic representation is shown in Figure 11.1. The teachers' thinking about their own actions normally refers to four concepts: determinants of the action, the action itself, the action's goal and the action's outcome, which might be a determinant for the next action. These determinants are of special interest here. If you ask a teacher 'What do you normally do in this situation?', her answer will often be 'It depends on . . .', and then she mentions certain conditions, which, in her view, possibly are crucial determinants of her actions.

For a given teacher's thinking the real graphic structures are much more complex. An example is given in Figure 11.2. For the moment I should add that a first proposal of the graph presented by the interviewer is revised through an intensive dialogue with the

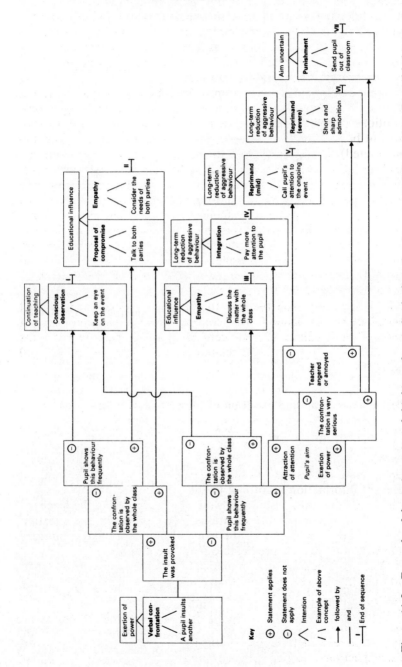

Figure 11.2   *Example of the action-oriented thinking of an individual teacher in respect of an aggressive pupil-behaviour*

teacher, who is encouraged to alter and supplement the draft until he can fully agree with its content. Apart from this helping role the interviewer's part during this dialogue is intentionally restricted to the correctness of the formal aspects of the graphic design by following clearly defined rules. This procedure is referred to as 'communicative validation' of subjective theories.

Based on graphic displays from twenty-three secondary teachers, Krause (1986) analysed how these teachers describe their cognitions, emotions and actions in response to several categories of disruptive student behaviour. For example, for the teachers' first actions the (attributed) 'characteristics of the target student's behaviours or personalities' (such as easy–difficult to handle, ringleader–follower, high–low intensity of offence) turned out to be the most important determinants (63 per cent). 'Self-related cognitions and emotions' (such as afraid of losing face, feeling angry–relaxed) and 'external circumstances' (such as first–last hour, gym lessons–mathematics) are less frequently seen as influential (21 per cent and 16 per cent respectively). All kinds of teachers' actions – neutral, punitive and social-integrative – are most frequently preceded by determinants of the type 'characteristics of the target student's behaviour' (39, 37 and 39 per cent respectively). In the second place, neutral and social-integrative actions are contingent on 'characteristics of students' personalities' (25 per cent each), while punitive reactions are especially linked to 'self-related cognitions and emotions' (20 per cent).

The Action-Regulating Function of Subjective Theories

Of course, dialogue consensus does not guarantee that the cognitions are really relevant for actions. We therefore visited our teachers during classwork for a second week (Dann and Krause, 1988). New aggression-relevant episodes were observed, and all relevant information according to the graphic representations was collected. From this, predictions were made concerning the teachers' new actions in comparable situations. More precisely, the question to be answered now is: does the teacher under specified conditions behave in the manner predictable from the graph?

Correct predictions of systematically observed behaviour turned out to be much more frequent than could be expected by chance and knowing the event probabilities of the several behaviour categories (goodness-of-fit-values of a log-linear model: likelihood ratio $\chi^2 = 161.4$, Pearson $\chi^2 = 223.9$, df = 110, $p < 0.001$). On a more illustrative level, the degree of consistency between predicted and realized actions, ranging between 0 and 1, is informative, too. Sixty-four per cent of the predictions reached a degree of consistency-value of at least 0.66, 43 per cent a value of 1.0. The average value of all the predictions is 0.67 or 0.75, depending on the exact nature of the consistency measure.[3] Wahl et al. (1983) in a similar study, using only yes–no decisions instead of degrees of consistency, found 38 per cent correct predictions, which were also highly significant above chance. The results seem to indicate that post-actional interview and graphic-representation techniques with communicative validation have a substantial degree of validity in assessing action-relevant subjective theories.

Again, the prediction studies do not prove in a strict sense that subjective theories have an action-regulating function. But the evidence that subjective theories do not only serve a justifying function for otherwise guided behaviour is now much better than that founded on the correlational studies alone. Even stronger evidence should be reached by modification studies: if subjective theories are at least co-determinants in action-regulation processes, then a modification treatment of subjective theories should result in corresponding changes of behaviour. Studies of this type have not been conducted thus far. However, even in this case it could be argued that any modification of a subjective theory simultaneously modifies behaviour, the two aspects being as closely connected as two sides of a coin. But as long as the thesis of the action-regulating function of subjective theories is embedded in a theory of action, there is no reason to abandon it in view of the existing data.

From a developmental point of view we most probably have to assume an interdependent relation: within a continuous interchange certain constellations are built up with specific subjective theories and corresponding actions. In this continuing socialization process cultural and subcultural influences as well as actions and their consequences lead to certain subjective theories which in turn regulate actions and exert their influence on cultural conditions. In accordance with this position subjective theories can be considered as individually modified social representations, in which societal knowledge is organized (von Cranach, Mächler and Steiner, 1983). This argument shows that in this area the issue of simple causality is not one which can be applied because there is a dialectic relation between subjective theory and action.

According to these theoretical assumptions one should expect that teachers who differ in their conflict-management capabilities have also different subjective theories. This was exactly what we found in our teaching-success study (Dann et al., 1987). More successful teachers are quite different from less successful teachers: the subjective theories of successful teachers are more complex, more efficiently organized and more consistent with overt behaviour. Certainly, subjective theories are not always used in the regulation of actions. There are conditions under which they lose their action-regulating function. From action theory (especially Tomaszewski, 1978) it can be expected that this is the case when the person is in an unusual emotional state. In their prediction study, Dann and Krause (1988) found the degree of consistency between subjective theories and behaviour to be especially low if teachers were very angry and felt hindered in pursuing their goals. It can be shown that hostile goals within an aggression motive are activated in such situations (Kornadt, 1982). Under certain conditions this leads to aggression-motivated actions, in this case to more punitive and escalating measures towards disruptive students. It is important to note that even such cases of inconsistency between subjective theory and action can easily be explained in action-theoretical terms.

Improving Teachers' Subjective Theories and Actions

It is clear from the analysis above that subjective theories fulfil important action-regulating functions and that emotional processes are also very significant in the regulation of action. From these considerations we developed an intervention method to be used in teacher training called the 'Konstanzer Trainingsmodell' (KTM) (Tennstädt, Krause, Humpert and Dann, 1987).

The main question we started with could be formulated as follows: how can psychological knowledge be adapted for teachers in such a way that they gain the capability of solving their problems in a personally responsible manner? The answer from Hunt's (1976) ideas mentioned earlier is: we should activate teachers' existing knowledge and problem-solving capacity and begin with this. As a first step this can be realized by reconstructing teachers' subjective theories about their problems and their corresponding actions in the problem situations.

The target group of the KTM are teachers who, according to their own opinion, have special problems with aggressive and disruptive students and teachers who generally want to strengthen their educational impact. The KTM is designed as a self-help programme, with two teachers working together in tandem, that is mutually visiting each other's lessons, discussing their respective problems and working out possible solutions according to selected parts of the programme.

According to our action-theoretical approach, a teacher action may be split up into several components or sub-processes, especially the understanding of the situation, the development of an action programme, the processing of the programme and the evaluation of the action's outcome. Ten training elements are assigned to these sub-processes (Tennstädt, 1987). Depending on the individual nature of his problems every teacher makes his selection of these training elements. For this purpose the training begins with diagnostic steps consisting of the interview and graphic-representation technique (Krause and Dann, 1986) and the observational system (Humpert and Dann, 1988), which have been described above.

A central training element contains several proposals of action strategies with a number of concrete measures which are described in detail and which may be adapted to the trainee's special needs. These strategies and measures are grounded on communication theory as well as on principles of group dynamics and social-cognitive learning. Other training elements are concerned with, for example, strategies of social perception, attribution patterns, action goals and situational pressures. Special attention is given to emotional processes which may disturb co-operative forms of dealing with aggressive and disruptive students. Altogether the KTM is intended to support more professional conflict resolution and management in classes.

An initial empirical evaluation (Tennstädt, 1987) shows a number of positive changes during the training process in observable behaviour as well as in self-perception of students and teachers. A comparison of the KTM with more traditional forms of in-service training (Tennstädt and Dann, 1987) suggests stronger results for the KTM in several respects. In view of these results the state government of Baden-Württemberg decided to implement the KTM in its secondary schools of the type *Hauptschule*.

Conclusions

Teachers' subjective theories are obviously, as our studies show, subject to change within a cultural context. Such changes influence the type of actions teachers engage in, that is they effect a change in teaching activities. As a consequence, subjective theories do not only serve a justifying function for otherwise guided behaviour; together with emotional processes they also fulfil important action-regulating functions. However, teachers' actions and their consequences will introduce changes in subjective theories as well.

Because of these interdependent relations it is impossible to make simple causal statements in this domain. Moreover, 'scientific' theorizing without taking into account subjective theories in this area of educational psychology is a vacuous undertaking. Last but not least our results yielded so far seem to show that using subjective theories as a central concept allows the performance of psychological research and educational practice according to the same principles and to a certain extent even with the same methods.

Notes

1 Collaborators have been Dr W. Humpert, Dr F. Krause and Dr K.-Ch. Tennstädt. Financial support has been given by the Deutsche Forschungsgemeinschaft to the Sonderforschungsbereich 23: Educational Research.

2 From this, five groups of teachers were built according to their degree of success by means of non-hierarchical cluster analysis. The cluster membership served as success variable in the above-mentioned correlation with 'external variable explanations' of aggression.

3 In establishing a measure of consistency between predicted and realized actions two different algorithms were followed which, however, lead to quite similar results. The details are documented in the original research report (Dann and Krause, 1988).

References

Bromme, R. (1987) Der Lehrer als Experte – Entwurf eines Forschungsansatzes. In H. Neber (ed.), *Angewandte Problemlösepsychologie*. Münster: Aschendorff. pp. 127–51.

Bromme, R. and Brophy, J. (1986) Teachers' cognitive activities. In B. Christiansen, A.G. Howson and M. Otte (eds), *Perspectives on Mathematics Education*. Dordrecht: Reidel. pp. 99–139.

Calderhead, J. (ed.) (1987) *Exploring Teachers' Thinking*. London: Cassell.

Clark, Ch.M. and Petersen, P.L. (1986) Teachers' thought processes. In M.C. Wittrock (ed.), *Handbook of Research on Teaching* (3rd edn). New York: Macmillan. pp. 255–96.

Cranach, M. von, Mächler, E. and Steiner, V. (1983) *Die Organisation zielgerichteter Handlungen: ein Forschungsbericht*. Bern: Universität, Psychologisches Institut.

Dann, H.-D. (1983) Subjektive Theorien: Irrweg oder Forschungsprogramm? Zwischenbilanz eines kognitiven Konstrukts. In L. Montada, K. Reusser and G. Steiner (eds), *Kognition und Handeln*. Stuttgart: Klett-Cotta. pp. 77–92.

Dann, H.-D. and Humpert, W. (1987) Eine empirische Analyse der Handlungswirksamkeit subjektiver Theorien von Lehrern in aggressionshaltigen Unterrichtssituationen. *Zeitschrift für Sozialpsychologie*, 18: 40–9.

Dann, H.-D., Humpert, W., Krause, F., Olbrich, Ch. and Tennstädt, K.-Ch. (1982) Alltagstheorien und Alltagshandeln. Ein neuer Forschungsansatz zur Aggressionsproblematik in der Schule. In R. Hilke and W. Kempf (eds), *Aggression. Naturwissenschaftliche und kulturwissenschaftliche Perspektiven der Aggressionsforschung*. Bern: Huber. pp. 465–91.

Dann, H.-D., Humpert, W., Krause, F. and Tennstädt, K.-Ch. (eds) (1984) *Analyse und Modifikation subjektiver Theorien von Lehrern*, 3rd rev. edn. (Sonderforschungsbereich 23. Forschungsbericht 43.) Konstanz: Universität, Zentrum I Bildungsforschung.

Dann, H.-D. and Krause, F. (1979) Berufstheorien von Lehrern über aggressives Verhalten in der Schule. In B. Schön and K. Hurrelmann (eds), *Schulalltag und Empirie. Neuere Ansätze in der schulischen und beruflichen Sozialisationsforschung.* Weinheim: Beltz. pp. 204–17.

Dann, H.-D. and Krause, F. (1988) Subjektive Theorien: Begleitphänomen oder Wissensbasis des Lehrerhandelns bei Unterrichtsstörungen? *Psychologische Beiträge*, 30: 269–91.

Dann, H.-D., Tennstädt, K.-Ch., Humpert, W. and Krause, F. (1987) Subjektive Theorien und erfolgreiches Handeln von Lehrern/-innen bei Unterrichtskonflikten. *Unterrichtswissenschaft*, 15: 306–20.

Feldmann, K. (1979) MEAP – Eine Methode zur Erfassung der Alltagstheorien von Professionellen. In B. Schön and K. Hurrelmann (eds), *Schulalltag und Empirie. Neuere Ansätze in der schulischen und beruflichen Sozialisationsforschung.* Weinheim: Beltz. pp. 105–22.

Füglister, P., Born, R., Flückiger, V. and Kuster, H. (1983) Alltagstheorien von Lehrern. *Bildungsforschung und Bildungspraxis*, 5: 47–58.

Groeben, N. (1981) Die Handlungsperspektive als Theorierahmen für Forschung im pädagogischen Feld. In M. Hofer (ed.), *Informationsverarbeitung und Entscheidungsverhalten von Lehrern. Beiträge zu einer Handlungstheorie des Unterrichtens.* Munich: Urban & Schwarzenberg. pp. 17–48.

Groeben, N. and Scheele, B. (1984) Einige Sprachregelungsvorschläge für die Erforschung subjektiver Theorien. In H.-D. Dann, W. Humpert, F. Krause and K.-Ch. Tennstädt (eds), *Analyse und Modifikation Subjektiver Theorien von Lehrern.* (Sonderforschungsbereich 23, Forschungsbericht 43.) Konstanz: Universität, Zentrum I Bildungsforschung. pp. 13–39.

Hofer, M. (1986) *Sozialpsychologie erzieherischen Handelns. Wie das Denken und Verhalten von Lehrern organisiert ist.* Göttingen: Verlag für Psychologie Dr C.J. Hogrefe.

Humpert, W. and Dann, H.-D. (with T. von Kügelgen and W. Rimele) (1988) *Das Beobachtungssystem BAVIS. Ein Beobachtungsverfahren zur Analyse von aggressionsbezogenen Interaktionen im Schulunterricht.* Göttingen: Verlag für Psychologie Dr C.J. Hogrefe.

Hunt, D.E. (1976) Teachers are psychologists, too: on the application of psychology to education. *Canadian Psychological Review*, 17: 210–18.

Kohler, J. (1987) Das Konstanzer Trainingsmodell (KTM). Überprüfung der impliziten Annahmen. Unpublished Diploma thesis, Universität Konstanz.

Kornadt, H.-J. (1982) *Aggressionsmotiv und Aggressionshemmung.* Vol. 1: *Empirische und theoretische Untersuchungen zu einer Motivationstheorie der Aggression und zur Konstruktvalidierung eines Aggressions-TAT.* Bern: Huber.

Krause, F. (1984) Vorschlag zu einer handlungstheoretisch gestützten Erfassung subjektiver Theorien und der Bedingungen ihrer Handlungswirksamkeit. In H.-D. Dann, W. Humpert, F. Krause and K.-Ch. Tennstädt (eds), *Analyse und Modifikation Subjektiver Theorien von Lehrern.* (Sonderforschungsbereich 23, Forschungsbericht 43.) Konstanz: Universität, Zentrum I Bildungsforschung. pp. 91–9.

Krause, F. (1986) Subjective theories of teachers: reconstruction through stimulated recall, interview, and graphic representation of teacher thinking. In M. Ben-Peretz, R. Bromme and R. Halkes (eds), *Advances of Research on Teacher Thinking.* Lisse: Swets & Zeitlinger. pp. 159–71.

Krause, F. and Dann, H.-D. (1986) Die Interview- und Legetechnik zur Rekonstruktion kognitiver Handlungsstrukturen ILKHA. Ein unterrichtsnahes Verfahren zur Erfassung potentiell handlungswirksamer subjektiver Theorien von Lehrern. (Projekt 'Aggression in der Schule', Arbeitsbericht 9). Konstanz: Universität, Sozialwissenschaftliche Fakultät.

Scheele, B. and Groeben, N. (1984) *Die Heidelberger Struktur-Legetechnik (SLT). Eine Dialog-Konsens-Methode zur Erhebung subjektiver Theorien mittlerer Reichweite*. Weinheim: Beltz.

Tennstädt, K.-Ch. (1987) *Das Konstanzer Trainingsmodell (KTM): Ein integratives Selbsthilfeprogramm für Lehrkräfte zur Bewältigung von Aggressionen und Störungen im Unterricht.* Vol. 2: *Theoretische Grundlagen, Beschreibung der Trainingsinhalte und erste empirische Überprüfung*. Bern: Huber.

Tennstädt, K.-Ch. and Dann, H.-D. (1987) *Das Konstanzer Trainingsmodell (KTM): Ein integratives Selbsthilfeprogramm für Lehrkräfte zur Bewältigung von Aggressionen und Störungen im Unterricht.* Vol. 3: *Evaluation des Trainingserfolgs im empirischen Vergleich*. Bern: Huber.

Tennstädt, K.-Ch., Krause, F., Humpert, W. and Dann, H.-D. (1987) *Das Konstanzer Trainingsmodell (KTM): Ein integratives Selbsthilfeprogramm für Lehrkräfte zur Bewältigung von Aggressionen und Störungen im Unterricht.* Vol. 1: *Trainingshandbuch*. Bern: Huber.

Thommen, B. (1985) *Alltagspsychologie von Lehrern über verhaltensauffällige Schüler*. Bern: Huber.

Tomaszewski, T. (1978) *Tätigkeit und Bewußtsein. Beiträge zur Einführung in die polnische Tätigkeitspsychologie*. Weinheim: Beltz.

Wagner, A.C., Maier, S., Uttendorfer-Marek, I. and Weidle, R.H. (1981) *Unterrichtspsychogramme. Was in den Köpfen von Lehrern und Schülern vorgeht*. Reinbek: Rowohlt.

Wahl, D. (1981a) Psychologisches Alltagswissen im Unterricht. In H.-J. Fietkau and D. Görlitz (eds), *Umwelt und Alltag in der Psychologie*. Weinheim: Beltz. pp. 67–90.

Wahl, D. (1981b) Methoden zur Erfassung handlungssteuernder Kognitionen von Lehrern. In M. Hofer (ed.), *Informationsverarbeitung und Entscheidungsverhalten von Lehrern. Beiträge zu einer Handlungstheorie des Unterrichtens*. Munich: Urban & Schwarzenberg. pp. 49–77.

Wahl, D., Schlee, J., Krauth, J. and Mureck, J. (1983) *Naive Verhaltenstheorie von Lehrern. Abschlußbericht eines Forschungsvorhabens zur Rekonstruktion und Validierung subjektiver psychologischer Theorien*. Oldenburg: Universität, Zentrum für pädagogische Berufspraxis.

Index